INSTITUTE LECTURES.

LECTURES

ON

MENTAL AND MORAL CULTURE.

BY

SAMUEL P. BATES, A.M.,

SUPERINTENDENT OF PUBLIC INSTRUCTION,
CRAWFORD COUNTY, PENNSYLVANIA.

'Whatever career you embrace, propose to yourselves an elevated aim, and put in its service an unalterable constancy."—*Lectures on the True, Beautiful, and Good.* M. VICTOR COUSIN.

"Knowledge is acquired with difficulty, with the sweat of the brow, at the price of humanity's perpetual labor. Spontaneity is innocence, the golden age of thought; but virtue is worth more than innocence, and virtue requires a continual struggle."—*History of Modern Philosophy.* ID.

A. S. BARNES & COMPANY,
NEW YORK AND CHIGACO.

1873.

Entered, according to Act of Congress, in the year 1859, by
A. S. BARNES & BURR,
In the Clerk's Office of the District Court of the United States for the Southern
District of New York.

CONTENTS.

PREFACE.

The following Lectures, as the title indicates, were prepared for the use of Teachers' Institutes, and have been delivered at intervals, before these bodies, during the past five years. They were intended to be addressed to an assembly of teachers and citizens, such as are usually found at the evening sessions; consequently, they are not designed for the exclusive reading of teachers.

The attempt has been, to make the opinions developed thoroughly accord with the fundamental principles of our institutions and form of government. The necessity to the safety and prosperity of the State, that every child should be educated, and that the wealth of the country should pay for this education, has been made a prominent feature.

There will not be found in this volume a

systematic treatise for the special guidance of the teacher, but those motives and incentives to preparation, which may serve to awaken inquiry and stimulate thought. In the hope that it may contribute to the development of our noble school system, it is submitted to the public.

MEADVILLE, June 6, 1859.

LECTURE I.

DIGNITY OF THE TEACHER'S PROFESSION.

EVERY man should regard his profession with pride. He should see in it something to challenge his admiration and win his affections. He should seek to view it on its sunny side and in its fairest aspects. He should feel that love and regard for it that inspires him with energy and enthusiasm in its pursuit, that enables him to triumph over its difficulties, and to glory and revel in its charms.

He who looks upon his profession with disfavor, who thinks meanly of its labors, and speaks disparagingly of those who belong to it, will inevitably be a drone. His labor will press upon him as drudgery. The action of all his powers will be sluggish, and in despising the pleasures of professional pride, he misses the finest enjoyment of active life. There is no feeling more degrading to a man, than the thought that he is engaged in a business of which he is ashamed; than to feel that other men look upon him with contempt because he labors in it. It stifles every attempt to excel. It obscures every spark of genius and sinks him to the rank of a slave.

In one sense there is no calling that possesses claims to dignity above another. The man who is engaged in the most menial occupation that is honest, may possess as pure a heart, as he who has won for himself the greatest earthly fame. The humblest laborer, that lugs bricks upon his back the day long, may possess the spirit and honor of a nobleman. " If two angels," says John Milton, " were to be sent from heaven, the one to be monarch of an empire, and the other to be a chimney sweeper, the difference in their minds would not be the value of a straw." Earthly and outward distinctions would have no weight. To do the will of Him who sent them would be their only care. To perform with fidelity the duties of the occupation to which, for the time, Providence has called us, should indeed be the object of our solicitude.

But when we compare the results which the different callings in life are capable of producing, we discover that there are different degrees of dignity to which each is entitled. Aside from the purity of a man's heart, and the fidelity with which he discharges his duties, there are the effects which his labors may produce upon those about him and upon society. The members of the human body are all equally necessary to its life and symmetry, but in the results of their action we readily admit the superiority of some in dignity and importance. The callings of life also have their comparative value, and exert their respective influences in the economy of the world's progress. Beyond the claims of the personal dignity of the individual, and of integrity and honor which should be cultivated in every profession, there are grounds of distinction in the results of his labors. It makes very little difference with the progress of humanity, whether a shoemaker displays great skill in his craft, or whether he be an awkward fellow. The result in either case will be the commendation or curses of a few dozen pimps and dandies. But the man on whose skill and energy the permanent improvement, the mental growth of large numbers of human beings depends, has a higher destiny.

The noblest object for which any man can live is, without doubt, the cultivation of that part of him which is imperishable. It is the mind that governs and directs us in all things, and if we would have our lives well ordered, and would be wisely governed, we should seek first of all, generous mental culture. The many ills to which we are subject, and the troubles and vexations with which our lives are beset, result principally from ignorance. If we look abroad in the world, we see those classes of society enjoying least of the rational pleasures of life who have least knowledge. Those nations and tribes are most barbarous and brutish who are the most ignorant. Self interest and present gratification, if these only were consulted, would confirm us in this opinion.

The teachings of Providence point us to the same conclusion. We are created with the special design of improving our gifts. Had this not been the purpose of our existence, the Creator would have endowed us with instinct, and thus have put us for ever under the control of an iron necessity, like the beast of the field, the bird of the air, and the insect that flutters in the sunbeam. These can not improve their gifts, and they have no need of improvement. The cattle of to-day know no more than the cattle in the time of Abraham. The bird builds her nest, and the bee fashions its cell, as they did at creation's dawn. Were these to live a thousand years they would develop no new faculties, they would make no improvement. Their knowledge is just sufficient for their needs. They eat, and sleep, and then lie down to die. But not so with the soul of man. It is endowed with faculties susceptible of indefinite expansion and improvement. At the earliest dawn of existence development begins, and from infancy to trembling age, he may by diligence and judicious culture, add strength and knowledge to his increasing stores. The accumulations of the fathers may be handed down to the sons, and thus from generation to generation, and from age to age, the soul of man, profiting by all that has been before it, may go on growing in strength and increasing in knowledge to the last syllable of recorded time.

Nor does development cease here. There is a more exalted view that opens beyond. The teachings of Nature and the direct testimony of Revelation unite in proof, that the mortal life of man is but the beginning of his mental training. It is only the childhood to that more perfect development which shall succeed. It will be the business of eternity to unfold the height and depth of that knowledge which we can here see but dimly, and with a vision obscured by all those weaknesses to which flesh is heir. Our best acquirements are comparatively infantile and weak. The farther we advance in knowledge only makes our weakness and folly more apparent; for the light which we gain, serves to show the boundless extent of that which remains to be learned, and leads us to that which it is not possible for us to know with our present light. The shortness of life prevents us from prosecuting at length those subjects even which our present powers and helps fit us to pursue. The great majority of mankind are prevented by their position in society, by the necessity they are under of toiling early and late for the maintenance of themselves and families, from devoting the small space of this life to the development of their spiritual natures. But the man who gives his life to study is only able to master a few of the elements of knowledge. Look at the mind of such a man as Lord Bacon! Possessed of a comprehension and a grasp which seemed to look upon the laws of the material world as with the eye of a God! which seemed to range the universe at will, and pointed out those sound rules of investigation which have conducted to the splendid triumphs of modern science, and have reared so proud a trophy to his name! And yet he felt when he died that he had but just entered the vestibule of knowledge; that he had only torn aside a few of the obstructions from the field of discovery, and had set up an occasional landmark to point the way; that he had only picked up a few pebbles upon the sea-shore, while its great caverns were full of hidden things and mysteries, which his earnest mind was thirsting to discover when he was called away! And does God create for naught? Does that Being bestow such gifts without granting the means for their improvement? Though we but commence their cultivation in the brief period that is alloted to us in life, we are impelled to the belief by every principle of human judgment, that abundant opportunity will be afforded for the full development of all our faculties, and the comprehension of unbounded knowledge. What more worthy occupation can employ our mental powers in a future state? Our physical needs will then be at an end, for our employments will only pertain to pure spirit. There will then be no occasion for all that labor which is bestowed in acquiring lands, and houses, and costly furniture, and in answering those demands which are made upon us by fashion and the eyes of other people. For, if our lives have been consistent with His will, we shall live in mansions that are prepared for us, we shall need no protection or rest, for it is eternal sunshine and summer; we are dressed in the white robes of purity, and the only occupations in which we can be engaged will be such as pertain to us as pure intelligences.

We see then that the cultivation of the mind is the noblest work we can accomplish for ourselves; that its results are unlimited in extent and unending in duration; that we derive from this the highest gratification which a human being is capable of enjoying; that we thus begin that work of development and improvement, for the attainment of which we are without doubt expressly created; and that we thereby secure the approval of Him, whose will it is our life and light to obey. For upon the faithful servant, who used the talents with unceasing diligence, were bestowed the cheering words of praise; while he who hid his talent in a napkin, was sent away in disgrace with merited reproach.

If what has been said be true, we must conclude that the profession, whose business it is to train the faculties and energies of mind,—to have under control the spirits of childhood, fresh from the Creator's hand,—to impart knowledge which shall be the basis and key to other knowledge,—to lay burdens that will make strong the mental sinews,—to draw out and set in operation all the latent faculties,—to unfold those laws immutable which exist in the physical, the mental, and the moral,—to plan conquests and execute designs where the agencies are immaterial and spiritual,—and to be the instrument of developing character that shall outlive the years of mortal life, such a profession can not be excelled in dignity. In our short-sighted judgment we are likely to lose sight of the importance that should be attached to it. The spiritual is too often obscured by the material and the tangible.

When Æneas was crossing the seas, as it is given in Virgil's beautiful poetic account, he landed upon that island sacred to filial affection, and ordered games to be performed about the tomb of his father Anchises. Among others he instituted prizes for those who would try their "skill with the swift arrow." The mark was a dove, tied high up upon the mast of the vessel. But when he came to award the prize, it was not bestowed upon him who hit the mast with his arrow, nor upon him who severed the string, nor yet upon him who pierced the dove in her upward flight; but it was given to that aged chieftain whose far ascending shaft kindled amid the clouds of heaven, and marked its track with flame.

We are apt to forget that we are created with other faculties than those which pertain to us as animals,—which minister simply to our physical necessities. Surrounded as we are by the strife of men fast to be rich and eager to lay up goods where moth corrupts and where thieves break through, we lose sight of the fact that we have hearts and an emotional nature which demand our care and culture. Digestion is not the highest order of development of which this being of ours is susceptible. Had growth been the end of our existence, we could have been created without the means of locomotion, and stood with our arms extended like the oak of the forest. Had we simply been designed to fulfill the conditions of animal life, we could have been made like the lion who devours his prey and then sleeps by his lair till he needs more. But how different in purpose and destiny is the creation of man! What powers of thought and action is he not capable of displaying, how generous in impulse, how lofty in purpose, how sublime in virtue is he capable of becoming! Who can fully realize the invention displayed by Homer, the analytic acuteness of Aristotle, the sublime virtue of Socrates, the intuitive perceptions of Bacon, the broad generalizations of Newton, the incomparable acquaintance with human thought and feeling displayed by Shakspeare, without entertaining a more exalted view of man's nature and man's destiny, and unceasing delight in the thought that he is himself a man, possessed of a spirit akin to these?

That we may have a just conception of the dignity and value of teaching, and the relation it sustains to the world's thinking, let us compare it with some of the other professions which are most highly esteemed among men, and are usually looked upon as the most honorable and dignified.

It is indeed a noble occupation to till the soil. What glorious triumphs has the hand of the husbandman achieved! He indeed eats the bread of labor,—he toils early and late,—and his garments at times are worn and dusty. But what shapes of beauty and magnificence does the earth take beneath his hand! He hews down the heavy forest, and lets the warm sunlight in upon the damp, mouldy earth. He breaks the stubborn and rocky soil, and clothes it with verdure. He digs deep trenches and plants the vine,—with careful hand he prunes the too luxurious growth, and hangs beneath the broad green leaves long clusters of purple grapes. Orchards of mellow fruit glow in the autumnal sunshine, and along the hills are ridges of golden corn. In summer time the choicest varieties of stock graze in the meadow beside the cool brook, and in winter they delight in warm shelter, and pure water, and unstinted feed; and he rejoices to see them eat and thrive. It was that great lawyer and statesman, Cicero, who said, when contemplating amid the cares of state, the freedom and ease he enjoyed when surrounded by the labors of his farms, that it was his greatest delight to see his ewes eat and his lambs suck.

But beyond this limited view, to the husbandman the volume of nature is wide open. He is in the very midst of the Creator's laboratory. It is indeed ennobling to be a tiller of the soil, and to see the work of creation that is constantly going on,—to witness the changes that are taking place in the vegetable, and mineral, and animal kingdoms, whereby the subtle and unseen elements take forms of beauty and magnificence—the fragrant shrub, the stately tree—the diamond, and the ruby—the graceful turns and curves in the contour of the horse, the stately bearing of the king of beasts, and the strong wing of the king of birds. And yet, what is the purpose of the husbandman's work? What the end of all his labors? Why! that when the seed time has passed and the harvest has come, he may furnish the market a few score bushels of grain,—that he may fit for the sacrifice a dozen bullocks, and half as many swine,—that he may store up in cellar and granary enough to feed himself and family till harvest shall come again.

The life of the teacher is spent in a different sphere. There are none of the elements of natural beauty about him, that light up the path of the tiller of the soil. The herds lowing for their keeper, barns filled with plenty, the fruitery groaning with the orchard's bounty, the broad, rich acres of nicely cultivated land,—are not his. His home, it may be, is an up-stair tenement in some obscure court. His mornings and his evenings are spent in study, preparing for his daily task. If by chance he catch a breath of fresh air, laden with the fragrance of new-mown hay and apple blossoms, or the "sound of bees' industrious murmur," it is when wafted to him as he passes the garden wall of the farmer. His days are spent in the toil of the class-room. Patient and unceasing he must instruct the pupils committed to his charge. One may be quick to apprehend, and ready and attentive in all his tasks, while others are drones and laggards. But he must adapt himself to all. He may be obliged to repeat again and again, processes and explanations the most simple in their nature, and still realize the disheartening truth that he has failed in making them understood by dull and indolent members of his class. He may see his instructions disregarded, and his good advice thrown away. But he must be meek and patient still, and renew his attempts as though all were equally apt to learn and teachable in spirit, and never yield and never tire in his exertions for the improvement and welfare of the company that are gathered around him. Indulgent parents may pour into his ear the complaints of pampered and fault-finding children, who have perhaps escaped unwhipped of justice, which, but for the kindness of his heart, would have been meted out to them. But he must take it all in sympathy and meekness, and still strive to go on in harmony. Who can tell the heart-eating cares that beset the life of the teacher in his accustomed round of tasks? Who can recount the burdens that he bears on his bosom during his waking moments, and the perplexities that disturb his midnight slumbers?

Such is a picture of the daily life of the teacher. As an occupation, as a means of support and pastime, it can not compare in independence and comfortable living with that of the cultivation of the earth. But what is the end of his labors? The work which the teacher accomplishes is unending in its results. Eternity will alone suffice to measure the fruits of his industry. He works upon a material that will never perish. When he labors to bring into operation all those faculties with which the minds of his pupils are endowed, and inspires by his enthusiasm their young hearts with a love for learning, and a reverence for the truths of science, and the beauties of literature, he wakes to action the energies of a living soul,—he tunes an instrument strung by the hand of the Creator, that will never cease to yield harmonious sounds. He disciplines, and trains for usefulness in life, those who come under his charge. But the influence of that training is not confined to those who received it. They go forth into life to impart to others in turn what they have realized;

> "And each, as he receives the flame,
> Will light his altar with its ray."

What calling merely secular can equal in dignity a work like this? What profession in which the responsibilities are so great, in which the future teems with results so momentous? The teacher is no less a personage than a co-worker with the Creator in the highest manifestations of his power. Without development, the mind of man is naught but a blank, a waste without beauty and without use. But when the hand of culture is laid upon it, it praises alike the handiwork of the Creator, and the developments it receives from him who trains it. So that the work of the latter approximates in dignity to the former.

There is a grandeur in the profession of the law which is hardly equaled among the callings of life. Though so often sneered at and despised, for the reason that no profession is more shamefully abused by many of the class who should defend its honor and uphold its dignity, yet in its true purpose, and in its legitimate results it challenges our respect and veneration. It is the business of the lawyer to search out the facts which shall show innocence or guilt, and thereby establish justice. The notion of a judgment for the purpose of establishing right, is one that inheres in the human mind, and is essential to veracity and honor. We can scarcely conceive a more exalted idea than that of a general judgment, when all the wrongs of ages shall be righted, when the rights of the abused and long-suffering shall be vindicated. But such is the daily labor of the lawyer. His office is to correct the wrongs which man suffers at the hands of his fellow-man. The idea very generally prevails, that an advocate can not take up on the side of the guilty without compromising his honor and his integrity. But even the culprit has rights which should be respected and defended. Because he is in the hands of the law and powerless, he should not be abused by the party that is interested to crush him. He should not be made to suffer for more than he is guilty of. It is quite as honorable to defend and protect conscientiously the rights of the accused, as to be engaged in the prosecution, and even more creditable to a man's heart:

> "For earthly power shows likest God's
> When mercy seasons justice."

The honest advocate does not agree to prove a man innocent when he is guilty,—to misrepresent and falsify to gain the suit of his client; but to see that no more than justice be done,—that the rights and privileges of that client are respected, and that he secure "even-handed" justice. In this light, the profession of the law is noble and dignified. It awakens the finest feelings and sensibilities of the heart to feel that one is the vindicator of the injured, and taxes the noblest powers of the intellect to search out and set in order the facts that shall inevitably conduct to justice. To feel that the life or death of the client, the happiness or misery of an innocent and dependent family may hang upon his words, is sufficient to arouse him to the utmost of his capacity, and to inspire him with unwonted vigor.

But the genuine faithful teacher does more than this. He is not only a vindicator of justice and a defender of truth and virtue, when trampled on by the offender, but he performs this labor prospectively. He labors to establish in the character, principles that are antagonistic to vice and crime, and to nurture in the heart sentiments and feelings which shall direct in the paths of rectitude and honor. His office is to smooth and polish the gem whose ragged corners would otherwise tear and lacerate whatever it chanced to come in contact with. He subdues the spirit of contention, he inculcates the universal brotherhood of man, and lifts his pupils up above the petty spirit of jealousy and revenge, which leads to those endless and harassing difficulties that principally occupy the time of the lawyer. The dignity of these duties is apparent. They supersede in spirit the necessity of the legal profession, and hence rise above it in honor. Whenever the mission of the schoolmaster shall be made perfectly successful, then the lawyer's "occupation 's gone."

We prize beyond the value of gold those masterpieces of art scattered over Europe, which attract the connoiseur of every land. From generation to generation, and from age to age, they are preserved with almost a religious veneration. We pronounce the name of the artist with a thrill of feeling which his own lofty genius alone can inspire. But he labors to produce the form and features of these frames of ours upon canvas and in marble; and though he inspire these, dumb and cold as they are, with the grace and beauty of the moving, speaking form, yet it is but a shadow that he creates. Scarce has he put the final touch of his pencil, or has struck upon his chisel the last tinkling blows, ere time's effacing fingers are busy on its surface, and the canvas fades and moulders, and the marble is crumbling into dust. Not so with the work of the teacher. He draws the lineaments and features of life upon a human soul, warm with emotion and radiant with heavenly beauty. His work does not fade and crumble, but is more enduring with years. Every line from his pencil takes deeper and brighter color as time wears on, and every stroke from his chisel lays bare veins of beauty which grow richer with age, and take a higher polish from use.

In every age the teacher has been held in honor. He is the interpreter to his own time of all the generations of thinking men that have preceded him. He is the exponent of all cotemporary thought. He is the chosen representative in the republic of letters. The men of every profession seek to read and understand what he has written, and his books, like the books of fate which the Sibyl presented to the Roman emperor, are preserved with religious care, and are studied with pious veneration. As we look back through the ages that are past, the eye rests on many nations that have, in their day, shone forth with transcendent glory, and have served as beacon lights to those which followed. There are Troy, and Thebes, and Athens, and Argos, and Sparta, and Carthage, and Rome. They have achieved universal fame. Though existing in those remote ages, the mellow light of their glory rests down upon them in unclouded serenity. And what among all their grand achievements and boasted honors have they bequeathed to us that we prize the most? The books of their schoolmasters. There is no other of their possessions that have come down to us, which can be compared to these. Without them the glory of those nations departs, for it is their books that form the title-deed of their renown.

When the Goth and the Vandal uncouth and savage, invaded Rome, and trampled out the last remaining spark of Roman genius, the night of barbarism settled down upon Europe and the civilized world. Rome was the last of the great heathen nations, and when the light of her civilization was extinguished, a period of gloom and ignorance succeeded, which was significantly called the dark ages. Generation after generation passed, and we nowhere see any marked achievement of mind. There were no triumphs in literature, in science, in art, and consequently, there was no lofty impulse, no aspiring purpose, that anywhere moved the national heart. A universal gloom brooded over the nations. And what was it amid this thick darkness that gave presage of the approaching dawn? What was it that stimulated thought and kindled that flame which was soon to flood the world with light, and burn with increasing splendor? It was the books of a few schoolmasters, that had been hoarded up, and were now scattered to the four winds. Upon the fall of the Western Empire the writings of the Grecian and Roman scholars were collected at Constantinople, and during that long period of intellectual darkness they were preserved and reproduced with vigilant and unceasing care. But at the breaking up of the Eastern Empire, and the overthrow of the power there concentred, the books that had been collected were scattered over the whole face of Europe, and the energies of the nations, which had lain dormant for more than three centuries, were inspired with new vigor. The compass was invented, which sent Columbus in search of a new world. The discovery of the explosive nature of gunpowder civilized the profession of war; and the invention of the printing-press scattered thought as the wind drives the chaff of the summer threshing-floor. The dozing millions over all Europe were aroused, like the giant waking from his long slumbers and girding himself for great labors. The national pulse beat with new vigor, for an element of life and activity was poured into its veins. And this mighty revolution which followed was achieved by the books of a score or two of schoolmasters, who, centuries before, had lived and died in peace on the shores of the Mediterranean.

In the same volume in which we read the history of Alexander the Great, we read that of Socrates. Alexander is recognized as one of the leading military chieftains of any age. His conquests extended over half of the civilized world. He was worshiped by his subjects as a demigod. While he lived he walked the earth in glory, but he died a miserable death, in a fit of beastly intoxication, surrounded by a circle of drunken revelers. Scarce was he cold in his grave, before the captains whom he had raised to power quarreled over his tomb for the spoils of empire. And whenever we utter his name, there is no thrill of gratitude and veneration.

Socrates, on the contrary, was an humble teacher; who spent his days in the groves of the Academy, among his pupils, and dwelt beneath a "low-roofed house."

> ——" But from his mouth issued forth
> Mellifluous streams, that watered all the schools
> Of Academics old and new, with those
> Surnamed Peripatetics, and the sect
> Epicurean, and the Stoic severe."

His life was so pure and unsullied, and its closing scenes were characterized by such sublime virtue, that his praise has been upon the tongue of all succeeding ages. His pupils gathered around him at his death, filled with unutterable grief, preserving with religious care every word that escaped his lips. The mention of his name thrills the heart with love and admiration for his character. The thoughts which were matured in his brain will never die so long as there are admirers of virtue,—and the consistency of his life, like the jewel on the brow of beauty, sheds unfading luster on his name.

Socrates indeed lived to a great purpose. His power of intellect, the acuteness of his thoughts, and the logical correctness of his reasonings, have made him the teacher, not merely of the pupils gathered about him in a Grecian city and speaking the Athenian tongue, but he is the teacher of all time, and in every polished language of the earth. And yet, his intellectual greatness has achieved for him the least part of his fame. Many philosophers of his own time, in mental vigor and acumen would compare favorably with him. But in moral excellence he stands alone. And when the teachers of other times have lectured to their pupils on the principles of virtue and moral rectitude, and have sought amid the records of the past for some example which should inspire them with enthusiasm in the pursuit and practice of it, they have pointed to Socrates, to the integrity and honor of his life and the sublimity of his death. It is only after the lapse of ages, that we can point to a life so pure and unsullied,—that of our own Washington.

But even more intimately connected with the life of the great warrior Alexander, is that of his tutor—the companion of his younger days. When Philip of Macedon desired a teacher, who should conduct the education of his son, he sought the services of Aristotle, an humble citizen of Stagira, who by his skill in the art of teaching had created for himself a reputation that attracted the attention of the king. And though the pupil became the hero of his time, and achieved a glory that rivaled in brightness and splendor the brilliancy of the noon-day sun, and cast for the time in shade and obscurity the teachings of the humble tutor; yet the period was not far distant when the deeds of the warrior were regarded as mere bold and daring exploits, brutal and bloody in execution, and unimportant in their results, so far as they related to his design, upon the progress of humanity; while the teachings of the tutor have increased to an importance that far transcends that of any other man of ancient times. The systems of Aristotle became universal. In the domain of thought he was the monarch. His philosophy ruled the world for centuries, and even now his treatise on logic is the basis of the text-books in all our colleges. Up to the time of Bacon his philosophical systems bore undisputed sway, and in the field of criticism he can never be supplanted.

Such is the profession, my brethren, to which we belong. Such are the men who have labored in it, whose teachings have been lights to the world that are still clear and bright as time wears on, and with whom we can now claim companionship. Such are the labors which this profession performs among those great agencies that work out the problem of civilization. In its results upon the race every other profession sinks into insignificance beside it. Mr. Carlyle has quaintly but very pointedly asked, "The great event, parent of all others, is it not the arrival of a great thinker in the world?" It is surely the thought of the world that directs and controls its energies, and it is no less sure that the teacher directs and controls its thought. Those nations that have been most respected and honored, and have left their impress upon the progress of the race, have shown their appreciation of the profession of the teacher.

There are many events in the history of the past, that have for the time excited the most absorbing interest, and have engrossed the attention of prince and people, which have long ago been forgotten, and were not considered of sufficient importance to posterity to form a part of the annals of the times. But if a king has invited to his court an humble schoolmaster, the fact is trumpeted to the ends of the world, and the historian is careful to record it upon his page. The best period in the history of every civilized nation has been that in which the reigning power and the people at large have shown most emphatically their appreciation of the teacher's profession. And well they may; for it is by letters that the glory of a nation is perpetuated. In letters is its memory embalmed.

We have thus far considered the profession of teaching absolutely, irrespective of the character of those who fill its ranks. The object has been to show its dignity from the results which it is designed to accomplish. The dignity of the profession is always and everywhere the same. It is unchanging as truth. The ignorance or imbecility of its disciples may tarnish its luster and obscure its brightness, and society may be prevented from reaping those fruits which it is capable of bearing. But still the fault is not in the profession.

I am aware that many whom I see about me are the teachers of our common schools. It may be proper, before concluding, to inquire how the common school teacher, even in his humble sphere, may uphold its dignity and honor.

The first claim which he should seek to establish is that of capacity. No man can put confidence in another and intrust to him important duties without assurance of his ability. He should therefore seek first of all liberal culture. He should never be content with proficiency simply in those studies which he is required to teach. The grade of his school may be such that only the common English branches are comprised in the list; but a knowledge of these, however elaborate, should never satisfy him. He can better illustrate to a child the first lessons in arithmetic who has a thorough acquaintance with the higher mathematics, than one who has no knowledge beyond the simple acquirements of the class he instructs. The light of liberal culture throws its rays back upon even the rudiments of knowledge, and makes them appear brighter and clearer. The resources for explanation and illustration are at hand, and he has the discretion and judgment to use them intelligently. The teacher who is satisfied with a certificate of perfect qualification in the branches required by law to be taught will soon fall into a stereotype process, and will ere long be left to mediocrity and obscurity, by his more enterprising and ambitious brethren, in a profession whose fundamental idea is progress and development.

There are difficulties and trials which the teacher is constantly obliged to encounter. It is eminently a profession of labor and vexation of spirit. Perplexing questions, involving the knowledge he ought to possess in order to inspire and hold the confidence of scholars and patrons, are constantly arising. But if amid all these harassing cares he has liberal culture, if his mind has felt the strengthening influence of a thorough course in the gymnasium, he has a place on which to stand, from which he can not be moved. He has the spot of solid ground for which Archimedes sighed.

The teacher who expects to become eminent, will also be thoroughly versed in works of a professional character. In each of the other learned professions there are books detailing the theory and the practice of the art, and the young man who desires to enter either of them must become proficient in the principles upon which it is based. This should be expected of the teacher. The bare acquaintance with the several sciences should not constitute the maximum of his knowledge. He should in addition to this be familiar with professional books particularly devoted to the practice of his calling. His success mainly depends upon the conception he forms of the duties which his position brings with it. If he has no preconceived plans and purposes, then he will have none to execute when he arrives at the schoolroom, except such as are drawn forth by the emergency, and must be adopted or rejected without meditation. Those methods of governing and interesting scholars, which the best instructors have employed are unknown to him, and he must follow on the old beaten track, which those who taught him employed. But if his mind be thoroughly imbued with the true spirit of teaching, if he has acquainted himself with the opinions of those who have thought and written upon this science, his plans can be formed upon a basis of knowledge and mature deliberation. He has the theory of his profession, and he can weigh the value of different methods, and adopt or reject according to his faith in them. He will have at his command the experience of those who have had eminent success, and have had a life-long acquaintance with its duties. His mind will be rendered fruitful in expedients for managing a school, for conquering the stubborn, for winning back the disobedient to filial respect and submission, for arousing the indolent to a sense of their shame, for quickening the powers of the dull and unthinking, and for animating all with the spirit of enquiry. He learns, instead of the dull routine of enforcing lessons at the point of the rod, to substitute the "waking up process." He experiences the most grateful reward of his labors which a teacher can know, that of seeing his pupils love to learn, and delight most of all to be about him. To this end he should also have the leading educational periodicals, and thus familiarize himself with the improvements which are being made, and those methods which are practiced by our most distinguished educators. He should, in a word, acquaint himself with the last best thoughts which the world has produced upon the subject, and thus keep even with the times.

Finally, the teacher who desires the respect and confidence of cultivated and thinking men, should possess extensive general information. Many of our young men who aspire to this position are shamefully ignorant of the most common and familiar facts. A teacher once enquired of me if Benjamin Franklin lived in Boston now. And that young man was a proficient in Latin and mathematics, and was a splendid scholar in the Greek. Another, when, in conversation with him, I chanced to mention the name of Alexander Hamilton, wanted to know if he was not the president of Princeton Theological School. When I told him that it was Dr. Alexander to whom he probably had reference, "Oh! yes," said he, "that is the man I meant." This young man was about to graduate from college, and was actually making inquiries about a subject suitable for his graduating oration. Such shameful ignorance of the commonest facts in our history is unpardonable. It is the fruitful source of that derision in which many of our class are held.

Let every teacher possess himself of a few books on history, and especially the history of our own country, so as to be able to trace out our national origin, and the statesmen who have taken a prominent part in public affairs. He should be minutely acquainted with the constitution of the United States, and with the opinions of those who framed and adopted it. He should know something of the history of politics, and the positions which parties have held in the past. He should pursue a course of reading in general literature, acquaint himself with the best authors, and become familiar with their style and peculiarities. Let him study the poetry of the great masters, and be able to converse intelligently in a company of educated people upon any topic connected with its structure and allusions. If any young man thinks this too much for him to accomplish, then he had better quit the profession.

To the genuine, whole-souled teacher, nothing is impossible. He will never submit quietly and tamely to pass in the company of well-bred people, as a boor and a novice. He will work when others sleep. He will gather his knowledge from every source, from conversation, from his daily walks, from his scholars, and from his own quiet meditations. He will forego the gratification of sense and the pleasures of the passing hour, for that higher pleasure which flows from the consciousness of intellectual superiority.

The life of the teacher is not one of ease. Though his labors are not apparent, and he does not create so much noise and stir in the world as some who are engaged in other occupations, yet they are not on this account the less arduous and real. A few of the elements of success have been named. It is only by possessing these, and indeed vastly more, that the teacher can claim any part of that dignity which is inherent in the profession. He must never expect that it is to endow him with any honors if he has not first earned them. If he depends upon the profession for his dignity, without any real claims, he will be of all men the most undignified. For the more honorable the profession, the more shame to the man who proves himself unworthy of belonging to it. If we are scholars and play the man, we shall at least merit the reward. The great lights of the past are the companions of our labors. The future teems with opportunities. The field is already white for the harvest. We have only to thrust the sickle in. He who is worthy shall wear the crown, and vindicate the dignity of the Teacher's Profession.

LECTURE II.

THE BOYHOOD OF NAPOLEON.

A TRUTHFUL history of the youth and education of one, who in manhood has manifested transcendent powers of mind, must always be of interest. If the conduct and glory of his life has attracted unusual attention, there is a natural desire to be acquainted with that portion of it which transpired before he had come to public notice. But to the rising generation, to those who are now receiving that education which is to guide and support them through life, the early history of such a man is of vital importance. If a certain course of training has conducted him to success in what he has undertaken, it is fair to infer that similar training will exert a corresponding influence. If a well-spent youth has been rewarded with fortunate results, it will yield encouragement for others to go and do likewise. If his education has borne rich fruits in mature years, it will be profitable for us to inquire, what was the course of studies that he pursued, and what was the manner of pursuing them. When a man has arisen from poverty and obscurity to such a brilliant career as that of Napoleon, the force of his early example speaks to us in a voice that commands universal attention.

We are apt to look upon every marked achievement of human effort as having been secured by genius—by gifts the special manifestation of Providence. The young especially, are ever ready to believe that labor and genius are incompatible. They would transfer that halo of glory, that surrounds the reputed feats of the gods of antiquity, to the real heroes of history. There can be no belief more fatal to the claims of true greatness, and at no period of life is it more disastrous to entertain it than in youth.

Sir Sydney Smith has appropriately observed, that "it would be an extremely profitable thing, to draw up a short and well authenticated account of the habits of study of the most celebrated writers with whose style of literary industry we happen to be most acquainted. It would go very far to destroy the absurd and pernicious association of genius and idleness, by showing that the greatest poets, orators, statesmen, and historians—men of the most brilliant and imposing talents, have actually labored as hard as the makers of dictionaries and the arrangers of indexes; and that the most obvious reason why they have been superior to other men, is that they have taken more pains than other men."

Could such a collection be made, it would but add another proof to the many which already exist, that the only true glory of man is labor; and that so far from labor being incompatible with genius, it is in fact the creator of it. The most brilliant powers with which Heaven is pleased to endow men, must inevitably grow weak under the blighting influence of sloth and inactivity. While labor makes the five talents ten, and secures those habits of mental action which are absolutely indispensable to the loftiest achievements. Let no youth despise labor, and court the position of a luxurious life who hopes to walk the paths of glory. The muscles pine, and the strong sinews perish beneath the withering touch of inactivity; while the smith at his sooty forge can show a brawny arm and sinews like the steel he has wrought. The faculties become weak and the purpose wavering when pampered with inglorious ease, but the mind that is accustomed to bend steadily to its tasks will be ready to seize with firm grasp the object of its labors.

It is common for us to think of Napoleon only as a warrior, as General Bonaparte. At the mention of his name the presence is a lofty form, with a sword flashing by its side, and a plume bending from its lordly brow. We would as soon draw the picture of the lion without his claws and teeth, as Napoleon without the trappings of war. Does he cross the Alps? He is seated upon a black charger with fiery eyes and rearing form. Does he force the bridge of Lodi? He is amid the thickest of the fight, his saber drips with blood, his enemies flee at his approach as from the genius of war. Is he banished to Elba? He must still be an emperor, and the commander of a military establishment. He was put in his grave at Helena in the habiliments of war, and when they brought him back to France, his tarnished sword surmounted his sarcophagus.

We seem to forget that he ever had a boyhood; that he was once an infant muling in his nurse's arms; that he began in the world with as little knowledge as any of us; that he was obliged to resort to the same means for the attainment of it that we were all under the necessity of doing; that he encountered the same difficulties which perplex the mind of the youth who are to-day in our common schools. Because he was a giant in manhood we do not realize that he was in youth like other boys, subject to their weaknesses, captivated by their pleasures, and joining with equal zest in their sports, and that the only difference was, that he from his earliest years had his faculties under the control of his own will, while they suffered theirs to be led by their desires and passions.

Of the moral tendency of Napoleon's life we have nothing to say. Whether his career was a blessing or a curse to the world, is not material to the subject which we are considering. There are those who have stigmatized him as a demon, and others with equal zeal have praised his patriotism and his devotion to the welfare of his country. Upon this question we are not called to pass judgment. We do not desire by any praises we may bestow on his talent and industry in youth, to encourage a taste for military glory, or unholy ambition. He was a noble pattern of a scholar, and as such we wish to present him as an example to those who would become eminent in learning.

About five years previous to the opening of our Revolution, in 1769, Napoleon Bonaparte was born. His parents were Italian, and there consequently coursed in his veins some of the old Roman blood. We discover in his character many of the Roman traits. War was the profession of the Roman people. Peace was to them an abnormal state. We see in his nature that boldness and energy, that iron will and unconquerable perseverance which so signally marked his progenitors.

He was born in the midst of a revolution. Corsica, though an insignificant island in the midst of the Mediterranean sea, happened at the time to be the theater of a bloody strife. The French had invaded the island to subdue the Corsicans and to make it a French province. It was the scene of wild disorder. Families were broken up and scattered. His mother was at the time following her husband in the camp. Her womanly and tender spirit was disturbed by all those passions which the dangers of conflict must arouse. With him she fled to the wild retreats of the mountains, and shared in the alternate hopes and fears which the varying fortunes of their party inspired. But two months previous to his birth the Corsicans were beaten, and the dominion of the island passed into the hands of the French. Thus at the very dawn of existence Napoleon was nursed from a bosom convulsed by the wild disorders of the times —the privations of the camp—the dangers of the battle-field—and all the horrors of a most sanguinary struggle. He was born with the sounds of war ringing in his ears; and though in infancy he could neither know nor appreciate the state of affairs, yet he doubtless inherited the feelings which at the time inspired the mother; and the conversations and tales of heroic daring to which the conflict gave rise, were repeated to him and gave bias to his opening mind. We are told that he always listened with the greatest eagerness, in the most tender years, to the stories about General Paoli, and to those heroic incidents with which the accounts of the revolution abounded. The mother, as she had shared in these scenes, was fond of relating them to her boy, and was thus unconsciously fostering in his young soul a taste for arms and conflict. The character and future conduct of the man, is greatly affected by the influence which the mother exerts during the first few years of life. If the mother possesses a strong mind, with marked characteristics, we almost invariably find them impressed upon the spirit of the child, as the seal leaves its impress upon the wax. The mother of Washington was eminent for her moral virtues and her deep-toned piety, and the man, amid the temptations of early life, the vicissitudes of the camp, and the cares of state, was steady to the teachings of his youth;

> "Nor constant more the needle to the pole."

Napoleon was true to his lessons; and we find him in danger always brave, and in times of trouble always heroic, pursuing with an eastern devotion the love of glory which his mother's lips had inspired.

The island of Corsica is filled with scenery the most wild and romantic. In the midst of this, Napoleon passed his youth. To a mind cold and unappreciative, dumb and unthinking, scenery can have few attractions, and over such a mind can exert but little influence. But a soul alive to the tones of nature's many-stringed harp, a soul that is stirred by the echoes of caverns, the voices of the winds, the roar of ocean and the stillness of the wood, is greatly moved by sublime scenery. Such a mind had Napoleon. From his earliest years he was reserved and contemplative, delighting in solitary walks and silent musings. A seat by the overhanging rock was more congenial to his tastes than youthful sports with a band of noisy companions. Alone he wandered upon the breast of the rugged mountain, and through the deep ravine; he sought the foaming cataract and the rocky cavern; he stood by the sea and mused on its lonely shore. There was, near his mother's house, a quiet retreat embowered in trees, in which he particularly delighted to pass his time. Here he spent many of the hours of boyhood, in silent meditation, or in reading, which at this early period was his chief delight. Even now, when a stranger visits the island, this spot is pointed out to him, and he can imagine the pale, thoughtful boy pursuing his meditations as of yore.

Napoleon's first efforts at mental improvement were made in reading history. The aged and venerable Paoli, the general-in-chief of the Corsicans, whose fortunes the father of Napoleon had followed, was accustomed often to visit the family, and our young hero was never tired of hearing from the lips of him who had been a chief actor in the scene, the accounts of those thrilling adventures with which that fierce struggle abounded. In these early years his spirit was fired with enthusiasm for deeds of noble daring, and often his feelings became so much excited that he would break forth in those short, impassioned sentences, for which in after years his addresses to his soldiers were remarkable. Such was the depth and penetration which was sometimes evinced by his remarks, that Paoli was filled with admiration at the sagacity which he displayed, and treated him more as a companion than as a child. He soon became familiar with all the history of the island, the claims of the contending parties, and the character of the leading men. Later in life, when he was about closing his studies at the military school at Paris, he prepared a history of Corsica, which he was on the point of publishing, when the opening scenes of the French Revolution called on him to lay aside the pen and take the sword. Thus perhaps fortune made him a warrior, rather than an author.

Akin to the stories which he heard of the Corsican

revolution, were the accounts of the fortunes of other nations which he found in history and biography. His passion for hearing stories from the lips of his friends, was transferred to searching for stories in the records of the past; and thus early in life was established a taste for reading which was the foundation of his future fortunate career. His appetite was fed by his daily acquisitions. He devoured books, such was his eagerness to know their contents. The surprising amount of knowledge which he had early in life obtained, and the habits of reflection and studiousness which he thereby acquired, were the means, as we shall soon see, of his promotion.

After the island had come into the hands of the French, governors were sent from France to preside over its political affairs. Among them was Count Marbœuf, who became intimate in the family of the Bonapartes. The thoughtful and studious air of Napoleon attracted his attention. His conversation seemed to be that of a person much beyond his years. He was surprised at the extent of his acquirements. He became convinced of the strong natural abilities and studious habits of this strange boy. He accordingly recommended him for promotion to one of the national schools.

There were at this time twelve provincial military schools in France, which were annually supplied by the most promising youth to be found in the kingdom. Through the recommendation of the governor, Napoleon was sent to the school at Brienne, near Paris. In this promotion of the Corsican boy, is found one of the most striking lessons that can be impressed upon the minds of the young. He was promoted because he deserved to be promoted; because by his own efforts and zeal he had prepared himself to be promoted; because he had convinced his superiors about him whose attention he attracted, that he desired to know more, and that he had the resolution and the will to distinguish himself. The idea too often obtains, that some meet with eminent success because fortune favors them. But fortune generally favors those who work hardest and most merit success. The youth waits for some grand opportunity, when, by one long stride, he will acquire knowledge and correct habits of thought. He lets the little golden chances for improvement which each day brings with it, pass by unimproved, until sluggishness and imbecility of mind, and careless habits utterly preclude the possibility of his advancement.

Not so with the youthful Napoleon. He commenced a brilliant career for himself. He did not wait for a rare opportunity, when some one should commence it for him. He was studious, he was at tentive, he was thoughtful. He began early to make acquirements in knowledge, and persevered with zeal and energy in the course upon which he had entered; and when the time came he was not obliged to seek for the situation, but he was sought to fill it. Had his time been spent as most children spend theirs, in play, and sports, and frivolous amusements, with no thought, no aim, and no effort for improvement; had he not displayed the knowledge and qualifications necessary for the place, he would not have been recommended to the military school at Brienne.

The world is full of opportunities, but the trouble is we are not ready to embrace them. He was prepared for this which now presented itself, and entered at once upon the fulfillment of his destiny. Had the preparation been wanting, he might have lived and died in the island of Corsica, an obscure follower of some trade or profession, and the world never known of Napoleon Bonaparte.

It was at the age of ten, in 1779, that Napoleon was transferred to the military school. He shed bitter tears on leaving his mother whom he tenderly loved, and separating from his brothers and sisters, and the home of his childhood. On his way he passed through Paris, and saw the splendors with which that city abounded· the monuments, the temples, the palaces, the parks and fountains, and the throngs of people. Little did the poor boy then dream of the destiny which awaited him; that the proud city would one day resound with his name; that all that grandeur and magnificence would ere long be his; that kings and emperors, the proudest in Europe, would eventually be suppliants at his feet.

It was about the middle of our Revolution that this event transpired. From the part which the French people took in the contest, and the lively interest which they ever felt in the defeat of the British arms, it is probable that Napoleon now began to acquaint himself with the events transpiring among the American colonies. The new position in which he was placed would naturally favor the acquisition of such general knowledge of events, as would best fit him for that career which Providence had marked out for him. About this time Lafayette returned from America, to arouse the French people and the French king in behalf of the feeble colonies in their almost hopeless struggle. This gallant young Frenchman everywhere inspired the liveliest interest. His youth, his devotion, his manly attainments, the romantic project of aiding the weak and feeble in the wilderness, in a far off land, excited the warmest sympathies of his countrymen, and wherever he appeared in public he was received with bursts of enthusiasm. The story of his adventures was repeated upon the stage. This feeling was not only felt by the people, but was shared by the king; so much so that the old Count de Maurepas remarked "that it was fortunate for the king that Lafayette did not take it into his head to strip Versailles of its furniture to send to his dear Americans —as his majesty would have been unable to refuse him." There is perhaps no class of people in a nation so quickly or so strongly moved by an incident like this, as the students in its schools. The slightest variation in the rise and fall of public feeling is discernible in them. It is not unlikely that Napoleon shared in this feeling, and was incited to renewed exertions, that he might himself one day become a hero.

The entrance of Napoleon to the school at Brienne was the beginning of a new life. He had been accustomed to the quiet and seclusion of the island of Corsica, removed from the stir and commotion which increase as we approach the capital. None of the luxuries of wealth, or the refinements of courts, or the allurements to vice with which the more favored circles of society abound, had yet made his acquaintance. During that critical period in the life of every boy, he was secluded from the corrupting influences of a great city, by which many a youth, ere he has passed the age of ten, is hopelessly ruined. But in his new home every thing was changed. He was in close proximity to the metropolis of France, where beats the heart of the nation, and where the strong pulsations are quickly felt. He found himself surrounded by a company of young Frenchmen, the sons of noblemen and of the aristocracy of wealth. They had plenty of money, and all those habits of luxury and refinement which are cultivated in the best society of the most polite nation in Europe. Of these Napoleon could not boast. Money he had not, for his widowed mother had seven children beside himself to support, and of refinement he had only that which his strong native sense on every occasion supplied. He was therefore looked upon by his companions with contempt. They had been accustomed to consider every person in any way dependent upon his own labors for support, as beneath them in rank, no matter how exalted the occupation in which he might be engaged. Hence they derided him for being the son of a Corsican lawyer. These reproaches, for which he could in no way be answerable, stung him to the quick. The scorn of those young noblemen sunk deep into his heart. Friendless and alone, far away from his home, with no one to bestow upon him sympathy and kindness, his only alternative was to digest in silence their contempt. But the spirit which they displayed taught him to hate every pretension to superiority founded on wealth or birth. He felt himself their equal in every mental and moral gift, and he could perceive no ground for the distinction which they saw fit to make in the circumstance that they had inherited wealth and he had not. The reflections which this treatment gave rise to were undoubtedly the basis of those broad republican principles which he afterwards asserted. The sense of injustice and oppression is never so strong and deep-seated as in youth. The heart has not then been wrung by cares, and troubles, and hopes crushed. It expects every thing to conform to its intuitive sense of justice, and when it perceives the right trampled out by the wrong, the shock is more keenly felt than in after years, when the feelings have become callous by oft repeated agonies and injuries. It was an important lesson, and if he had learned no other while at this school he would not have left home and friends, and endured the scorn of his associates in vain. Thus early in life he imbibed and cherished that democratic doctrine, that there can be no claims to superiority not founded on merit. It was upon this principle, that in after years he made all those distinctions in his army, from the lowest subaltern, to him who wore the cross of the Legion of Honor.

Napoleon was of Italian parentage, and Italian was his vernacular tongue. He could scarcely speak a word of French when he entered the school. On this account he was more isolated than he would otherwise have been. But this circumstance may have been fortunate for him. He was looked upon as a plebeian and a foreigner, and he was of necessity driven to seek for society and amusement in books. Thus, at the outset of his career as a scholar, he was forced to adopt studious habits. Had he been received with open arms by his companions, and been petted as a brilliant young fellow, and formed loose and irregular habits, which are the almost inevitable result of excessive convivial entertainment, he might have come out a very ordinary man.

The course of studies in these military schools embraced an extensive range, including the languages and the abstract sciences. But the branches which received most special attention were history and the mathematics. In these Napoleon particularly excelled. By his indefatigable energy and studiousness he immediately rose to the front rank in his class, and at once secured for himself the reputation of a scholar among his teachers and his companions. He was indeed the plebeian and the foreigner; but he soon taught those about him, that in mental powers and accomplishments, the plebeian and the foreigner was far superior to them all, and that so far from poverty and obscurity being an impediment to mental development, it is in reality one of the most favoring circumstances, and that no one can become a scholar till he entertains the spirit which it induces.

Napoleon had a particular fondness for the mathematics. In this branch he excelled. And this is perhaps of all others most needful to the military man. The habits of mind which it cultivates, the precision of thought which is required in conducting the processes, the practice of confining the deductions to the legitimate results of our reasoning, the habit of admitting only known elements as the basis, the foundation on which we build the superstructure, is of infinite value in the training of a military commander. Those elements of mind which are required in conducting the various processes of the demonstration of a proposition in the mathematics, are the same as those employed in conducting a campaign. The elements of the reasoning alone differ. In the one case, they are first truths and the deductions therefrom. In the other, they are the varying facts and probabilities of the case, wherein the conclusions can never be more certain than the elements on which they are based. In that department of mathematics which embraces mechanics, civil engineering, and gunnery, the military man derives that practical knowledge which serves him in times of difficulty. Napoleon became a perfect master of these branches, and was never obliged to depend upon the knowledge of his subordinates in forming his great plans, for his own acquirements were superior to the experts of the army.

He delighted also in the study of history. The fabulous accounts of the origin of the nations recorded in profane history, and the veritable accounts of the daring spirits who figured in those early times, possessed for him indescribable charms. Plutarch's Lives were his delight. In reading these he was introduced to the choicest spirits that have ever lived, who acted their parts in the sunniest days of civilization, and who contributed, by their wisdom and bravery, to perpetuate the glory and renown of their respective nations. He was fond of heroic poetry, and read with the utmost avidity the great masters of the art. Even at this early age he wrote to his mother, " With my sword by my side and Homer in my pocket, I hope to carve my way through the world." The conduct of heroes and the fabled feats of gods, as they were conceived in the glowing imaginations of the poets, nursed in his bosom the spirit for lofty achievement. The enthusiasm with which he was inspired by his reading was manifest in all his thoughts and conversation. "Oh Napoleon," exclaimed the old Count Paoli, "you do not at all resemble the moderns. You belong only to the heroes of Plutarch."

He was at this period of his boyhood intensely studious. He was never eminent for his social qualities, though he was fond of the society of those who could converse on topics that interested him. He was always pointed and abrupt, and impatient with those who could not be equally so. On this account his companions never regarded him as a favorite, though his commanding abilities soon inspired respect. He was looked upon as too morose and secluded in disposition for a Frenchman. His habits of study contributed to this result. The usual boyish sports and amusements at this period had no attractions for him. He was rarely found upon the play ground. He preferred to spend his noon and evening hours in the library. The games of his companions could hardly rival the sports of gods and heroes of which he could there read, or the bloody encounters of contending hosts in their strife for victory, which he pursued with breathless interest. He not only mastered with surprising alacrity all the studies of his class, but he devoured with eagerness every thing upon history, politics and the practical arts that came in his way. He was thus enabled to commence life with the experience of all past ages at his command. The remembrance of failures and successes in other times, was the light by which his feet were guided in pursuing the uncertain paths to empire.

His studiousness and his laborious youth, bore their proper fruits. His habits became confirmed, and when in after years his position required of him intense devotion to business, it was easy and natural for him to apply himself, and accomplish almost superhuman labors. The power which he acquired of the undivided application of all his faculties to any subject, gave him the ability to make every question simple, and to decide with promptness in the most critical circumstances. All his vast energies of mind were by these means marshaled into the most complete subjection to his will, and like the battalions of his army they were under entire control. The acquisitions which he made during his school days must have been very great; for his career in the field commenced when he had scarcely arrived at the age of manhood, and the ardor with which he pursued it left little time in later years for study; and in whatever position he was placed he evinced unbounded knowledge. When he was made general-in-chief of the army, his associate consuls believed that he would be satisfied with the management of affairs in the field. But at their first meeting he convinced them that he could and would do every thing himself. Education, government, finance, were as familiar to him as the tactics of a campaign.

The remark has often been repeated that the child is father of the man. Those traits of character which we notice in the youth, are usually the ones which mark the conduct of mature years. It is related that Dr. Franklin, when a small boy and was assisting his father to salt a barrel of meat, asked him, when it was finished, if he could not ask a blessing on the whole barrel at once, and thus save the time of doing it every meal at the table. The mind that in tender years could devise so ingenious a plan for economizing time, is the same that in maturity taught us as a people the practice of economy, and has stamped it upon us as a national peculiarity. One of the playthings of Napoleon, when a child, was a little brass cannon weighing about thirty pounds, whose report probably sounded louder in his boyish ears than the whole park of heavy ordnance that played upon the field of Waterloo. We can fancy the great plans of battle and conquest which he executed with that single little cannon. His late biographer, Mr. Abbott, relates an incident that occurred while at the military school which marks his boyish propensities.

"The winter of 1774," says he, "was one of unusual severity. Large quantities of snow fell, which so completely blocked up the walks that the students at Brienne could find but little amusement without doors. Napoleon proposed that to beguile the weary hours, they should erect an extensive fortification of snow, with intrenchments and bastions, parapets, ravelins, and horn works. He had studied the science of fortification with the utmost diligence, and, under his superintendence, the works were conceived and executed according to the strictest rules of art. The power of his mind now displayed itself. No one thought of questioning the authority of Napoleon. He planned and directed, while a hundred busy hands, with unquestioning alacrity, obeyed his will. The works rapidly rose, and in such perfection of science as to attract crowds of the inhabitants of Brienne for their inspection. Napoleon divided the school into two armies, one being intrusted with the defense of the works, while the other composed the host of the besiegers. He took upon himself the command of both bodies, now heading the besiegers in the desperate assault, and now animating the besieged to an equally vigorous defense. For several weeks this mimic warfare continued, during which time many severe wounds were received on both sides. In the heat of the battle when the bullets of snow were flying thick and fast, one of the subordinate officers, venturing to disobey the commands of his general, Napoleon felled him to the earth, inflicting a wound which left a scar for life."

Napoleon remained five years at Brienne. It was the custom to send annually from the twelve provincial schools, three of the best scholars in each, to the military school at Paris. Napoleon was one of the three, from his school, selected for that purpose. From the fact that at the age of fifteen, the earliest age at which any are admitted to this, the highest military school of the nation, it is conclusive evidence of his great proficiency as a scholar. The selection of these candidates was made after a thorough examination. The following entry in the minutes of the examiners may be found in the records of the Minister of War:—"State of the king's scholars eligible to enter into service, or to pass to the school at Paris: Monsieur de Bonaparte (Napoleon) born 15th August, 1769; in height five feet six and a half inches; has finished his fourth season; of a good constitution, health excellent, character mild, honest, and grateful; conduct exemplary; has always distinguished himself by application to the mathematics; understands history and geography tolerably well; is indifferently skilled in merely ornamental studies, and in Latin, in which he has only finished his fourth course; would make an excellent sailor; deserves to be passed to the school at Paris."

At the early age of fifteen the plebeian and the foreigner had won his way to the highest military school of France. This school had been founded expressly for the sons of the nobility. It was furnished with every appliance for the ease and luxury of the young noblemen who were members of the institution. "Each of the three hundred young men assembled in this school had a servant to groom his horse, to polish his weapons, to brush his boots and to perform all other necessary menial services. The cadet reposed on a luxurious bed, and was fed with sumptuous viands." Such refinement as this was by no means congenial to the spirit and habits of Napoleon. Had they been offered him earlier in life, before his principles had become fixed by reading and meditation, and before those habits had become confirmed by necessity, he might have been won by them. But it was now too late. He regarded such luxury and effeminacy in a place where young men were to be trained for one of the most arduous and exposed professions known among men, in which hardships and privations are unceasingly encountered, as a shame and a disgrace to the nation. He yielded to none of the blandishments that were thrown about him, but established the same Spartan habits which he practiced in his more humble position at Brienne. He rose early and retired late. His maps, and charts, and scientific books were constantly before him. Here, as formerly, the mathematics were his favorite studies. "On one occasion, a mathematical problem of great difficulty having been proposed to the class, Napoleon in order to solve it secluded himself in his room seventy-two hours; and he solved the problem." I mention this circumstance, to illustrate the resolution and the will which characterized him as a scholar. This same unflinching, unwavering determination which he manifested in conquering difficult problems in the mathematics, characterized his efforts in solving many a knotty problem in his life's career. Many a day of darkness and difficulty dawned upon him, whose shadows were dispelled by that iron will.

While at this school he was introduced to some of the best society in Paris. The advantages which he derived from this source were very great. The student, ambitious of success, faithful to his tasks, deaf to the claims of society, shut up in his cell, and shut out from the world, is apt to neglect that very important part of his training which can only be acquired by mingling in the company of the educated and refined. The habit of managing a conversation with taste and ability, a becoming address, and ease and unaffected suavity of manners, are among the most important parts of an education, and no young man should ever make any claims to culture till he has acquired these. Napoleon was fond of elegant society, though he felt that he could only spend a limited portion of his time in it. He delighted in the company of the learned who were capable of conversing upon those vital questions which are felt in a nation's pulse, but he had no taste for dancing and cards, and the so called fashionable amusements. He believed that these were proper for those persons whose minds were not big enough to find entertainment in any thing higher, but for him they had no interest. In the circles in which he moved, he began to make his influence felt. Whoever came in contact with him, and saw the flash of his eye, and felt the fiery energy of his bearing, and heard the opinions which he had to advance upon any subject that chanced to be broached, never failed to perceive the superiority of his mind, and the immense extent of his attainments.*

* One evening, in the year 1790, there was a very brilliant party in the drawing-rooms of M. Neckar, the celebrated financier. His en-

The Abbé Raynal, one of the greatest philosophers of the age, was among the first to perceive and recognize the mature reflections and great acquire-

---

tertainments, embellished by the presence, as the presiding genius, of his distinguished daughter, Madame de Staël, were brilliant in the extreme, assembling all the noted gentlemen and ladies in the metropolis. On the occasion to which we refer, the magnificent saloon was filled with men who had attained the highest eminence in literature and science, or who, in those troubled times, had ascended to posts of honor and influence in the state. Mirabeau was there, with his lofty brow and thunder tones, proud of his very ugliness. Talleyrand moved majestically through the halls, conspicuous for his gigantic proportions and courtly bearing. Lafayette, rendered glorious as the friend of Washington, and his companion in arms, had gathered around him a group of congenial spirits. In the embrasure of a window sat Madame de Staël. By the brilliancy of her conversational powers she had attracted to her side St. Just, who afterwards obtained such sanguinary notoriety; Malesherbes, the eloquent and intrepid advocate of royalty; Lalande, the venerable astronomer; Marmontel and Lagrange, illustrious mathematicians, and others whose fame was circulating through Europe. In one corner stood the celebrated Alfieri, reciting with almost maniacal gesticulation his own poetry to a group of ladies. The grave and philosophical Neckar was the center of another group of care-worn statesmen, discussing the rising perils of the times. It was an assemblage of all which Paris could afford of brilliance in rank, talent, or station. About the middle of the evening, Josephine, the beautiful, but then neglected wife of M. Beauharnais, was announced, accompanied by her little son Eugène. Madame de Genelis soon made her appearance, attended by the brother of the king; and, conscious of her intellectual dignity, floated through that sea of brilliance recognized wherever she approached by the abundance of perfumery which her dress exhaled. Madame Campan, the friend and companion of Marie Antoinette, and other ladies and gentlemen of the court, were introduced, and the party now consisted of a truly remarkable

ments of Napoleon; and though but a boy the Abbé delighted in his company, and often invited him to his table, where he met many of the leading literary

---

assemblage of distinguished men and women. Parisian gayety seemed to banish all thoughts of the troubles of the times, and the hours were surrendered to unrestrained hilarity. Servants were gliding through the throng, bearing a profusion of refreshments, consisting of delicacies gathered from all quarters of the globe.

As the hour of midnight approached, there was a lull in the buzz of conversation, and the guests gathered in silent groups to listen to a musical entertainment. Madame de Staël took her seat at the piano, while Josephine prepared to accompany her with the harp. They both were performers of singular excellence, and the whole assembly was hushed in expectation. Just as they had commenced the first notes of a charming duet, the door of the saloon was thrown open, and two new guests entered the apartment. The one was an elderly gentleman of very venerable aspect and dressed in the extreme of simplicity. The other was a young man, very small, pale, and slender. The elderly gentleman was immediately recognized by all as the Abbé Raynal, one of the most distinguished philosophers of France; but no one knew the pale, slender, fragile youth who accompanied him. They both, that they might not interrupt the music, silently took seats near the door. As soon as the performance was ended, and the ladies had received those compliments which their skill and taste elicited, the Abbé approached Madame de Staël, accompanied by his young protégé, and introduced him as Monsieur Napoleon Bonaparte. Bonaparte! that name which has since filled the world, was then plebeian and unknown, and upon its utterance many of the proud aristocrats in that assembly shrugged their shoulders, and turned contemptuously away to their conversation and amusement. Madame de Staël had an almost instinctive perception of the presence of genius. Her attention was instantly arrested by the few remarks with which Napoleon addressed her. They were soon engaged in very animated conversation. Josephine and several other ladies joined them. The group grew

men of the metropolis. This afforded him a rare opportunity for improvement, and one to which boys of his age are not often admitted. He heard the

---

larger and larger as the gentlemen began to gather round the increasing circle. "Who is that young man who thus suddenly has gathered such a group about him?" the proud Alfieri condescended to ask of the Abbé Raynal. "He is," replied the Abbé, "a protégé of mine, and a young man of very extraordinary talent. He is very industrious, well read, and has made remarkable attainments in history, mathematics, and all military science." Mirabeau came stalking across the room, lured by curiosity to see what could be the source of the general attraction. "Come here! come here!" said Madame de Staël with a smile, and in an undertone. "We have found a little great man. I will introduce him to you, for I know you are fond of men of genius." Mirabeau very graciously shook hands with Napoleon and entered into conversation with the untitled young man without assuming any airs of superiority. A group of distinguished men now gathered about them, and the conversation became in some degree general. The Bishop of Autun commended Fox and Sheridan for having asserted that the French army, by refusing to obey the orders of their superiors to fire upon the populace, had set a glorious example to all the armies of Europe; because, by so doing, they had shown that men by becoming soldiers did not cease to be citizens.

"Excuse me, my lord," exclaimed Napoleon, in tones of earnestness that arrested general attention, "if I venture to interrupt you; but as I am an officer I must claim the privilege of expressing my sentiments. It is true that I am very young, and it may appear presumptuous in me to address so many distinguished men; but during the last three years I have paid intense attention to our political troubles. I see with sorrow the state of our country; I will incur censure rather than pass unnoticed principles which are not only unsound, but which are subversive of all government. As much as any one I desire to see all abuses, antiquated privileges, and usurped rights annulled. Nay! as I am at the commencement of my career, it will be my best policy, as

best conversation which the capital afforded. He made the personal acquaintance of those men who were to guide the thought of the nation, and whose

well as my duty, to support the progress of popular institutions, and to promote reform in every branch of the public administration. But as in the last twelve months I have witnessed repeated alarming popular disturbances, and have seen our best men divided into factions which threaten to be irreconcilable, I sincerely believe that now, *more than ever*, a strict discipline in the army is absolutely necessary for the safety of our constitutional government, and for the maintenance of order. Nay! if our troops are not compelled unhesitatingly to obey the commands of the executive, we shall be exposed to the blind fury of democratic passions, which will render France the most miserable country on the globe. The ministry may be assured that, if the daily increasing arrogance of the Parisian mob is not repressed by a strong arm, and social order rigidly maintained, we shall see not only this capital, but every other city in France thrown into a state of indescribable anarchy, while the real friends of liberty, the enlightened patriots, now working for the best good of our country, will sink beneath a set of demagogues, who, with louder outcries for freedom on their tongues, will be, in reality, but a horde of savages worse than the Neros of old."

These emphatic sentences, uttered by Napoleon with an air of authority which seemed natural to the youthful speaker, caused a profound sensation. For a moment there was a perfect silence in the group, and every eye was riveted on the pale and marble cheek of Napoleon. Neckar and Lafayette listened with evident uneasiness to his bold and weighty sentiments as if conscious of the perils which his words so forcibly portrayed. Mirabeau nodded once or twice significantly to Talleyrand, seeming thus to say, "That is exactly the truth." Some turned upon their heels, exasperated at this fearless avowal of hostility to democratic progress. Alfieri, one of the proudest of aristocrats, could hardly restrain his delight, and gazed with amazement upon the intrepid young man. "Condorcet," says an eye-

literary productions "future generations will not willingly let die." He became familiar with the correct opinions of the actors in the scenes in that great drama which had already begun.

Napoleon remained but one year in the military school at Paris. As the result of his first examination he was recommended for promotion, and was consequently appointed an officer in the French army at the early age of sixteen. The mathematical section of the examination was conducted by La Place, the author of the Mécanique Céleste. To come out successful before such an examiner, was indeed no ordinary honor. In history, Monsieur Karruglion, after listening with admiration to his answers, and the elucidations which he gave of the various topics which were broached, wrote in the

---

witness, "nearly made me cry out by the squeeze which he gave my hand at every sentence uttered by the pale, slender, youthful speaker." The young Napoleon, then but twenty-one years of age, thus suddenly became the most prominent individual in that whole assembly. Whereever he moved, many eyes followed him. He had none of the airs of a man of fashion. He made no attempts at displays of gallantry. A peaceful melancholy seemed to overshadow him, as, with an abstracted air, he passed through the glittering throng, without being in the slightest degree dazzled by its brilliance. The good old Abbé Raynal appeared quite enraptured in witnessing this triumph of his young protégé.—*Abbott's Napoleon*, vol. i., page 36.—*Narrative communicated to Chambers' Edinburg Journal by an Italian gentleman who was present at the interview at M. Neckar's.*

records after the entry of Napoleon's name, "A Corsican by character and by birth. This young man will distinguish himself in the world if fortune favors." He might have written with greater propriety, "This young man will distinguish himself whether fortune favors or not." He had thus far in life been successful at every point, and he had not shared very bountifully in fortune's favors, and in after years he never left any thing for fortune to do for him. That qualifying phrase might have been very appropriately placed after the names of some young men, but it stands with an ill grace after the signature of Napoleon Bonaparte.

At this point closes the boyhood of Napoleon. He is no longer a scholar of fortune, fighting his way up from obscurity, but a lieutenant in that army of Frenchmen whose glory has sounded through the world. He now lays aside the humble garb of the student, and assumes the military costume of an officer, the heavy boots, the cocked hat, the buttoned coat and epaulettes. There was much in the position to which Napoleon had now attained to flatter the pride and satisfy the ambition of a youth of seventeen, and it is feared that there are few, who would not have considered their education complete, that the object of their strife was now attained, and that they might give themselves up to the ease and enjoyment which their position as officers would yield. But this honor was far from satisfying the ambition of Napoleon. His habits of study had been laborious and austere, he labored with indefatigable zeal, he had made vast acquirements, he was petted and flattered, and his company was sought by some of the first literary men in the world. But there was yet more that he wished to learn, and when he was ordered with his regiment to Lyons, no sooner were the troops quartered, than he sought out a room where he would be secure from interruption, and renewed those habits of laborious study which he had been accustomed to while at school. Instead of parading the streets to show off his plume and his epaulettes to the young and the admiring, he bent as steadily to his tasks as he had done previous to his promotion.

The education of Napoleon teaches the world one useful lesson, one which our youth especially need to learn. We are apt in pursuing a course of study to dally and procrastinate. Some one has said that "man is naturally indolent, as lazy as he can be." At no time in life do we yield so readily to ease as during the period of mental and physical growth, and this is the time usually allotted to study. Tasks to be wrought out by brain work, look formidable, and we often shrink from them on very slight pretexts. Not so with Napoleon. He shrunk from no tasks, he left no duty undone, and he has shown the world the virtue of working while the day lasts. Had Napoleon known his destiny from the outset, he could not have labored more faithfully in preparation for its accomplishment. This example speaks to every one who hopes to be a leader in the world, "Go and do thou likewise."

In concluding this survey of the boyhood of Napoleon, there are some reflections which naturally flow from the subject that may be of interest to us as teachers who have much yet to learn, and whose business it is to direct the education of others. If the mariner on an unknown sea can pick up the chart of a fellow navigator who sailed those seas before him, he feels a degree of assurance that he can go forward in his voyage in safety. The education of Napoleon was a success. It is not often that we know the history of one so triumphant. There are some important lessons to be drawn from it.

From the beginning the probabilities of success were all against him. He was a poor boy, an orphan, and a foreigner, unable to speak the French language, and without influential friends to advocate his cause. There were only twelve of the military schools in a population of thirty millions. The number of applicants would naturally be very great, and the sons of the rich and powerful would be most likely to succed in obtaining the place. The same motives and influences would operate against his advancement to the school at Paris, where the difficulties would be still greater on account of the aristocratic and exclusive style in which it was established. But notwithstanding the apparent obstacles that stood in his way, he invariably triumphed over them, and the merit of his triumphs is due to himself. He won his way from one position to another because he had first deserved the promotions. He was sent from the humble island of Corsica to the school at Brienne, because the culture he had already acquired attracted the attention of the governor and convinced him that the boy would honor the place. Again, he is selected as one of the three from among all his associates for a place in the highest school at Paris; and here he is promoted because of his great proficiency in his studies, and the unusual maturity of his mind. When we become familiar with his history during those five years, we feel satisfied that if the selection were made according to merit, the choice wisely fell upon Napoleon. At the age of fifteen, that very critical period in the life of youth, when most boys are "sowing their wild oats," we find him the companion of philosophers and sages. Without any other influence to recommend him or secure an introduction to the company of the learned, than that which his own intelligence had created for him, he wins his way to the best of French society. A foreigner and of obscure birth though he be, and in the midst of the nobility who are ever inclined to look upon those beneath them with contempt, he is welcomed with open hands to their circles, because his good sense and great learning made him the light and ornament of any society which he chose to grace. And finally, at an age when most young men are thinking about beginning their education, he is examined by some of the first scholars that the world has ever produced, is pronounced a proficient, and is recommended for appointment as an officer in the army. We feel satisfied, when we read this account, that there was no favoritism, or under current influence to which he owed his advancement,—for the poor boy had no means of securing such interests in his behalf,—but that he received his just deserts.

In this simple recital of the fortunes of this obscure boy, we witness the happy issue of a faithful discharge of duty. It is the most complete and triumphant illustration of the success which follows unremitting studiousness that we have on record. He is noted for being a bright boy, because he has improved the feeble talents of childhood, and has got a little more knowledge than other boys of his age. He moves among his fellow students, inspiring their veneration for him as a prodigy of learning, because he toiled when they slept, and he meditated when they squandered time. He acquired the respect and friendship of his superiors in knowledge and years, because he had diligently pursued those researches in which well cultivated minds delight. And those habits of study and toil which we see rewarded with success in the boyhood of Napoleon, are the habits that will be rewarded with success in any boy of fair ability. There is no well directed exertion which does not sooner or later bear its proper fruits. This law of toil and recompense holds good in the physical world, in business, but especially is its veracity vindicated in the history of distinguished scholarship. There is no man of ordinary mental endowments, who can possibly fail of becoming eminent as a scholar, if he puts forth eminent exertions.

We hear much about the genius of Napoleon, and we are treated to flaming dissertations on this undetermined specimen of the human species, which naturalists are unable to classify, whose creation was looked upon as a miracle of creative power, and which was especially demanded by the French nation, as though he had come upon this earth,

"Summoned direct from chaos and old night,
By Jove's power fledged, and ready for the flight."

But when we become familiar with his boyhood, the genius of Napoleon ceases to be a mystery. We wonder from whence his power and his success, but the wonder is how the result could have been otherwise. The fact about the genius of Napoleon is simply this: he possessed by nature good common sense, an unusual degree of physical and mental endurance, and an insatiable ambition. And only this. He seemed to think* and never tire, to labor† and

* It was nearly midnight when Napoleon, accompanied by Josephine, entered the darkened streets of Paris on his return from Vienna. He drove directly to the Tuilleries, and ascended the stairs, with hasty strides, to his cabinet. Without undressing, or even throwing himself upon a couch for a moment of repose, he sent for the Minister of Finance. The whole of the remainder of the night was passed in a rigid examination of the state of the bank of France. The eagle eye of the emperor immediately penetrated the labyrinth of confusion in which its concerns were involved. The next day at eleven o'clock the whole Council of Finance was assembled. Napoleon kept them incessantly occupied during an uninterrupted session of nine hours. Thus energetically, without allowing himself a moment for repose, he entered upon a series of labors unparalleled in the history of mankind.—*Abbott's Napoleon*, vol. i., page 487.

† The miseries of his progress in Egypt were extreme. The air is crowded with pestiferous insects; the glare of the sand weakens most men's eyes, and blinds many; water is scarce and bad; and the country has been swept clean of man, beast, and vegetable. Under this torture even the gallant spirits of such men as Murat and Lannes could not sustain themselves; they trod their cockades in the sand.

never be weary. These elements of character secured him success in every step of his career, from early boyhood to the last of his great deeds. There is no mystery about his wonderful fortune; for there is not a position in the whole course of his life, to which, if we become acquainted with the steps that led him to it, we must not acknowledge he was above all others the best entitled. His knowledge, his energy, and his perseverance so far excelled those who might be considered to come in competition with him, that the scale at once turns in favor of Napoleon, and there is no propriety in questioning the decision.

Of the moral and religious training of Napoleon, we know but little. Indeed I am inclined to the opinion that he never had much. We know that he had a kind mother, who cherished with masculine austerity, probity, and honor, and virtue. "Left

---

The common soldiers asked with angry murmurs if it was here the general designed to give them their seven acres? He alone was superior to all evils. Such was the happy temperament of his frame that while others, after having rid themselves of their usual dress, were still suffused in perpetual floods of perspiration, and the hardiest found it necessary to give two or three hours every mid-day to sleep, Napoleon altered nothing; wore his uniform buttoned up as at Paris; never showed one bead of sweat on his brow, nor thought of repose except to lie down in his cloak the last at night and start up the first in the morning.—*Lockhart's Life of Napoleon*, vol. i., page 116.

without a guide, without support," says Napoleon, "my mother was obliged to take the direction of affairs upon herself. But the task was not above her strength. She managed every thing, provided for every thing, with a prudence which could neither have been expected from her sex nor from her age. Ah, what a woman! Where shall we look for her equal? She watched over us with a solicitude unexampled. Every low sentiment, every ungenerous affection, was discouraged and discarded. She suffered nothing but that which was grand and elevated to take root in our youthful understandings. She abhorred falsehood, and would not tolerate the slightest acts of disobedience. None of our faults were overlooked. Losses, privations, fatigue, had no effect upon her. She had the energy of a man combined with the gentleness and delicacy of a woman." During the time that he was at the military schools, France had no religion. The French people worshiped at the shrine of base Indulgence under the name of Liberty. The Sabbath was abolished and the Bible burned, and every tenth day was appointed by the government as a day of rest. The guillotine was in active operation, and the blood of her best patriots flowed unceasingly from it. The king was sent to the block. Anarchy was rampant. Disorder reigned supreme. Amid all this confusion, Napoleon remained steady at his tasks, and did not suffer this frenzy to disturb the equanimity of his mind or bate one tittle of his devotion to his studies; and amid the corruptions of that corrupt age he escaped unstained. His mother's instructions in his youth were the guiding principles of his manhood. He had an intuitive sense of honor and justice, upon which he acted.

It is good to trace the life of one who has been successful. It is instructive to go back to boyhood, and examine the education and habits which serve as the foundation stones on which the superstructure is built. Demosthenes has very pointedly observed, "that in common life success is the greatest good, and that the next is conduct, without which the first must be of short continuance." It is certainly the best fortune for which we can hope, to be successful in our efforts. Often, as the world goes, the good is left to obscurity and the undeserving triumphs. But it is still a source of satisfaction to have the assurance in one's own breast that he has deserved success. It serves to cultivate a good companionship with self. It enables us to merit our own esteem and confidence. But he who never makes one honest effort, and feels no enkindling aspiration that can inspire a hope, who is satisfied to live without success and without deserving it, is of all men the most brutish and miserable. He neither enjoys the applause of his fellow-men nor of himself. Few men have been so successful as Napoleon. His was indeed a brilliant career. His triumphs in the cabinet and in the field, are among the most remarkable examples of the sublime in action. The iron will of that one man aroused all Europe in arms to oppose him, and in the terrible struggles which he inspired is seen the "compacted might of genius." But there are other fields for triumphs than those of war; and whenever we would encourage the youthful mind to put forth effort in preparation for triumphs, we can point with pride and confidence to the Boyhood of the humble Corsican

LECTURE III.

THE POWER OF SPOKEN THOUGHT.

MANY years ago, the streets of London were filled with people, wending their way to Kensington Common. The gathering multitudes were composed of a motley throng from every class in that crowded city. The rich and the poor, the philosopher and the sweating mechanic, the poet and the street singer, proud lords and gay ladies, peers of the realm and ministers of state,—all eager and anxious, were there. The trees and fences, and stages built for the purpose, and chariot wheels, and the backs of gaily caparisoned horses, were crowded with the living throng. The eager countenances of these waiting thousands betokened some great occasion. The pride of dress and the beauty of countenance added gayety to the scene. Yet there was no sound of martial music or rolling drum. There were no soldiers with gay plumes and epaulets, and red coats and glistening bayonets. There were no "white-winged" tents; no amphitheater as at ancient Rome, where the wretched captive chiefs were brutally murdered in gladiatorial contests for the sport of a Roman holiday. This throng were attracted by no motives like these. They had come to hear a plain man preach. They had come to hear Whitefield preach.

Patiently they stand in the open field, in God's first temple, whose only canopy is the blue vault above, whose inlaid floor is the bright green earth, and encounter the press and the crowd, to hear the accents from the lips of him who was thought unworthy of gorgeous churches, where the worshipers recline upon velvet cushions, and where the mellow light streams through richly stained windows. They had come to hear a very common subject, but from the lips of no ordinary man. The words from his tongue reach every ear, touch every heart. What is in his countenance is reflected in theirs. Now indignation burns on every lip. Anon their streaming eyes attest the violence of their emotions. And now hope smiles through their tears. Thus he sways that vast assembly to and fro upon the stormy waves of his eloquence. It is not alone the tender-hearted girl that weeps, but the stout heart shares unrestrained the feeling which moves prince and peasant alike. That emotion that comes unbidden, that susceptibility which nature has given all her children, responds to the touch of that master spirit. And the voice of an eternal Providence, which for a time infidelity may be deaf to, and which debauchery and crime may drown, must still be heard.

The power of Mr. Whitefield's preaching was very great. It is unusual that we meet with an exhibition of the force and attractions of eloquence, and of its despotic power over every class of mind and character, such as was displayed by this wonderful man. It illustrates the influence which spoken thought is capable of effecting. In general, it is far superior to written thought. If a speech of unusual interest has been delivered on some public occasion, the report of that speech, when published in the journals of the day, will attract attention, when an article of equal interest, and penned with the greatest care, is passed by without notice.

The reason of this preference is obvious. We are fond of identifying the thoughts with the speaker who uttered them, and the occasion which called them forth. Abstract thought, unaccompanied with the incidents of its origin and promulgation, has few attractions except for those who are fond of pure intellections. The laws of God, when written upon tables of stone, were dead and powerless. The nations soon fell back into idolatry; they became oblivious to every element of religious feeling, and worshiped and served the creature more than the

Creator. But when God in the personation of Jesus Christ came upon earth, and in the likeness of man, "spake as never man spake," and went about doing good, then the will of our Maker became a living power, before which the pride of philosophy and the blindness of superstition yielded, and gave place to religion pure and undefiled. "It was," says Macaulay, "before Deity embodied in human form, walking among men, partaking of their infirmities, leaning on their bosoms, weeping over their graves, slumbering in their mangers, bleeding on the cross, that the prejudices of the Academy, and the pride of the Portico, and the fasces of the lictor and the swords of thirty legions were humbled in the dust."

The feeling which inspires the orator, is the most exalted of any that sways the bosom of man. In the moment of sublime conception and overwhelming emotion, he feels, in common with his hearers, more than words can express. At such a moment words become powerless, and feeling, rising above such poor exponents of thought, reigns supreme. This is the sublime. For "the sublime," says Longinus, "not only persuades, but even throws an audience into transports. In most cases it is wholly in our own power to resist or to yield to persuasion. But the sublime, endued with strength irresistible, strikes down and triumphs over every hearer. The sublime when seasonably addressed, with the rapid force of lightning has borne down all before it, and shown at one stroke the compacted might of genius."

The faculties which eloquence calls into exercise are the most exalted of which a human soul is possessed. Reason, imagination, taste,—those powers that are last developed, and which are the crowning graces of the mind,—are the agencies of the orator. But even these, without the inspiration of a spirit burning with an ardent purpose, are powerless. These faculties must arouse corresponding ones in the minds of those who are addressed. The thoughts which are in the spirit of one man, must be transferred to the bosoms of other men. The electric chords which vibrate so musically in the breast of the speaker must telegraph to those addressed. The flashing eye, the burning lip, the beating heart, between speaker and hearer must be reciprocal.

Rhetoricians have attempted to define eloquence. But the most truthful and refined definition can have little relevancy to him who has not felt it. Dr. Campbell defines it as "that art by which the discourse is adapted to its end; and that all the ends of speaking are reducible to four; every speech being intended to enlighten the understanding, to please the imagination, to move the passions, or to influence the will." This is the definition of a critic, rather than that of a master of the art. It is eloquence adroitly quartered and carefully dissected. It is a definition which may be abstractly appreciated but one which would convey no idea to him who had never felt it. Quintilian says that eloquence is "*Scientia bene dicendi*," the art of speaking well, which is as dull and lifeless as it is brief. This is also the definition of a critic. But Cicero says, "*Optimus orator qui dicendo, animos audientium, et docet, et delectat, et permovet*"—he is the best orator who in speaking, both teaches, and delights, and greatly moves the minds of his auditory. This is the definition of one who has felt all that he describes, who has portrayed the impression drawn from his own consciousness. It was inspired by the remembrance of stirring scenes in which he had been a leading actor; the courts of justice where he had plead, the struggles of the commonwealth for life when surrounded by conspirators, and the senate house where Cæsar fell.

But there is no definition, however pointed or life-like, that can convey any adequate idea. The best of them are merely formulæ, to which he who has heard and felt may refer his impressions. When Washington, after having led the feeble army of his country for eight long years, struggling on against every disheartening circumstance, and hoping even against hope, at last had triumphed over his open foes in the field, and the more dangerous ones who in secret were plotting his overthrow, when peace at length came, and he felt that his services were no longer needed, he went to the hall of Congress to deliver up his sword. He saw about him those who had stood by him with their counsels through many dark and troublous days. With a voice faltering with emotion at the remembrance of the past, he spoke those sublime and pathetic words that are dear to every lover of his country. But when he came to take leave of his officers, those who had been his companions in arms, who had shared with him the privations of the camp and the carnage of the battle field, and had been faithful to the last, the struggling emotions quivered on his lips; he could not speak, his feelings were too strong for utterance, and he pressed the hand of each in silence and departed. This was eloquence. It was speaking without speaking. It was the height of the sublime.

But one month from the time Bossuet pronounced his funeral oration over the corpse of the royal mother, he was called to perform the same solemn rite over the young and beautiful Princess Henrietta, "so highly stationed, so greatly gifted, so widely admired, and so generally loved. The idol of the world! The pride of her august family! The delight of all who approached her!" As he described the short but brilliant career of the princess, every heart was borne along upon the full tide of his words. But the interest which the successive events of her life excited, when portrayed in the lovely light of his well-known eloquence, only served to make the catastrophe to which he was approaching more terrible, and as he came to utter that passage, "when like a peal of thunder, the dreadful words—'Henrietta is dying—Henrietta is dead,'—burst upon us, nothing was discernible but grief, despair, and the image of death;" the effect was overwhelming; the whole audience rose from their seats, and Bossuet himself was so much affected that for some moments he was unable to speak.

It is only by experience in those emotions which eloquence is capable of producing that we can form any conception of its nature. He who has felt it, and has a heart to appreciate it, alone has the key that unlocks the mystery of its power. There are certain tones of the voice that have a wonderful effect upon the human soul. It is said that the singing of the Marseilles Hymn in the streets of Paris brought on the French Revolution. Those electric tones which thrilled the nerves of the young Frenchman, which filled his heart with desire for glory, which fired his passions with hatred and revenge for his oppressors, and which inspired a love for liberty and equal rights, nerved his soul to fight in their defense—to bare his bosom to that terrible death-storm that swept the continent of Europe—and with his dying breath exclaim—

"Ye sons of France, awake to glory!"

The speaker is but the exponent of the thoughts and feelings of those whom he addresses. If his feelings are thoroughly aroused, if he is fully in earnest, he will be likely to imbue the breasts of his hearers with the emotions of his own heart. "A clergyman of our country states that he once told an affecting incident to Mr. Whitefield, relating it, however, with but the ordinary feeling and beauty of a passing conversation; when afterward, on hearing Whitefield preach, up came his own story, narrated by the preacher in the pulpit with such native pathos and power that the clergyman himself, who had furnished Whitefield with the dry bones of illustration, found himself weeping like a child."*

It is interesting to observe with what varied effect different men may pronounce the same sentence. Every school-boy has read how Demosthenes, after having been unsuccessful in his first attempt at public speaking, retiring from the assembly in despair, was

* Todd's "Girl at School," page 141.

met by a friend who spoke to him some encouraging words, and requesting him to recite a few sentences of a familiar poet, repeated them in tones so distinct, and with such force of utterance, that Demosthenes could not believe it the same passage.

There are some public speakers who come before us and read beautifully written pieces. The argument is well planned, and constructed upon sound principles. The reasoning is perfectly accurate. The imagery is beautifully wrought, and introduced where Archbishop Whately himself would approve. Combined, it is a perfect piece, and its delivery is well toned. And yet, faultless as it is, it fails to attract attention. No interest is excited. The speaker does not enlist our sympathies. We strive in vain to accompany him upon the velvet lawn he treads. The monotony induces stupor. It is by an effort that we arouse to a sense of the proprieties of the occasion, and we are relieved when the speaker closes his discourse,

"So coldly sweet, so deadly fair."

The contrast is agreeable when we are brought into sympathy with one who inspires us with a fervor of feeling which we can not resist. His words come warm from a feeling heart. He is full of passion as well as argument and imagery. He not only teaches, but he greatly moves the minds of his hearers. That feeling which he possesses he transfers to them. Our minds are taken captive; we hear every word; we watch every action; we laugh when he laughs; we weep when he weeps. We feel no fatigue, no weariness, and we regret when he is through that he has no more to say.

Thought in the hands of such a man has life and power. We feel in his presence as though he were the ruling spirit; we realize the value of his thoughts as he does himself. But it often happens that the impression is felt among those who are endeavoring to listen, that the speaker himself is not interested in what he is saying, that he does not appreciate the force of his own words, and leaves it doubtful whether he believes them. It is related that a farmer in the country once had a friend visiting him from the city, and on the Sabbath took him to church with him. When they were at home again and seated by the fire, the old man, fond of having his minister praised, asked his guest how he liked the preaching. The friend replied, "tolerably well." The old man, piqued at the slur cast upon the minister, turned with some warmth and inquired, "Did he not tell the truth?" "Yes," answered his friend, "he told the truth, and he would have told the truth had he got up and declared all the forenoon that his name was John."

The minister of the gospel has, perhaps, of all other classes of public speakers, the most difficulties and discouraging circumstances to encounter. Dr. Campbell, in his Philosophy of Rhetoric, lays down this general principle: "that the more mixed the auditory, the greater is the difficulty of speaking with effect; and that we may justly reckon a Christian congregation in a populous and flourishing city, where there is a great variety in rank and education, of all audiences the most promiscuous." When the Spirit of God moves the heart of the preacher of the gospel, when he fully appreciates the greatness of his calling, when he feels the stirring nature of the message which he is delegated to proclaim to the world, and the consequences which must result from his labors, there can be no mission on earth more inspiring. But this inspiration does not always operate upon the followers of the humble fishermen. The ministry are human, and are subject to the weaknesses and depressions of spirit that are incident to us all; and the trials and difficulties which they have to encounter often press upon them with overwhelming power. Mr. Giles, in his essay on the pulpit, observes that "the necessity of periodical composition is, in itself alone, no slight aggravation of ministerial toil. Who, that has ever experienced the necessity of stated intellectual preparation, will not understand this? The head may be heavy with bodily disease, or the heart sick with inward grief; the pen may tremble in the hand, and the eye grow dim with sorrow; but the shadow is already upon his imagination and the weekly sermon must be ready. Alas! the tale of brick must be forthcoming, and often there is not wherewith to make it."

If the preacher of the gospel is highly educated, his task may seem to be easy. But even education acts as a clog upon the passions. Protracted contemplation wears the brain, and eats away upon the vital energies. Intense application of the mental faculties sometimes operates to smother emotion, and to deaden the sympathies. The fastidious cultivation of the style may depress the devotional affections. Of the other professions in which public speaking forms a part of the duties, there are circumstances which render the labor less arduous and trying. The pleader at the bar has only a bench of judges, or a jury of twelve men to address, whose characters he may individually study, whose prejudices he may appeal to, whose vanity he may flatter, and whose sympathies he may enlist. The circumstances of the case awaken interest, and the anxiety of the client spurs him on to exertion. When the excitement of a term of court is over, which has served to quicken his powers, he enjoys periods of relaxation from the drudgery of public speaking. The legislator has a body of equals before whom he speaks, who can readily apprehend and digest his opinions, and whose attention he can easily secure. The excitement of debate is admirably fitted to arouse his talents, and draw forth the fires of eloquence. Often he knows not when he is to speak till the emergency is upon him, and the principles of his party, with which he is at all times familiar, demand his aid.

But whatever may be the character of the audience, the subject of discourse, or the circumstances of the speaker himself, it is a matter of the first importance that he should thoroughly feel and understand what he has to say. For we always conclude, whether it be the minister of the gospel or the member of Congress, the lawyer or the lecturer, if he fails to impress his hearers, that the divinity does not move in his own soul. It is necessary for a speaker to realize fully the importance of what he has to communicate, to be desirous that the minds of his hearers may be precisely in that state in which he finds his own. When he can open his discourse with this feeling, he may consider it as a sure indication that he is to succeed, that he will in some way reach their hearts with his words. But there are too many men who attempt to perform the offices of public speaking, like the character whom

Shakspeare describes, "Who speaks an infinite deal of nothing, more than any man in all Venice. His reasons are as two grains of wheat hid in two bushels of chaff; you shall seek all day ere you find them; and when you have them they are not worth the search."

He who would influence men and make them of his mind, in these days so characterized by hurry and commotion, of point blank directness and lightning speed, must speak from a full heart. He must pour forth his words as though he meant men should believe them. The hearer expects this, and he will not be induced to take his attention from those thoughts which haunt his brain, unless the speaker presents him something of sufficient importance to recall him from wandering meditations. Listlessness and inattention on the part of the hearer speak in a language no less audible than words,

"If you would have me weep, begin the strain."*

It has often been remarked, that it is not the speaker whose opinions are most weighty, or whose speech has most intrinsic merit, that always produces the greatest influence. It is an observation that is

* "———Si vis me flere, dolendum est
Primum ipse tibi."

often repeated, that if Mr. A's address could have been delivered by Mr. B, it would have been excellent. There is a happy combination of gifts which seem to fit some men to be eloquent. We listen with admiration to whatever they have to say, if it be but a simple announcement. If we seek for the secret of their skill, we must find it, if at all, in our emotional nature. Eloquence is the work of the emotions. A thought, to deserve the name of being eloquent, must originate in emotion and must terminate in emotion. The voice is the agency by which this effect is produced. The tones of the voice, though they do not express words, are still capable of being understood, and of producing an effect upon the mind. Every person in this assembly might speak in a language unknown to the others; and yet we could readily distinguish whether it were in joy or anger. A screech of anguish or of fear causes every one to start. The infant too young to talk, will make its wants and feelings known quite as successfully by its varying tones of voice,—from those of unbounded pleasure to uncontrollable grief,—as it can in later years by the use of words.

These tones constitute the language of emotion. It is by means of these that feelings of extreme delight or anguish are made known. The man who is overjoyed does not give utterance to his feelings in words, but he bursts forth in the full tones of laughter. Whereas he who is suffering intense pain expresses it by moans and weeping. This language of the emotions is easily communicated. We may hear a person laugh. He laughs from a soul full of the risible emotion; and although we know not the occasion of his joy, yet we feel like laughing too. On the contrary, we always feel sad when we approach the bed of a sick person and hear the voice of anguish from the sufferer. In the skillful use of these tones of emotion lies the secret of the orator's power.

Perhaps no man ever understood the compass and expressiveness of the human voice better than David Garrick. His quick, intuitive spirit had threaded all the secret mazes and windings of the human heart. And by those silver tones of his, as by the wand of the magician, he could "make the past present, and the distant near." He could take the minds of men and lead them on in what track he would. It was true he was an actor, and spoke the thoughts of others. Yet it was praise enough for him, that he drew from those productions which graced the stage, sparks of genius, which to the reader's eye would have ever remained unappreciated. In him was seen the character which he represented, in greater grandeur and majesty than it had ever appeared to the poet's eye rolling in its finest frenzy. The delighted author saw his thoughts take shapes which he had never himself fully realized. The verse of Shakspeare was his delight. And those beautiful and majestic words would never have fallen upon the ear with half their sweetness and their power, had it not been for the tongue of Garrick. And yet he once declared that he would give a hundred pounds, if he could only speak the word "Oh!" as Whitefield did. In this he was conscious of his inability. The training and course of thought of the two had been widely different. Garrick was indeed familiar with all the horrors of life. He could feel and act and express the agony and madness of Lear, the jealousy of Othello, the writhings of Macbeth under the consciousness of guilt, and the imperial majesty of Cæsar. But the imagination of Whitefield had traveled on beyond the grave. He had not only contemplated the passions which rend the bosom while living, and the agonies and struggles of the death scene, but he could in fancy accompany the soul to its destiny in the eternity beyond. In view of the tortures of the lost, which were to him ever present realities, he could but warn the living in exclamations deep-mouthed and awful.

Few men of modern times have produced so great an effect by preaching the gospel as did Whitefield.

It is related that on a certain occasion when he was speaking to an immense assembly in the open air, Lord Chesterfield came to hear him. He drove as near to the speaker as he possibly could, and remained seated in his carriage. Whitefield was describing the condition and final fate of the sinner, who refused to listen to the warnings and entreaties of his friends, and compared him to one who is suspended over a yawning gulf, reaching forth for whatever object meets his view, regardless of his peril. Chesterfield was leaning forward from his carriage to catch every syllable; and the preacher represents the friends of the deluded man coming to show him his danger. They point him to the chasm below and the brittle thread by which he is suspended. But he refuses to hear them, and struggles and grasps for the objects about him that please his fancy. The thread wears away and begins to break, till he is held but by a single fiber. His friends beg and entreat; he turns from them for his pleasure—the thread snaps —he falls. At this word, Chesterfield exclaimed, "My God, he's gone!"—forgetting the proprieties of the occasion, with all his sympathies enlisted for the poor deluded being whom he sees suspended by a brittle thread before him, and shuddering as he beholds the fibers loosen,—it breaks—he is lost—and the great man utters the exclamation as though it were all real. It is rare that one acquires such a command over his hearers, such a power that all is forgotten, save the creations of the speaker's fancy. Place and circumstance are unnoticed, and the hearer bends forward spell-bound to catch the syllable glowing from his lips.

We have had one man in our own country who possessed this power in an eminent degree. That man was Patrick Henry. The opening scenes of the Revolution were well fitted to arouse his passions, and to work upon a mind so susceptible to emotion as was his. Many of his speeches then made on political questions, were characteristic of the skill which he possessed. But his true sphere, or rather the sphere in which he could be most effective, was without doubt before a jury as a criminal lawyer. This was the stage on which he delighted to act. On one occasion a clergyman was prosecuted in Virginia for violating some sectarian law of the State, and in the indictment there occurred this clause—"for preaching the gospel of Jesus Christ." Henry volunteered to defend him. The indictment was read and laid upon the table. The prosecuting attorney delivered a labored argument to prove the charge and secure a conviction. When he was through, Henry arose, grasped the indictment, swung it about his head and exclaimed "My God! prosecuted for preaching the

Religion of Jesus Christ! What did our fathers come to this country for?" He swung it again about his head,—dashed it upon the floor,—stamped upon it with his feet and took his seat. Such an effect did those few words have upon jury and audience, that they were seized with indignation against the man who could prefer such a suit. Without retiring from their seats a verdict of "not guilty" was rendered.

The power of Mr. Henry's eloquence in many of his early efforts seems past belief and well nigh miraculous. From early youth he was quiet and contemplative in his deportment, and possessed a peculiar tact for relating striking facts and anecdotes. He was particularly fond of argument, and often drew the neighbors, who frequented the store where he was employed, into wrangling discussions, that he might observe the working of their passions or come to the relief of the beleaguered party. He was much given to meditation. And when he came to plead causes, he made his argument from an original and elementary analysis of the case,—paying little regard to precedents,—with illustrations drawn from his own fancy. He had not much reverence or use for law books, and had his causes been decided according to precedent, the result would have been very damaging to his success as a lawyer. But a jury of common men will hear eloquence when they will pay little regard to the dry details of co-ordinate cases.

In the management of a discourse Mr. Henry was signally successful. All his powers of mind and of body seemed to flock about him when he entered the arena. His approach to a cause was like the war-horse "that paweth in the valley and rejoiceth in his strength; and goeth on to meet the armed men." His frame dilated. The features of his face took new relations. His head was erect. The whole bearing of his person was noble. His biographer, in narrating the circumstances connected with the celebrated "Parson's case," has given a glowing account of the trial, and in alluding to the plea of Mr. Henry he says, "No one had ever heard him speak, and curiosity was on tiptoe. He rose very awkwardly, and faltered much in his exordium. The people hung their heads at so unpromising a commencement; the clergy were observed to exchange sly looks with each other; and his father, who was upon the bench, is described as having almost sunk from his seat. But these feelings were of short duration, and soon gave place to others of a very different character. For now were those wonderful faculties which he possessed, for the first time developed; and now was witnessed that mysterious and almost supernatural transformation of appearance, which the

5*

fire of his own eloquence never failed to work in him. For as his mind rolled along, and began to glow from its own action, all the exuviæ of the clown seemed to shed themselves spontaneously. His attitude by degrees became erect and lofty. The spirit of his genius awakened all his features. His countenance shone with a nobleness and grandeur which it had never before exhibited. There was a lightning in his eyes which seemed to rive the spectator. His action became graceful, bold and commanding; and in the tones of his voice, but more especially in his emphasis, there was a peculiar charm, a magic, of which any one who ever heard him will speak as soon as he is named, but of which no one can give any adequate description. They can only say that it struck upon the ear and upon the heart, in a manner that language can not tell. Add to all these his wonder-working fancy, and the peculiar phraseology in which he clothed his images; for he painted to the heart with a force that almost petrified it. In the language of those who heard him on this occasion, 'he made their blood to run cold and their hair to rise on end.'"

It is not often that the power of intensely moving the emotions, is found united with the highest order of dignified and manly eloquence. It requires a mind constructed on the grandest scale. The faculties need to be nicely balanced. The judgment must be broad and firm; the sense of justice and integrity thoroughly inwrought into the mental constitution. Providence rarely bestows such gifts. We find them perhaps more perfectly combined in the mind of Daniel Webster than in any other in the history of our nation. There are few positions in which a public speaker can be placed, in which he had not the talents to succeed. His power was equally felt whether he spoke in presence of a bench of learned judges, or before a promiscuous assembly of ten thousand people. Nor does he, to accomplish this result, adopt a method peculiar to the audience whom he addresses. All his great efforts are marked with that plain but lofty style, which identify it as the stately steppings of his giant mind; and it is equally characterized by a pathos and sublimity which move the passions of his hearers. When he argued the cause of Dartmouth College *versus* the State of New Hampshire, before the Supreme Court of the United States, composed of Chief Justice Marshall, associated with Washington, Livingston, Johnson, Story, Todd, and Duvall, men the most venerable and august that ever graced that bench, it is related by one* who heard him on the occasion, that

* Before going to Washington, which I did chiefly for the sake of

for upwards of four hours he detailed to the court, in the most clear and lucid style, the features of the case, without apparent effort to himself or his

---

hearing Mr. Webster, I was told that, in arguing the case at Exeter, New Hampshire, he had left the whole court-room in tears at the conclusion of his speech. This, I confess, struck me unpleasantly—any attempt at pathos on a purely legal question like this, seemed hardly in good taste. On my way to Washington, I made the acquaintance of Mr. Webster. We were together several days in Philadelphia, at the house of a common friend; and as the College question was one of deep interest to literary men, we conversed often and largely on the subject. As he dwelt upon the leading points of the case, in terms so calm, simple, and precise, I said to myself more than once, in reference to the story I had heard, "Whatever may have seemed appropriate in defending the college at *home*, and on her own ground, there will be no appeal to the feelings of Judge Marshall and his associates at Washington." The Supreme Court of the United States held its session, that winter, in a mean apartment of moderate size—the Capitol not having been built after its destruction in 1814. The audience, when the case came on, was therefore small, consisting chiefly of legal men, the *élite* of the profession throughout the country. Mr. Webster entered upon his argument in the calm tone of easy and dignified conversation. His matter was so completely at his command that he scarcely looked at his brief, but went on for more than four hours with a statement so luminous, and a chain of reasoning so easy to be understood, and yet approaching so nearly to absolute demonstration, that he seemed to carry with him every man of his audience without the slightest effort or weariness on either side. It was hardly *eloquence*, in the strict sense of the term; it was pure reason. Now and then, for a sentence or two, his eye flashed and his voice swelled into a bolder note, as he uttered some emphatic thought; but he instantly fell back into the tone of earnest conversation, which ran throughout the great body of his speech. A single circumstance will show you the clearness and absorbing power of his argument. I

auditory, and that in the few pathetic sentences, with which he closed his argument, he so wrought upon the feelings of his hearers that he left them

---

observed that Judge Story, at the opening of the case, had prepared himself, pen in hand, as if to take copious minutes. Hour after hour I saw him fixed in the same attitude, but, so far as I could perceive, with not a note on his paper. The argument closed, and *I could not discover that he had taken a single note.* Others around me remarked the same thing, and it was among the *on dits* of Washington, that a friend spoke to him of the fact with surprise, when the judge remarked, "Every thing was so clear, and so easy to remember, that not a note seemed necessary, and, in fact, I thought little or nothing about my notes." The argument ended. Mr. Webster stood for some moments silent before the court, while every eye was fixed intently upon him. At length, addressing the Chief Justice, Marshall, he proceeded thus:—"*This, sir, is my case.* It is the case, not merely of that humble institution, it is the case of every college in our land. It is more. It is the case of every eleemosynary institution throughout our country—of all those great charities founded by the piety of our ancestors to alleviate human misery, and scatter blessings along the pathway of life. It is more. It is, in some sense, the case of every man among us who has property of which he may be stripped; for the question is simply this: shall our State Legislatures be allowed to take *that* which is not their own, to turn it from its original use, and apply it to such ends or purposes as they, in their discretion, shall see fit? Sir, you may destroy this little institution; it is weak; it is in your hands! I know it is one of the lesser lights in the literary horizon of our country. You may put it out. But if you do so, you must carry through your work. You must extinguish, one after another, all those great lights of science which, for more than a century, have thrown their radiance over our land.

"It is, sir, as I have said, a small college. And yet, *there are those who love it*——."

Here the feelings which he had thus far succeeded in keeping down,

and even that grave bench of judges, moved with the strongest emotions, and eyes suffused with tears.

It was my lot to have heard Mr. Webster but once.

---

broke forth. His lips quivered; his firm cheeks trembled with emotion; his eyes were filled with tears; his voice choked, and he seemed struggling to the utmost, simply to gain that mastery over himself which might save him from an unmanly burst of feeling. I will not attempt to give you the few broken words of tenderness in which he went on to speak of his attachment to the college. The whole seemed to be mingled throughout with the recollections of father, mother, brother, and all the trials and privations through which he had made his way into life. Every one saw that it was wholly unpremeditated, a pressure on his heart, which sought relief in words and tears. The court-room, during these two or three minutes, presented an extraordinary spectacle. Chief Justice Marshall, with his tall, gaunt figure, bent over as if to catch the slightest whisper, the deep furrows of his cheek expanded with emotion, and eyes suffused with tears; Mr. Justice Washington at his side, with his small and emaciated frame, and countenance more like marble than I ever saw on any other human being—leaning forward with an eager, troubled look; and the remainder of the court, at the two extremities, pressing, as it were, towards a single point, while the audience below were wrapping themselves round in closer folds beneath the bench to catch each look, and every movement of the speaker's face. If a painter could give us the scene on canvas—those forms and countenances, and Daniel Webster as he then stood in the midst, it would be one of the most touching pictures in the history of eloquence. One thing it taught me, that the *pathetic* depends not merely on the words uttered, but still more on the estimate we put upon him who utters them. There was not one among the strong-minded men of that assembly who could think it unmanly to weep, when he saw, standing before him, the man who had made such an argument melted into the tenderness of a child.

Mr. Webster had now recovered his composure, and fixing his

He had been secured by a "Library Association" to deliver an address. The occasion was one of simply ordinary interest—the usual weekly lecture. But long before the time announced, the spacious hall was filled to overflowing. I was so fortunate as to secure a favorable seat, and waited patiently for hours that I might fully satisfy the desire of seeing and hearing the American Cicero. At a few moments before eight o'clock the side door opened, and a hale, well-formed man, something past the meridian of life, advanced unattended to the platform, which he mounted with a ready step, and advancing a few paces, retaining a kid glove upon the left hand in which he held his hat, he bowed gracefully to the audience, and retired to a sofa. Daniel Webster was before us! The grace and noble bearing of the man upon his entrance, which seemed to sit so easily

---

keen eye on the Chief Justice, said, in that deep tone with which he sometimes thrilled the heart of an audience:—"Sir, I know not how others may feel," (glancing at the opponents of the college before him,) "but, for myself, when I see my *alma mater* surrounded, like Cæsar in the senate-house, by those who are reiterating stab upon stab, I would not, for this right hand, have her turn to me, and say, *Et tu, quoque, mi fili! And thou, too, my son!*" He sat down. There was a death-like stillness throughout the room for some moments; every one seemed to be slowly recovering himself, and coming gradually back to his ordinary range of thought and feeling.—*Choate's Eulogy on Daniel Webster*, page 35. *Incident communicated by Dr. Chauncey A. Goodrich.*

upon him, produced a favorable impression. The thought that came to my mind, as we were greeted with the bow, was, that if a being from another world were to come upon this earth and desire to see a specimen of the race, here is the individual I would present,—in form—in features—in full-souled bearing, so *entirely a man.* As he arose to speak, I could observe him more minutely. His cheeks were ruddy, his eye was clear and bright, his dress was simple but tasteful—a blue coat, a buff vest and black pants,—his usual dress for a public occasion. His hair, thin and sprinkled with the frosts of age, was brushed back as represented in the pictures.

His subject was the Constitution, that instrument which he first read, when a boy, printed upon his pocket handkerchief, and the theme which of all others he most delighted to speak about. The discourse was entirely *extempore*, and was mainly devoted to a history of the formation of the Constitution, and the opinions entertained of it by the framers. There was nothing particularly striking or original in the matter. Yet there were many facts which he had learned from the mouths of the men who took part in those grave deliberations, which were deeply interesting, and at times held the audience breathless. His voice was bold and majestic, like the full-toned bell of some lofty tower. It was the voice which could represent our race. But there was something in that presence which no pen can describe—a majesty which we attach to kings and emperors. Sometimes he faltered for an instant, and when the precise word or thought would not come at his bidding, that noble eye would invariably roll up in the socket as if in search, and he would pass his hand over his forehead as though to arouse it. His countenance rarely changed—lofty and majestic like the fabled countenance of Jove in the halls of the gods. Every feature was lit up with the brightness of a great mind filled with generous thoughts.

Once only during the discourse a smile was seen to play upon his countenance. The occasion of it was this: in that part of his lecture in which he alluded to Adams and Jefferson, he said that at their death he had, at the request of his fellow-citizens, delivered a eulogy; and in that part which referred to Mr. Adams,—that he might inspire it with life,—he was desirous of introducing his speech on the adoption of the Declaration of Independence. As Congress sat in secret session at that time, and no speeches were reported, the remarks of Mr. Adams were lost. He accordingly composed and inserted in the eulogy, what he thought Mr. Adams would be likely to have said, beginning, "Sink or swim, live or die, survive or perish, I am for the Declaration."

Since the delivery of that eulogy, Mr. Webster said that he had received, on an average, two letters a month, from 1824 to the time he was speaking, in 1851, from persons in various parts of this country and from Europe, asking where he found that speech of Mr. Adams, stating that they had searched the records and the archives of state, without being able to discover any trace of it.

My impression from this personal reminiscence of Mr. Webster, is, that our opinion of his eloquence is greatly modified by our appreciation of his overshadowing mind. At all events, it is a matter of consolation to have seen the man and to have heard his voice. It is good to look upon the face of one in whom commanding talents have been united with majesty of person, to behold grace and dignity where nature has set them, and to come into immediate contact and sympathy with one of the leading minds of the world.

Spoken thought is an instrument of great power. Its influence is confined to no sphere of action, and may be employed for purposes of evil as well as of good. It may be made to minister to virtue and happiness. It may be the instrument of wrong and incalculable sorrow. In the hands of the licentious villain, it may arouse in the breast of innocence the worst passions of which our nature is susceptible. From the lips of the earnest minister of the gospel, it may lift us up and transport us to the very gate of heaven.

At the tribunal of justice it may turn the scale in favor of wrong, trample upon the most sacred principles of honor, and crush the very heart of innocence; or it may inspire the evil doer with terror, and lead him in the way of virtue. It may paralyze the rights of the poor injured victim of that heartless man who would take advantage of weakness and ignorance; or it may pour into the wounded breast a balm, and convince mankind that there still is faith on the earth, and that the spirit of justice has not yet taken her final flight.

In the science of government it may serve the purpose of duplicity and personal selfishness; or it nay inspire the breast with undying courage in the defense of liberty and the rights of civil society. The man in whose heart burns not one generous aspiration for the public good, who would sell the liberties of his country for his own personal aggrandizement, may go on from court-house to court-house, from city to city, and from State to State, pouring out as it were his very heart in burning eloquence, and all that his particular friend may be elected President, and he be appointed a member of the cabinet, a minister to a foreign court, or the governor of a territory. Or it may be in the hands of the disinterested, noble-minded patriot, the power which sunders the bonds of the oppressed, which lights the torch of civil liberty, which rouses in a nation the spirit that has slept for centuries, and makes the heart of the abused and long suffering serf to leap for gladness. With the philanthropist it vindicates the brotherhood of man. It binds up the broken heart, and alleviates the sorrows and distresses of the unfortunate.

If there is any thing that can be achieved by forensic eloquence—by the spirit of man, which can be a source of pride in life, which can adorn the name when he who bore it lies mouldering in the tomb, it is the achievement of virtue. If a distinguished orator makes a speech on a topic which concerns the public interest, what is the judgment of mankind concerning it? If he has appealed to the sense of right and justice, if he has shown a clean heart and a disinterested purpose, and moves with power upon their feelings, he is honored and revered, and his memory is sweet to them. But if he displays the traces of a low, mean ambition, if he attempts by smooth words to create an under current, which shall some day carry him into some position of emolument, the universal sense of mankind is to damn and execrate him for it. The orator, and especially the political orator, is too often captivated by present honors and gratifications than the more enduring fame; is better pleased with a green exotic than the fadeless laurel.

No state, either ancient or modern, ever yielded so much to the power of eloquence as did the Greeks. They lived in a tropical climate where warm and quick passions are nurtured. Theirs was the land of the orange and the olive—a pure atmosphere and balmy breezes. Their language, too, was the most accurate, comprehensive, and beautiful that has ever been invented by the ingenuity of man; capable of expressing the profound conceptions of Plato, the most accurate and exact rules of Aristotle, the resistless eloquence of Demosthenes, the playful fancies of Anacreon, and the liquid strains of Pindar. The art of printing among them was unknown; the freedom of speech was unbounded; and the passion of the people was to hear news, and witness theatrical performances. No wonder that eloquence among them had such unbounded sway. The Athenian assemblies were stormy and tumultuous, and Athenian oratory was of a corresponding character. Laws were made and public ordinances passed by the voice of the whole people. It will be readily perceived that such a deliberative body would be liable to be deceived and duped by the artful and designing demagogue, who possessed in an eminent degree the power of forensic eloquence. But what has been the judgment of succeeding ages respecting Athenian statesmen? The glory has not been awarded to him who best succeeded, but to him who best deserved success. The wrangling orator who sought for personal advancement, and opened unprovoked attacks upon the wise and virtuous to secure their banishment, has merited and received the scorn of all succeeding times; while he who was firm in his attachment to the prosperity of his country, and who would rather submit to banishment or even death than compromise its honor or his own veracity, has always been held in grateful remembrance. The demagogue may be successful for a time, and the good man may suffer deep wrong. But these circumstances only make us more thoroughly despise the former, and bind to our hearts more firmly the latter. Themistocles was eminently successful. Yet we never pronounce his name without thinking that he was a deep, designing politician, who was ever working to secure to himself some political end. But Aristides will ever be loved and venerated; and though he is banished from his country by the intrigues of Themistocles, and by those who were tired of hearing him called "the just;" yet as he steps upon the trireme that is to bear him away into banishment, he can drop a tear of pity for his enemies, and offer a prayer to the gods for the protection and prosperity of his native city,—that city for whose glory he had toiled so long and sacrificed so much.

When we see the blackness and perfidy that is wrapped up in the breast of Catiline, who does not tremble for the fate of Rome, and grow indignant over the story of this heartless villain? But will not those noble sentiments that burst forth from the soul of Cicero, make us better citizens and greater lovers of country? admirers not more of the beauty, elegance and resistless power of his eloquence, than the courage and fearless honesty of his heart? We scorn those tribunes who flattered the people with the promise of securing some rights for the public good, and when power was firmly in their grasp turned a haughty look upon the plebeians. But when we remember the honesty and devotion of Fabricius, and the noble death of Cato, it is pleasant to think that such men have lived.

Sir Joshua Reynolds once made the following remark to Mr. Burke: "I do not mean to flatter you, Mr Burke, but when posterity reads one of your speeches in Parliament, it will be difficult to believe you took so much pains, knowing with certainty, as you did, that it could produce no effect, that not one vote would be gained by it." "Waiving your compliment to me," was the reply, "I shall say in general that it is very well worth while for a man to take pains to speak well in Parliament. And if a man speaks well, he gradually establishes a certain reputation and consequence in the general opinion, which sooner or later will have its political rewards. Besides, though not one vote is gained, a good speech has its effect. The bill you oppose may pass into a law, but it will be modified and softened by it."

This little fragment of personal remark opens to our view the heart of the great statesman. We discover that principle in his character upon which he was willing to stake his reputation. It was not the rule of mere expediency, or party triumph, or personal advancement upon which he acted. But deep and unyielding devotion to those principles which in his judgment were right, a fixedness of purpose which no circumstance could change, obedience to conscientious conviction that no hope of reward could alter, were the elements which gave luster to the character of him who is the pride of British statesmen and civilians, and which will entwine about the name of Burke in perennial beauty.

In some respects civil society among us is similar to what it was among the Greeks. Ours is a confederated republic, and with us, as with the Greeks, the orator is at liberty to think what he pleases and speak what he thinks. Successful oratory is in high repute.

We pay great deference to the man who affects and moves us by the expression of his opinions. We are therefore, like the Greeks, as a people, liable to be deceived by him who has a false heart and a persuasive tongue. In many respects the prospects before our nation are flattering. It occupies the fairest portion of this western continent. It is situated in the most beautiful and productive region of the whole earth. It has ample territory, and boundless resources. For beauty and grandeur of scenery, salubrity of air, and serenity of sky, it is not surpassed. Its people are of that stock who are ever restless and unsatisfied. The arts eminently flourish. Intellectual culture is duly appreciated and patronized. But, alas for its fate if wicked men are suffered to control its destiny! Heaven grant that wisdom may direct, that virtue may prevail!

LECTURE IV.

VOCAL CULTURE.

A CORRECT and ready elocution can not be overvalued in a system of education. Speech is that one of our faculties which is in almost constant use. From the artless prattle of infancy to the last trembling accents of age, the voice rarely remains long unused. If it be employed for the purpose of public speaking, there is special need of a happy and effective utterance. But even in ordinary conversation it is pleasant to hear a musical voice equally removed from ignorant vulgarity and studied affectation. It is exhilarating to feel in the tone, the sentiments that glow in the mind of him who addresses us. An easy elocution is among the first of accomplishments, because it is one which constantly shows. They who labor so assiduously to maintain a claim to aristocracy in manners and dress should not neglect this.

When we speak, it is our object to convey to the minds of others the thoughts which we have in our own minds. We may fail to effect this purpose, either wholly or in part, from a defective or careless habit of utterance. We receive and retain the thoughts of some persons, because of the pleasant and striking style in which they are spoken, and we forget what another has said before he has done speaking, because his style of address is so repulsive and bungling. If we gain the attention of the one we address and his mind is in a receptive state, still we may fail to make him feel the force of a thought as we do, because we have not the faculty of throwing it fully into the words we speak. We have all observed that there is music, a magic in some voices that is charming and attractive, while others are capable of blunting our perceptions and forcing us to close our ears.

If we read aloud what another has written, the task becomes more difficult; for in addition to what has been named above, we have to learn and appreciate what was the idea of the author. Reading consists in conveying to the minds of those who listen, the thought as it originally existed in the mind of him who wrote it. If we fail to understand and fully appreciate the meaning of the piece as we proceed, then we do not read, but simply call words like the parrot. If we have a correct understanding of it, but still fail to communicate it by the words we use, then we do not read in the proper acceptation of that term. The requisites for reading are an appreciation of the thought of the author, and a correct and effective elocution which enables us to convey that thought to the hearer.

The first knowledge of the use of the voice we acquire by imitation. The child, before it is old enough to talk, will express its ideas by a correct modulation. In youthful play and sport we rarely hear an incorrect inflection, and if the example has been good scarcely a principle of elocution will be violated. But when the child learns its letters, and then to combine those letters into words, it usually fails to understand and appreciate the thought, and consequently fails to communicate it. Reading, according to the conception of the child, is a process of calling words more or less rapidily, and stopping to spell out only the more difficult ones. The habit is formed of reading and speaking in a set, measured tone, without any reference to the sense, and observing none of the principles of inflection and intonation which were in infancy correctly learned. As the boy grows up he often indulges in animated and impassioned conversation, and by using language rapidly and without care, the very bad practice is indulged of omitting many sounds, and of obscuring others, and the habit is soon formed of incorrect and imperfect articulation.

The object of vocal culture or elocution is to break up false habits and to establish those which are correct, and to arouse the emotional nature of the reader to a just conception of the thought to be communicated. It is not the province of this science to *create* an emotional nature, but simply to awaken and direct that which already exists. It can not bestow on the voice any new elements of power; but it may give to those which we have a new vital force by unburdening them of many false habits and imparting skill in correct ones.

In a systematic course of vocal culture, it is necessary to give attention, in the first place, to enunciation and pronunciation. It would be time lost to attempt to cultivate expression before the elements of expression have been corrected. A class in almost any academy or college, will illustrate the variety of habits to which they have been accustomed. A sentence of ten words may not be properly read by any one of them, and yet no two may have made the same mistake. It requires on the part of the teacher a quick and nice sense in detecting errors, and the power of imitating them, that the force of the criticism may be appreciated. It is only by a thorough drill that errors of long standing can be broken up, and that correct habits can be firmly fixed. The omitting or obscuring the consonant R, is one of the most common mistakes. The R should not be made so prominent and trilled as it is by the Scotch, but it should be full and distinct. It is an extremely pleasant sound when correctly given. It is one of the liquids, and adds much to the beauty and melody of a sentence. The consonant S is another of those letters that commonly receives very harsh usage. It has a soft, flute-like sound that is very agreeable. But most public speakers, and almost every one in conversation, substitute for this, a rough harsh one that tears the ear. The French exercise the greatest care in uttering all their nice and pleasant sounds, that they may produce by means of them a favorable effect. But we as a nation are unmindful of the rich treasury of the nicest and most exquisite elements in which our language abounds.

Pronunciation is not a matter which strictly pertains to vocal culture, and yet it can not be neglected. The standard of pronunciation, is the usage of that class of society the most refined by mental culture. There are provincialisms, and the style of speaking in different cities, which may prevail even in the best cultivated circles. But local peculiarities should be discarded. A dictionary is usually considered the standard; but it can not be authority unless it give what is good usage. A dictionary based upon any other plan than that of detailing present usage is worthless. The lexicographer can not make laws for language. But he must be the faithful chronicler of the custom of our best speakers. That dictionary should therefore be used, which most strictly conforms to this principle. The slightest variation of sounds from true pronunciation should be promptly corrected, and pupils should be taught to distinguish the errors to which they are liable with the nicest perception of what is correct, so that they may soon acquire the habit of watching with critical care every sound that escapes their lips. The child inherits many errors in pronunciation. Our population is so heterogeneous, being made up of representatives from almost every nation on the globe, that we not unfrequently find in the same school a variety of peculiarities traceable to the language of the people from which the family has descended. The greatest care on the part of the teacher is therefore needed. These peculiarities are to be dispelled, and the tongues of all nations made to blend in harmonious English, or, if you choose, American.

Pitch and inflection should next receive our attention. The best place for a boy to learn these is upon the play-ground. During a single intermission, a company of lads will give expression to almost every variety of pitch and inflection known to elocutionists. In the exuberance of youthful feeling, and the contentions for their privileges and rights, they have occasion to utter thoughts and emotions of every shade and degree,

"From grave to gay, from lively to severe."

In general these intonations will be correct. The feelings one cherishes, naturally prompt to a proper expression of them. But those same boys, at the call of the bell, will enter the school room and read a lesson from their books in their "reading tone," entirely different from that which they so appropriately used upon the play-ground. They observe the pauses, and give inflections according to some spelling-book rule, regardless of the sentiment to be communicated and the emotions which it is intended to awaken. They have an abundance of tones at command when surrounded by their companions, but when they have taken their places in the class, their command of voice forsakes them, and they have only one pitch for every variety of thought. There is a monotonous tone, uninterrupted by any species of modulation, which is characteristic of most youth at some period, and which many never abandon. Whether the sentiment be intended to awaken peaceful and gentle thoughts, like the words of Lioni in the night soliloquy in Venice:

"All is gentle: nought
Stirs rudely; but congenial with the night,
Whatever walks, is gliding like a spirit;"

or, bold and defiant as the language of Brutus, when chafed by the testy spirit of his friend:

"Fret, till your proud heart break—
Go show your slaves how choleric you are,
And make your bondmen tremble;"

it is all read to the same pitch, and upon that same unvarying tone. The spelling-book has made it his duty to keep the voice up at a comma, and to let it fall at a period, and to this he religiously adheres through all the storms of passion, and the peace and quiet of a summer evening and moonlight hours—through the wild shouts of "sentries' shriek," the clang of arms and the torrent's roar, or the gentle rippling of the brook and the soft sighing of the breeze.

To break up false habits and establish correct ones, can most easily be accomplished by employing for practice that species of composition which the pupils are accustomed to use in conversation, and which they naturally use correctly. If the scholar reads with an unnatural and drawling tone, let the teacher copy upon the blackboard a little fragment of talk which he has overheard in passing the play-ground, and let that be the lesson. By the reading of a familiar conversation, and giving the correct, the natural inflections and intonations, the identity of conversing and reading, of speaking and declaiming is established. For this reason, dialogue, carefully and correctly read, has great advantages over any other kind of composition. It is not well for a class to read continually in course. Those passages should be selected which illustrate the particular branch of elocution upon which instruction is being given. It is a great mistake, which many of our teachers make, in allowing their pupils to read on, piece after piece, day after day, as the squirrel turns the wheel of his cage, knowing no object or end, and only correcting the words called wrong; as though the calling of words were reading. A single passage thoroughly understood and correctly practiced may be of more service than carelessly calling the words of many pages. For the reading of that exercise is a pattern by which all others may be read of that class. A few such passages cover the whole ground of what is termed by elocutionists rhetorical thought, and he who has once mastered these is in the proper way to improvement.

We would not be understood by these remarks to discard extensive practice. The calling of words readily is the basis of good reading, and the pupil needs much exercise in acquiring the habit. But if he first understand the meaning of the words he calls, and enters fully into the spirit of the thought, the way, instead of being barren and gloomy, is joyous and delightful, cheered by the odors of flowers, the music of the grove and the companionship of nature, living and animated. A word whose meaning he knows and whose force he appreciates, is at once remembered, and is ever after hailed with familiarity; whereas a word or phrase which he fails to understand, is encountered a thousand times with the same vacant stare. We need reading books so graded and suited to the wants of scholars, that at every stage the pupil may have something adapted to his capacity and capable of interesting him. He can then appreciate the value of intonation in communicating thought, can practice calling words understandingly, and much time may be saved.

The final object of vocal culture is to make our reading and speaking effective. It may not make every one equally impressive, but no one can doubt that careful training improves the utterance of all. The proper modulation of the voice, adapting it to the sentiment and the emotions it is capable of awakening, and sustaining the tone with the proper degree of force and energy, may be to a person a source of very great power. The child, by a natural gift and by imitation, may learn many pieces of music. Its performances may be touching and pathetic and be tolerably correct, yet the lack of systematic culture in giving power and expression is at once detected, and the singing is pronounced *puerile*. In reading, as in music, it requires much practice to acquire great skill. The minstrel made many a disgraceful failure and discordant sound, and long

> "Amid the strings his fingers strayed,
> And an uncertain warbling made,"

before the hand had caught the cunning of the art, and

> "In varying cadence, soft or strong,
> He swept the sounding chords along."

What culture can do for the singer, it can also do for the reader and the speaker. It requires many lessons to teach a singer to open his mouth. He must know the value of a full round volume of voice, of loud and heavy strains, and of those which are soft and light. He must with many tedious strokes beat the air to right and left, and up and down, and with exactness measure time. It is equally necessary that the person who would read well should learn the use of all these elements, for it is these that give the speaker the command of force and power.

The value of systematic culture to the singer is now generally felt and appreciated. We have musical festivals and conventions, in which it is the business of the conductor to train the voices of the members in expression, to draw out those powers which have never been reached by the ordinary course of instruction. An impulse was given to the progress of this noble science by the visit of Jenny Lind to this country. The power which the human voice may be made to exert upon the mind when duly cultivated was admirably illustrated in her performances. Wherever she sang, crowds pressed to hear her. Sums of money, which for almost any other purpose would have been considered the height of extravagance, were freely paid. Captivated by those bewitching charms of voice which she displayed, breathless thousands gazed and listened with delight. Such wealth of variety, such melody of utterance, such sweetness of tone, and the inimitable command of the most delicate expression, is the rare attainment of mortals. Her songs,—at times mild as the morning zephyr, playful as the twitter of the swallow, soft as the cooing of the dove, at others wild and piercing as the shrieks which express the fancies that revel in the wild girl's brain,—summoned from almost every city in our nation delighted and admiring multitudes.

It is difficult to comprehend how it is possible for a mortal spirit to exert such unbounded sway. The secret will be found in the elaborate cultivation of the faculties to which her early life was given. Those melting tones did not burst spontaneous from her lips. It was not instinctive utterance, like the song of the young nightingale that for the first time opes its tender throat. That capacity which she possesses is the fruit of long hours of weariness and toil. Practice and unceasing effort were the elements of her success and enviable fame. While her young companions threaded the streets, or dozed upon their pillows, she was

> "——at her work and her stern hours."

Gifted by nature with a delicate ear, all those tones unusually sweet, expressive and forcible, which had pleased her youthful fancy, still lingered in her mind, and when alone with her worn instruments of sound, she varied, combined, and practiced them till the pallor of her cheek spoke her devotion, and her wasted energies cried for relaxation from intensity of toil. With a diligence scarcely paralleled, she pursued the vocation which she loved, till she drew forth from that voice of unknown and unmeasured power, her matchless songs

> "In notes, with many a winding bout
> Of linked sweetness long drawn out,

> With wanton heed and giddy cunning,
> The melting voice through mazes running,
> Untwisting all the chains that tie
> The hidden soul of harmony."

The counterpart of the visit of Jenny Lind to this country, was that of Hungary's unfortunate exile. Both were eminent examples of the power which the human voice is capable of displaying. Song was the instrument of the one, eloquence of the other. It was not the novelty of seeing and of hearing a foreigner, or merely sympathy for him in his misfortune, that drew crowds of our nation's proudest sons about him. But it was the resistless power of his eloquence—that marshaling of words into harmonious phrase which captivated the soul of the hearer—those bursts of passion for the rights of the injured and the oppressed—those withering words of satire, and exclamations of reproach and denunciation against the oppressor's wrong and the "proud man's contumely," which, could they have heard who had been guilty of grinding out with iron heel the last life spark of his native land, would have inspired the vain attempt to stifle the workings of their coward consciences, and caused

> "Their knotted and combined locks to part."

The young and the old, the grave and the gay everywhere, who heard, universally feel and express a satisfaction that it has been their fortune to have listened to those miraculous displays of eloquence which were exhibited by that unfortunate exile. His progress through this country was a triumph, prouder than that of a conqueror. It was a triumph of eloquence! A triumph of one mind over many minds! A triumph of the tongue! Nor was this the spontaneous and natural outburst of untutored, unbridled genius. It was the fruit of long, lonely hours of weariness and toil in the dungeons of his enemies. In a cold prison house, in a damp cell, with no books but an English grammar and a Shakspeare, he caught the inspiring breath of eloquence. There he familiarized himself with words of power and energy and might. During those dark and dismal hours, he gained the rudiments of the English tongue; and those conceptions,—endued with such pathos and sublimity as alone characterize the spirit of the great English bard, and which were so congenial to his own,—were the "studies" of his repeated brilliant efforts.

The objection is urged by some to any attempt at vocal training, on the ground that it induces an artificial and affected style of speaking. The principles of elocution are all discarded, and the rules for the government of the voice, and the notation for its guidance which are employed in many elementary reading books are wholly rejected. It is repulsive to many to hear the word culture in connection with that of oratory. It is more congenial to think of the orator as a genius, to believe him, like the poet, "born, not made." But such was not the experience of Demosthenes, beyond comparison the greatest orator of all ancient times. Without culture he was awkward and unnatural in his manners when speaking. He had the habit of throwing one shoulder higher than the other. The features of his face were distorted into unseemly grimaces. He stammered, and his voice was small and feeble. It would seem disheartening for a man with all these physical defects to attempt to excel in eloquence. Yet by systematic training, these seeming insurmountable obstacles*

* When Demosthenes was about sixteen years of age his curiosity was attracted by a trial in which Callistratus pleaded and won a cause of considerable importance. The eloquence which procured and the acclamations which followed his success, so inflamed the young Athenian, that he determined to devote himself thenceforward to the assiduous study of oratory. At the age of seventeen he appeared before the public tribunals, and pronounced against his faithless guardians, and against a debtor to his father's estate, five orations which were crowned with complete success. These discourses, in all probability, had received the finishing touches from Isæus, under whom Demosthenes continued to study for the space of four years after he had reached his majority. An opening so brilliantly successful, emboldened the young orator, as may well be supposed, to speak before the people; but when he made the attempt, his feeble and stammering voice, his interrupted respiration, his ungraceful gestures, and his ill

were overcome, and he rose to the first place in eloquence. His industry in breaking up bad habits, and in learning and cultivating correct ones, is such

---

arranged periods, brought upon him general ridicule. Returning home in the utmost distress, he was reanimated by the kind aid of the actor Satyrus, who, having requested Demosthenes to repeat some passage from a dramatic poet, pronounced the same extract after him, with so much correctness of enunciation and in a manner so true to nature, that it appeared to the young orator to be quite another passage. Convinced, thereupon, how much grace and persuasive power, a proper enunciation and manner added to the best oration, he resolved to correct the deficiencies of his youth, and accomplished this with a zeal and a perseverance which have passed into a proverb. How deeply he commands our respect and admiration by his struggles to overcome his natural infirmities, and remove the impressions produced by his first appearance before his assembled countrymen! He was not indebted for the glory he acquired either to the bounty of nature or the favor of circumstances, but to the inherent strength of his own unconquerable will. To free himself from stammering, he spoke with pebbles in his mouth, a report resting on the authority of Demetrius Phalerius, his contemporary. It also appeared that he was unable to articulate clearly the letter R, but he vanquished that difficulty most perfectly; for Cicero, says, "exercitatione fecisse ut plenissime diceret." He removed the distortion of features, which accompanied his utterance, by watching the movements of his countenance in a mirror; and a naked sword was suspended over his left shoulder while he was declaiming in private, to prevent its rising above the level of the right. That his enunciation might be loud and full of emphasis, he frequently ran up the steepest and most uneven walks, an exercise by which his voice acquired both force and energy; and on the sea shore, when the waves were violently agitated, he declaimed aloud, to accustom himself to the noise and tumult of a public assembly. He constructed a subterranean study, where he would often stay two or three months together, shaving one side of his head, that, in case he should wish to

as we always find associated with eminent success. The idea, that great ability is independent of faithful industry in accomplishing great results, is a relic of superstition which the light of a wiser faith has not wholly dissipated. The same argument, which is brought against the cultivation of the voice, might with equal propriety be urged against the cultivation of manners. It being desirable that our children should possess easy and natural habits of address, we might expect by this process of reasoning, that neglect would be the surest means of attaining this end. The absurdity of such a conclusion becomes apparent upon a moment's reflection.

go abroad, the shame of appearing in that condition might keep him within. In this solitary retreat, by the light of his lamp, he copied and recopied, ten times at least, the orations scattered throughout the history of Thucydides, for the purpose of moulding his own style after so pure a model. Whatever may be the truth of these several reports, Demosthenes got credit for the most indefatigable labor in the acquisition of his art. His enemies at a subsequent period of his career, attempted to ridicule this extraordinary industry, by remarking that all his arguments "smelt of the lamp," and they eagerly embraced the opportunity of denying him the possession of natural talents. A malicious opinion like this would easily find credit; for, since it is acknowledged on all hands, that all successful men who are naturally dull must be industrious, the converse of the proposition grows into repute, and it is inferred that all men who are industrious must be dull. The accusation against Demosthenes seems to have rested chiefly on his known reluctance to speak without preparation.—*Anthon's Article, Demosthenes.*

Transfer a rustic lad who has never seen much of life and society, but the disorderly kitchen scenes in a log cabin, and whose most familiar acquaintance extends only to his implements of husbandry, dressed in his best sheep's-grey, to a nice drawing-room where cultivated society is assembled, and the trepidation which he evinces and the awkwardness which characterizes every movement, show in his entire deportment and in every feature of his countenance the embarassment by which he is oppressed. His face glows with confusion, his hands instinctively seek the pockets, and his legs tremble and smite against each other as though they too would seek a place of concealment. In this picture we have none of the effects of culture. Nothing is artificial. It is the action of a spirit under the simple teachings of nature. But how is it with the boy who has been carefully instructed in the principles of good breeding, and in the practice of the best society? His deportment in company does not attract attention. His manners seem to set easily upon him. If he is introduced into a gentleman's drawing-room, he advances with an elastic step, and salutes the company with modest grace. His manners are pronounced easy and natural. But it is that kind of naturalness which is acquired by care and culture. It is the ease which flows from unremitting attention to the correction of errors, and the improvement of habits which nature has ungraciously imposed upon us. It is that ease, which though originally the effect of discipline, when it has once become habitual, has a more natural appearance than any movement which untutored nature can produce. The sentiment of Pope,

"That ease in writing flows from art, not chance,"

is equally true of manners, and of every accomplishment which we esteem.

The same principles are applicable to vocal culture. That ease and naturalness of expression which we so much admire in eloquence and in common conversation, is usually the result of careful culture, and that which seems the artless flow of language is itself the result of art. Our physical natures are subject to the same laws. Culture produces power. The athletæ, who contended for the prize in the great national games of Greece, understood its value and gave their lives to preparation. And he who engaged in the contests, soon learned that it was the boxer who had acquired most skill, and not the one who had the most brute force, who could deal the blow with the greatest effect. Every fact and every analogy teach us that culture of the voice, study of correct habits, admiration of the best models, and persistence in practice, will be rewarded with their legitimate fruits. Demosthenes by the sea shore, with the pebbles in his mouth, or clambering up the steep of some beetling cliff, or by his lonely lamp in his secluded cell, are world-renowned examples of devotion to eloquence, which will ever be connected with the merited success of that immortal orator.

In a piece which embraces many of the principles of rhetorical reading, there is special necessity of being able to enter into the spirit of it. It is impossible for us to read properly and with effect, that which we do not understand. There is no culture of the voice that can be of any avail, until we fully appreciate this principle. It has been observed, in the early part of this lecture, that reading or delivery consisted in communicating by the tones of the voice the thought as it was conceived by the author. The first object then to be accomplished is to become fully imbued with the thought and spirit of the writer. The voice at once indicates whether we feel intensely or not. An audience readily detect if we earnestly mean what we say. If then the voice so readily betrays the state of the feelings, it is of importance, in order to make it effective, that we study to place ourselves in the position of the writer. When we properly appreciate the opinions we utter, it inspires the whole person, and makes every look and feature speak for us. Demosthenes felt the force of this truth, for when asked what in his opinion was the first requisite in oratory, he replied *delivery*. And when asked what were the second and the third requisites, he made the same answer. Without doubt one of the principal elements of his success was his ability to enter fully into the spirit of what he said, of feeling with all the intensity of his nature those thoughts which he meditated with such elaborate care.

In this, probably, consisted the great power of Mr. Garrick. It is safe to say that he never made an audience intensely feel that which he did not first intensely feel himself. Tragedy is the highest order of rhetorical reading, and no person can properly read or speak it, till he feels the passions that fired the bosoms of the persons represented. Fielding, that faithful delineator of character, has aptly represented the effect of Mr. Garrick's speaking upon the common mind, in that passage in his "Tom Jones" in which Jones and Mrs. Miller are represented as taking Partridge, a young man from the country, to hear Garrick in the character of Hamlet.

"Partridge gave that character to Mr. Garrick which he had denied to Jones, and fell into so violent a trembling that his knees knocked against each other. Jones asked him what was the matter, and whether he was afraid of the warrior upon the stage. 'O, la, sir,' said he, 'I perceive now it is what you told me. I am not afraid of any thing, for I know it is but a play; and if it was really a ghost, it could do one no harm, at such a distance and in so much company; and yet, if I was frightened, I am not the only person.' 'Why, who,' cries Jones, 'dost thou take to be such a coward here, besides thyself?' 'Nay, an you may call me coward, if you will; but if that little man there, upon the stage, is not frightened, I never saw any man frightened in my life.' . . . Partridge sat with his eyes partly fixed on the ghost, and partly on Hamlet, and with his mouth open; the same passions that succeeded each other in Hamlet, succeeded likewise in him.

"At the conclusion of the scene, Partridge says to Jones, 'It is natural to be surprised at such things, though I know there is nothing in them; not that it was the ghost that surprised me neither; but when I saw the little man so frightened himself, it was that which took hold of me.' 'And dost thou imagine, then,' cries Jones, 'that he was really frightened?' 'Nay, sir,' said Partridge, 'did not you yourself observe afterwards, when he found it was his own father's spirit, how his fear forsook him by degrees, and he was struck dumb with sorrow, as it were, just as I should have been, had it been my own case.'

"Little more worth remembering occurred during the play, at the end of which, Jones asked him which of the players he liked best. To this, he answered, with some appearance of indignation, 'The king, without doubt.' 'Indeed!' answered Mrs. Miller, 'you are not of the same opinion as the town; for they are all agreed that Hamlet is acted by the best player that was ever on the stage.' 'He the best player!' cries Partridge, with a contemptuous sneer; 'why, I could act as well as he myself. I am sure if I had seen a ghost, I should have looked in the very same manner, and done just as he did. And then, to be sure, in that scene, as you called it, between him and his mother, where you told me he acted so fine, why, Lord help me, any man—that is, any good man, that had such a mother, would have done exactly the same. I know you are only joking, madam; though I never was at a play in London, yet I have seen acting before, in the country; and the king for my money; he speaks all his words distinctly, and half as loud again as the other. Anybody may see he is an actor.'"

In this excellent representation of character, is seen the effect produced upon the ingenuous mind, by one who successfully enters into the spirit of what he says;

who exnibits the same feeling and passion which would be produced upon one who should meet in real life what he experiences in the play. In this art, Garrick preëminently excelled. In his speaking, we see the effect of personating with fidelity the character which he represents. His words, the tones of his voice in harmony with the look, the features, the whole person, speak to us, and we are made to feel all the emotions that succeed each other in his mind, as the great poet himself first conceived them. Partridge, in the simplicity of his unsophisticated nature, is unable to keep up the distinction between fiction and reality. He trembles when he sees the little man upon the stage tremble. Like the child who weeps and sobs over the story of the Children in the Wood, he is moved with sorrow, as though the play were a passage in real life. For this reason, his judgment of the relative merits of the speakers is false. To his simple and untutored feelings, the performer who acts as though every thing in the scene were real, seems to him to show no skill or art, and exhibits no special excellence deserving of praise; but only speaks just as any one would speak who is afraid, or pleased, or angry. But the mouthing performer who personates the king, and speaks his words half as loud again as the others, and is the person whom we never meet in life, is to him the great actor. The agitation and trembling of Partridge are a lasting tribute to the eloquence and power of Mr. Garrick; but his criticisms must ever excite merriment for their simplicity.

We learn from this illustration, that to enter into the spirit of what we say, requires no seeming effort, but, on the contrary, the greatest ease. If culture of the voice induces a style like that displayed by the performer of the king's part, it can not be too much despised and discarded. To one who has not a mind capable of understanding the thought and feeling of an author, vocal training may produce this effect. The culture which we have advocated is not the universal panacea for imperfect delivery. It only operates favorably upon those who have souls to appreciate feeling and beauty. If it be made to serve as the curb to our passions, if it enables us to bring the voice, with all its energy and power, under complete control of a correct taste, if it yield us that fruit which is denominated skill, then it deserves our highest commendation.

It should be the aim in all our practice, to secure ease and simplicity in the style of speaking. Some of the greatest efforts of human genius, which are looked upon as masterpieces of eloquence, are conceived in the plainest style. Perhaps history furnishes no better example of the truth of this principle, than is presented by the poet in the funeral oration of Antony over the corpse of Cæsar. All Rome was in commotion. Cæsar had been stabbed, while sitting upon his throne in the senate-house in the presence of that august assembly, a Roman Senate. All business was stopped. The people were filled with consternation and horror at the perpetration of the bloody deed. Under these circumstances, Antony, the friend of Cæsar, carries the dead body, just as the conspirators had left it, to the forum, and in presence of a vast concourse of the people speaks in his funeral. He recounts the martial deeds of Cæsar, and what he has done for the greatness and the glory of Rome; and when he tells them of the love they once bore to Cæsar, his heart swells and chokes his utterance. He descends from the pulpit; raises up the dead body of his friend; shows them the rents in the bloody mantle; and tells them of the first time ever Cæsar put it on. It was a summer's evening in his tent, after that bloody day on which he had gained one of those signal victories which were the glory and the pride of Rome. He tears aside the bloody mantle and

> "Shows them sweet Cæsar's wounds, poor, poor, dumb mouths,
> And bids them speak for him."

He tells them of the will of Cæsar, and how he had

remembered the poor people and given them all his private walks and arbors, and new planted orchards on the banks of Tiber.

The effort is successful. The effect is overwhelming. The populace had come rejoicing at the murder of Cæsar; they go away bearing his corpse in triumph and swearing revenge and death upon the heads of the conspirators. They came burning with hatred and indignation at the very name of Cæsar; they go awav with such love and reverence for him,

> "That they would go and kiss dead Cæsar's wounds,
> And dip their napkins in his sacred blood;
> Yea, beg a hair of him for memory,
> And dying, mention it in their wills."

The elements of his success are apparent. Those qualities which have been presented are the basis of its merit. This passage in Shakspeare has always been admired as a choice specimen of eloquence on account of its homely simplicity. The topics are so artfully managed and so aptly chosen, that it seems to be the spontaneous, unpremeditated expression of his feelings. It is perfectly natural, and seems to be just what we ourselves would have said under those circumstances And yet it is that kind of naturalness that is the result of art. It is that facility and ease, apparently unattended by effort, which we denominate skill. It is characterized in all its parts by the utmost simplicity. The speaker keeps himself entirely out of sight of his hearers. They are not aware that he is the agent that moves their feelings. Like the glass that brings the star near to us, we are unconscious of its presence in our eagerness to view the object. He declares, and they believe it,

"I am no orator as Brutus is;
But, as you know me all, a plain blunt man
That love my friend;
For I have neither wit, nor words, nor worth,
Action nor utterance, nor the power of speech
To stir men's blood; I only speak right on,
And tell you that which you yourselves do know."

But in that very seeming simplicity of style, and that ease and naturalness in the choice of topics, he steals away their hearts, and leads them captive wheresoe'er he will. He rouses their passions, he nerves them to revenge,

"——and puts a tongue
In every wound of Cæsar, that would move
The stones of Rome to rise and mutiny."

In writing and in manners, the simplicity upon which we have dwelt is that quality that is last developed. The young composer acquires every other element known to rhetoricians before he learns that most important one of all, to use simple language in simple style. The youth who begins to move in company, makes many mortifying failures before he learns the golden mean between stiff and awkward manners, the result of diffidence, and that over-much politeness which characterizes the egotistic and self-satisfied spirit. So in the education of the voice. This simplicity and plainness of utterance which is always found in our most successful speakers, is the last grace of speech to be acquired.

The elements which we have now noticed, are the ones to which careful attention should be given in a systematic training of the voice. Speech is among the noblest of the gifts which Heaven has been pleased to bestow upon man; and it was not bestowed, as a wily diplomatist has observed, to conceal our thoughts, but to enable us to hold ingenuous and delightful communion with each other. It is that gift which distinguishes man from all other created beings, and enables him to fill up the measure of existence with sociality, and thus diversify and gladden its otherwise unendurable monotony.

The limit to the improvement of the voice, like that of the mind itself, is indefinite. It is an instrument of great power and compass, capable of exciting the most intense grief and ungovernable joy; of electrifying a people with patriotic enthusiasm, and of paralyzing the heart with appalling fear; of touching, as with an unseen hand, sympathies for the sorrowing and pity for distress, and moving the tenderest feelings of maternal love.

It is the duty of every one to give the voice the most careful training. It is a shame for a man to possess a gift so inestimable, and not be able, on account of a defect in early education, to use it with taste and propriety. Its culture should form a prominent part in the instruction imparted in all our schools. It should be constantly subjected during youth to that exercise which will strengthen it, and should not be left to neglect even to the latest years of life.

LECTURE V.

THE STUDY OF LANGUAGE.

DURING the latter part of the last century, a club of literary gentlemen in London were accustomed weekly to sup together. From my earliest reading, I have always been attracted by the charms which seemed to cluster about it. They were brought together because their tastes and their attainments were congenial. Their learning and discrimination were so far superior to the society which they encountered in the daily walks of the world, that it was cheering to meet with mutual appreciation and sympathy. They met for a social interchange of opinions. They cast, as into a common treasury, the curiosities of literature which they had chanced to pick up in their daily reading. They discussed the merits of authors. They talked of current events, and criticised with unrestrained freedom the measures of parties. They read to each other fragments of those literary productions upon which they chanced to be engaged, and commented upon their beauties and defects. Sometimes the party was convulsed with merriment, at others it was wrapped in the most profound attention, as they discoursed of the principles of morality, and those sublime truths which exalted intellects have searched out. The hours were agreeably varied by the light artillery of wit, and humor, and satire, and anon by the heavy ordnance of reason and solid argumentation. The members of that club were men of rare ability. Their writings have made and will keep the literature of England respectable throughout the world in all coming time.

The leading peculiarity, the crowning excellence of this school of literary men, was their great skill in the use of language. It is true, they had won distinction in their specialties. Every Englishman will point with pride to Burke, as the first of English orators. Johnson is the moralist and the lexicographer. Goldsmith is the pleasant bard; Reynolds the painter, and Garrick the actor. They are not, however, in these departments, preëminently models; but when we select for patterns of purity and elegance of English style, we unhesitatingly produce the genial writings of Goldsmith, the finished periods of Johnson, and the magnificent speeches of Burke.

For eminence in conversational power, for social entertainment, for enlightened opinions in the various departments of high art, that club has never been surpassed or equaled. Among its members, the acknowledged head was Dr. Johnson. Though mingling in social intercourse as equals, he acted the monarch. When he essayed to speak, all other tongues were silent, and while he had aught to say, no other entertainment was desired. This superiority was not due to him preëminently for the soundness of his opinions; for his notions were often eccentric, and his unconquerable prejudices frequently allured him into false positions. But his strength was in his great skill in the use of language. The art in which he excelled all others, and by which he inspired his friends and admirers with respect and reverence, was in his power of expression. It enabled him to invest his thoughts with unusual interest. There was a loftiness and a nobility in his style of conversation, which his companions could not assume. All his thoughts were marked with that peculiar charm which the great master painters, by a rare combination of colors, give to their pictures.

The importance of the gift of language, and the necessity of its study and cultivation, are frequently underrated. In the modern systems of education, the attempt is made to treasure up vast stores of knowledge, and to fathom the intricacies of the abstruse sciences at the expense of the study of language. Since the results of the recent researches in the natural sciences have been published to the world, and the unparalleled progress of the arts has caused increasing demands for knowledge in practical mechanics and civil engineering, the study of language has fallen into the background; and the use of the ancient languages as a part of a system of academic culture, which has had the countenance and approval of a long line of generations, is now scouted by many, as a barbarous relic of a bygone age.

The comparative importance of the study of language may be inferred from our wants as intelligent and communicative beings. There are two general purposes of education—to teach us to think, and to express our thoughts. The former is the basis; for if we use language without thought, we either speak well by accident, or we speak foolishly and bring shame upon ourselves by the use of the gift. The latter is equally essential, practically considered; for although we might learn facts and be able to construct arguments, we could not make use of them intelligibly beyond the narrow limits of our own minds. The cattle upon the hills may be burdened with many ponderous thoughts, but no one knows of them.

A successful system of education ministers to our wants in both these essentials. The study of the natural sciences acquaints us with facts. They give us knowledge of objects by which we are immediately surrounded in nature, and with which we have constantly to do in life. Much that is curious and wonderful in the designs of the Creator is brought to light through the disclosures which they make to us. We learn that the air we breathe is composed according to the nicest system of weight and measure; that its capacity for moisture, for heat and cold, and the more subtle fluids, is subject to fixed and invariable laws; that the fauna and flora upon the surface of the earth, are distributed through the different parallels of latitude, and the low and high elevations of the same latitude, upon the law of adaptation; that there is a correspondence in structure between the paw of the lion, the fin of the whale, the wing of the bird, and the hand of man. Nothing can be more useful or interesting to the human mind than such facts as these. They afford us fruitful materials for thought and contemplation. We may conceive of a human being using no other or higher powers of mind than those necessary for investigating and recording facts, for noting and observing such truths as these we have mentioned, and satisfied with these acquirements.

If we advance a step further, we come to the mathematics and logic, the latter comprising the theory and the former the practice of the same art. By these we are taught to use the reasoning faculties in passing from the known to the unknown. I have said that the natural sciences acquaint us with facts. The mathematics make us familiar with the process by which we pass from these facts to other and new knowledge. When to the faculty of searching facts, arranging them, and treasuring them as data, we add the power of syllogistic reasoning, we greatly enlarge the power and capability of the mind, and indefinitely extend the field of its operations.

But if the education to which we trust for the formation of our intellectual characters stop here, we perceive that it would be decidedly defective. A man may acquaint himself with all that has been observed in nature, or constructed in art; he may go back in the history of the world to the period of fog and vapor, and come on up through the slime and mud of the ages; he may be thoroughly skilled in all the processes of reasoning, and be familiar with the progress of philosophy and the history of opinions; and yet he may be unable to express the results of his studies with such taste, precision, and accuracy as to commend them to the minds of scholars. Dr. Johnson had no better judgment or more sound sense than many men of his own or succeeding generations; but his thoughts are embalmed in the English language, because the style in which he has expressed them has met with almost universal commendation.

Hence we conclude that no system of education is complete, which does not provide for the successful cultivation of language. There seems to be a tendency in arranging the courses of study in our institutions of learning, towards too great a preponderance of branches in physical inquiry, which are dignified by the name of sciences, but which are as yet vague and ill-defined. This remark is by no means intended to discredit the ardor of research in this direction, but to question the propriety of making these inquiries in their crude state the subjects for a course of mental discipline. A single illustration will show the progress of this tendency. Of the patronage which has been bestowed by the Smithsonian Institution "for the diffusion of knowledge among men," no considerable portion has ever been given for investigation in any other department of knowledge than the natural sciences. The whole management of the institution has been under the control of men who make these sciences their specialty. The memoirs of the several competitors have been disposed of upon this principle, and the public have received, as the yearly contributions of this mammoth institution for the "diffusion of knowledge among men," a *single volume* of indifferently written matter upon the shell-fish of some desert shore, or upon the language of a decaying tribe of Indians that has no literature, and can have no practical value to anybody. The committees of award have been selected with an eye to this department alone, which would seem to preclude competition in any other field of inquiry. If the books which the Smithsonian Institution have published should stand as an index of the progress of knowledge among men for the last ten years, it would show progress in only one direction, and a meager result at that.

The same spirit is manifested in many of our seminaries of learning. The time formerly given to the study of the languages has been shortened, or they have been entirely discarded, and a number of new branches in the natural sciences have been introduced. This latter step may be correct, but the former is at least questionable. If in the progress of knowledge new branches of study need to be employed, then let the time for completing the whole be proportionately increased, instead of enlarging the field of inquiry in one department at the expense of another.

Language originates in the necessities of our nature. We express our wants, we gratify desires by means of it. A national language is enlarged and perfected, as the wants of that nation become more numerous and the capacity for satisfying them is increased. It rises to its greatest perfection and beauty, where civilization has been carried to its highest point, and the systems of mental culture are most complete.

The branches of study which are most usually employed for the cultivation of language, are grammar, rhetoric, and foreign languages, both ancient and modern. Grammar and rhetoric belong to the same class, and may be considered rather as passive than as active agents in enabling us to give expression to thought. They are not so much for the cultivation of ease and volubility, as a means to test the accuracy of language. They are to the writer and the speaker what the square is to the joiner, the water-level and the plumb are to the builder. We sometimes meet with a man who speaks very grammatically who never saw the inside of a grammar—who composes with purity and elegance, and reasons logically, who knows nothing of the elements of style, of rhetorical tropes and figures—who hardly knows the meaning of logic, and never heard of the Dialectics of Aristotle. This is possible, and yet he may be guilty of gross blunders without knowing them to be such, and without the knowledge to correct them. The joiner may put work together without the square, and the builder may lay foundations without the level and the plumb; but he has no means to test the accuracy of his work.

On the other hand, we not unfrequently encounter those who know a text-book in rhetoric from beginning to end, and can describe every trope and figure known, and yet can not construct a tasteful sentence. This is doubtless true, and it points to a defect in the manner in which these studies are taught. Pupils have been made to repeat rules and formulæ, without having exercises in the practical use of them. They have been taught to give the part of speech of each word in the parsing lesson, the "government and rule for it," without ever dreaming that all this is to enable them to speak and write the English language correctly; and they would doubtless be unable to tell, if the question were propounded, whether man was made for grammar, or grammar for man. The great object of many a youth is to get through the text-book and into the Paradise Lost, and the height of his ambition is to be able to rattle off the lingo of what is termed a great parser.

There are two legitimate results of studying grammar. It enables us in the first place to perceive the elements of a sentence and their offices. It shows us how to take to pieces the thoughts of the best writers, and to discover the manner in which those sentences were made. It imparts a clear notion of the different shades of idea which successive added words and elements will give. We thus acquire a nice discrimination in the use of language, and thereby form the habit of expressing our thoughts with accuracy and point. This part of grammar is termed Analysis. It has been treated with a master hand by Professor Green, in his "Analysis of the English Language." It is indeed a philosophic work and one of great merit.

The second result of this study is to enable us to take those elements which we have found to exist in a sentence, and to recompose them, and thus make sentences for ourselves. It not only teaches us what offices the several elements are designed to fill; but what offices our own ingenuity can make them fill. Composition should be a much more frequent exercise than parsing, and should be interspersed with it.

Taking sentences to pieces that have been well written, and writing sentences well ourselves, should be the chief business in the study of this science. And the learner should be reminded by each recurring lesson, that the object is to learn to speak and write correctly, and that whatever does not conduce to this result is of but little value.

Rhetoric should likewise be made a practical matter. We sometimes think we have done well for a student when we make him recite the author used, and understand all the qualities of style and the figures of speech. But we are by no means sure that this will enable him to make a correct writer. He may have a very exact verbal knowledge of the concise and the verbose, of looseness and strength, of the comparison, the metaphor, the simile, synechdoche, ontonomasia and onomatopeia, and yet he may be entirely innocent of their use. If we were to teach a printer's apprentice to become a ready and skillful compositor, we would not tie his hands behind him, and then lead him round and explain the use of the various objects employed in the different parts of the work—the compositor's stick, the fonts of type, with the lines and leads. For although he might by this means understand what was necessary to be done, yet he would be little better prepared to execute a fine job of work than before our instructions commenced. But we would place the compositor's stick in his hands, put him to the font of type, and combine instruction with practice. When Monsieur Jourdain, in the French comedy, is told that he must bring his jaws very near together, and stretch the corners of his mouth towards his ears whenever he pronounced the vowel I, the direction seemed to the unsophisticated ignoramus like very profound learning. But whether the pupil was enabled to give utterance to the sound any better after he had heard that learned rule than before, we are not informed.

It may with safety be asserted, that a large majority of those who study grammar do not reap the proper, the legitimate results. A person who learns to recite all the definitions of terms in grammar—to repeat the rules for the government of words—and to parse fluently in some poem, may acquire thereby some discipline of mind and habits of attention; but these are only the subsidiary results. How many of those who study grammar improve in speaking and writing the English language, in any tolerable proportion to the time and effort expended, I submit to the good judgment of practical teachers to decide. The position which the study of grammar now occupies in many of our schools, is not very unlike that held by the steam engine in the early history of that invention, when nearly all the power was expended in moving the wheels and gearing necessary to its own motion. Until we as teachers, can learn to instruct in the branches of grammar and rhetoric in such a manner that our pupils can bring into practice what they learn, and shall have their energies directed to the great results which it is the design of those noble sciences to accomplish, we signally fail.

The second means employed in our schools for

improvement in speaking and writing, is the study of foreign languages. In the remarks which I am about to submit on the comparative value of the ancient languages, I shall not attempt to advocate the study of them on the ground of ancient prestige and renown; I shall take no advantage of the fact that Milton and Pope, and Newton and Johnson, and Burke and Macaulay, and Webster and Prescott, the acknowledged leaders of their respective generations, were all ripe classical scholars. No principle of aristocracy should be brought to bear in keeping any study in a system of education longer than the best good of the pupil demands it. If the ancient languages can not hold their place among the studies usually employed for acquiring a liberal culture, on their own merits, then let them give way to those which will better accomplish the purpose for which they are designed. Let every thing pertaining to a course of study rest upon this basis.

I have said that grammar and rhetoric were passive agents in enabling us to speak and write. These furnish us with rules and definitions by which we may determine whether our use of language be correct. The study of foreign languages, on the contrary, is an active agent, which exercises us in the expression of our thoughts. It gives us power and fluency in the use of words, and precision in the arrangement of them. It is frequently impossible to translate a sentence so as to make it into good pure English, by giving the meaning of each word as found in the vocabularies; but we can readily perceive what the meaning of the author was designed to be; hence our ingenuity is taxed to select from our stock of words, those which will best express the particular shades of idea which we find in the original. We not unfrequently meet with a sentence in a foreign language, where the idea is apparent enough, but which gives us quite as much difficulty to put into good English as to word an original thought. For this reason, I choose to call it an active agent in disciplining those faculties which are employed for the expression of our ideas. It affords us a rich experience in originating and framing forms of expression, and in adapting the words of our own language to choicest specimens of thought. Hence the advantage of studying any foreign tongue, is to enable us to use our own with greater ease and accuracy. This is the great object which should ever be kept in view; the end for the attainment of which our efforts should be directed. This so far transcends all others that it may be considered the only real purpose for which any language is studied. It is rare that a person studies a language for the immediate purpose of conversation.

Of the thousands who acquire the modern languages in schools and colleges, the number is comparatively small who ever speak them with tolerable propriety, unless they mingle with those nations which use them. The culture to be derived from the study of a modern language is the same in kind as that from an ancient, only differing in degree. The former is more simple, the order of the words more nearly resembles our own, and there are fewer idioms in its construction. There is therefore less difficulty in translating it. Our judgment is not so much brought into exercise in selecting words, and arranging them in our minds so as to express the particular idea of the author we read, as in the ancient. Hence the culture to be derived from its study is less severe, and as a consequence less powerful and abiding in its influence upon our habits of expression. If none of the propositions in Geometry were more difficult to prove than that the three angles of a triangle are equal to two right angles, the labor would be comparatively easy, and the mental culture to be derived therefrom would be correspondingly small. But if we want a higher order of discipline, we must grapple with those which are less elementary in their nature. If, therefore, a person only wants a limited amount of culture in expressing his thoughts, or has not the time and means for more extended studies, a modern language would, doubtless, be more serviceable than an ancient; and it is advisable for those who are intending to pursue the ancient languages to begin with some modern; especially for young persons and for ladies. The latter being easier, will serve as a stepping-stone to the more difficult. For this purpose there is probably none better than the French. It has the merit of precision and accuracy, and very much resembles in this particular the Greek. But it is not necessary to institute a comparison between the merits of the several modern languages—a subject rich in thought.

A perfect system of education, as has been already observed, acquaints us with facts, with the processes of reasoning, and with the use of language. If it fails in either, it is defective. There is an objection sometimes raised to the study of the languages, on the plea that much time is wasted in the attempt to learn them, which might be more profitably expended upon other studies; that innocent boys and girls are kept repeating the declensions and conjugations—the *hic, hæc, hoc,—bam, bo, bus,—j'ai, tu as, il a,* when the time might be employed upon studies more congenial and practical.* It is not difficult to excite

* The memory can be as well disciplined by treasuring up in its garner names of substances and their relations, which will be of real value in life, and without a knowledge of which, men and women

derision in the minds of the young and the uneducated, by representing the ultimate end of the study of the languages to be the learning and repeating these senseless sounds. Upon the same principle, we might excite equal derision in the minds of this class by the *cosines* and *abscissæ* in the Mathematics, by the *barbara*, *darii*, *ferio*, *baralipton*, in Logic, or the *Mollusks*, *Entomostraca*, *Tubulibranchiates*, *Gasteropods*, and *Rhizopods* in Zoology. Every science has its nomenclature. There are terms like these in all, which are constantly recurring, which sound like a barbarous jargon to those who know not their use. They are employed merely for convenience, and contitute no real part of the study. In a language, we do not look upon the declensions and conjugations as any part of the labor from which we are to derive the great advantage of studying it. They are the media through which we look at the thought. They are merely the A B Cs of the science. We learn these as a matter of course, as we

---

ought to be ashamed of themselves—as by repeating, till one is out of breath, *ode*, *tode*, or that sublime piece of philology and poetry—

From *o*, are formed *am* and *em*,
From *i*, *ram*, *rim*, *ro*, *sse* and *sem*:
U, *us*, and *rus*, are formed from *um*.
All other parts from *re* do come—
As *bam*, *bo*, *rem*.

Address of R. P. Stebbins, D. D.

learn the definitions of terms, and the rules in grammar, or as a mechanic learns the names of his tools, and the printer the places where his types are kept.

If by the objection (that time is wasted upon the ancient languages which might be more profitably spent upon some other studies), is meant that other studies designed to cultivate language should be substituted in their place, then, let the value of those studies be tested, and if they are better adapted to secure the end desired, let the languages give place to them. I do not know that any such claim is made. If it be meant that the study of the languages be discontinued* entirely, without any substitute, and the time devoted to the mathematics and

* "I will confirm my argument [in favor of the natural sciences] by the excellent and weighty authority of Professor Pierce, of Cambridge. In a letter written the last summer to Hon. Abbot Lawrence, founder of the scientific school connected with the university, in which he congratulates Mr. Lawrence upon the eminent success of the institution, he says (I quote from memory): 'The school has demonstrated that a good education can be gained without classical studies.' Such an opinion, coming from the shades of the oldest university in the country, is especially worthy of note. So far as mental discipline is concerned, I have shown that the natural sciences are more efficient and attractive than the study of the languages; that in studying the works of God we may do more for our intellectual culture than in studying the words of man. I now proceed to show that the knowledge which we gain in the study of the sciences is as much more valuable than that which we gain in the study of the languages, as its discipline is better."—*Address of R. P. Stebbins, D. D.*

the sciences, then the gift of language would be neglected, and that balance of mind which it is the business of education to strengthen and preserve, would be lost. Again, if it is meant that too great a proportion of time is spent upon the languages, then let the time be readjusted and equalized, so that each class of studies may have its due share. Let no power perish through neglect. If a man should keep either of his eyes shut continuously it would soon be enfeebled, and that beautiful and delicate organ would perish. We become culpable by neglect as much as by misuse. The cultivation of all the faculties should go on hand in hand. But, finally, if it be meant by this objection, that time is squandered in attempting to acquire a knowledge of the languages without attaining the true object for which they should be studied, or even understanding what that object is, if it be meant that those who pursue them study to no profitable purpose, then I join hands with the objector, and declare the saying worthy of all acceptation. As I have already stated, there are but few of those who study English grammar in the way in which it was formerly taught in our common schools, who are enabled thereby to speak and write the English language more correctly. So, of the vast number in our schools and universities who study the ancient languages, but a small portion of them reap the rich fruits which the classics may be made to yield. Indeed, there are very many college degrees that stand for a very small amount of philosophical knowledge of the languages. Students learn the declensions and conjugations, a few of the rules for construction, the vocabulary definitions of the words, and then, as the ultimatum, to garble the thoughts of the classic writers in horrid English. They hobble along through the remainder of their course upon crutches, or such a staff as they can pick up by the way.

We are aware that even this method yields a certain amount of advantage. The pupil learns the derivation of many words, and gets a discipline of the memory and other faculties. But these are merely the incidental results, and can be attained much more readily and economically in other ways. The great business of cultivating power and expression—of acquiring exactness in the use of language—of studying the classics for the purpose of enabling us to communicate thoughts in our own language with greater ease and accuracy, is left untouched. The skill derived from seeing a thought in a foreign tongue, and making an expression to match it in our own, is not appreciated. This class of students would be much better off without the ancient languages than with them. They squander and waste much valuable time, that might be devoted to labor in some useful and honest occupation. It is true that they absorb something of the caste and polish of the genuine students by mingling with them from day to day, but in the main, they get in lieu of a great good which they seek, nought but a glorious cheat. This shocking waste of time and money, and of mental energy in a few instances, is susceptible of explanation.

In the first place, a large number of those who fail are either persons of very moderate endowments, who have not brains enough to learn an ancient language, and would be much more usefully employed if they were at home swingling flax, or they are the sons of rich men, who do not want a college education, but whom the aristocracy of the family requires to take a degree at the university. A much larger number, who have fair talents, who are anxious to become good linguists, and who are honest and faithful in the application of their energies to the accomplishment of that purpose, make a signal and most shameful failure through the ignorance or negligence of teachers in not pointing out the true object of their labors, and the proper course to be pursued in order to attain it. The ghost of a good lady once appeared to her very dear friend, and on being asked if she was happy, replied that she had but one desire—that she might come back to earth and ask forgiveness for having attempted to teach what she did not know.

When the scholar begins the study of a language, he has no idea of the work to be accomplished. He sees before him nothing but the blackness of darkness, and often the shadows are very gloomy behind. He must therefore be governed in his efforts by his teacher. It is not in this study as in the mathematics, where a scholar by himself will, if he be honest and earnest in his endeavors, rarely fail in pursuing the true course to the end contemplated. But in a language, he may expend much useless time and labor before he finds the direct road. Here there is need of the ingenuity and judgment of the instructor. He must direct the efforts of his pupils in learning those things which he can put to immediate use, and thus fasten them in the mind. Pupils are not unfrequently compelled to begin the study of Latin, by learning from the grammar, principles, rules, exceptions—one indiscriminate mass, without the remotest conception of their application, and frequently not knowing the meaning of the terms used, or the examples which he is obliged verbally to commit. This usage is parallel with that of teaching the A B Cs by calling the child up and giving him a daily dose of twenty-six barbarous-looking characters, with unheard-of names, and requiring him to remember them.

Many of those who now denounce in unmeasured terms the study of the ancient languages, judge of the difficulties to be encountered in mastering the rudiments, by the senseless labors to which they themselves were once subjected. The faults of the systems of instruction are charged upon the studies themselves, upon which are bestowed curses loud and long. And it sometimes happens, that those very powers which have been acquired by the most elaborate classical training, are employed in condemning their use. Whenever I see such shameless ingratitude, I am forcibly reminded of the words of the dying Cæsar, "*Et tu, Brute!*"

There have of late been great advances made in conducting the study of the rudiments of the languages. There are two general systems now in use. One is called the Ollendorff method, from the fact that he first introduced the leading features of the system into practice in his classes, and afterward published them for the use of pupils in the German. Books upon that plan have since been prepared in nearly all the languages, both ancient and modern. The plan in that system is to put a thing into practice as soon as it is learned, and by constant repetition acquire the habit of using it correctly. As soon as the pupil has learned a half dozen words of Latin, he begins to translate into English and to compose Latin. When he has learned a declension, he is required to use the several cases till he has a practical knowledge of them. Each of the constructions peculiar to a language must be mastered, by the use of numerous examples in which they are found, and he is then obliged to make sentences in which those constructions shall be introduced. It will be seen at a glance that this is the most thorough and comprehensive course that can be pursued. By this, every thing is mastered as we proceed, and a pupil is prepared to read and compose at pleasure.

By the other system, the student first learns the grammar, and then begins at once to translate. By this method he is obliged to learn many things without seeing their immediate use. He obtains an acquaintance with the various constructions only as he recognizes them in the author which he reads. In thus learning a language, he will be enabled to translate a classic work in a much shorter time than by any other, and if pursued under the guidance of a skillful teacher, may acquire a thorough knowledge of it.

In deciding upon the comparative merits of the two systems, we should take into consideration the maturity of the faculties to be used. In acquiring a language, the memory is the one chiefly employed. We have all observed that in youth the memory differs from that in later years. In youth, we can readily remember facts; in manhood, we remember principles, facts being retained only as they are referred to principles. In youth, we gather the materials which we use when we come to the period of reflection. The mind in youth is more tenacious of facts than it is in manhood, while principles can scarcely be remembered because not comprehended; but in the prime of life we remember almost entirely by classifying our knowledge.

From these facts, it would follow that the Ollendorff method is better suited to youthful minds, and that of beginning with the grammar to minds which have arrived at the period of maturity. The latter method, however, should never be exclusively used. The pupil should be exercised as he advances, in putting the facts and principles into practice. He should be taught to write in the language which he is learning, such sentences as will illustrate the use of the cases in the declensions, the moods and tenses in the conjugations, and all the difficult constructions in syntax. He will thus fix his knowledge, and understand its value.*

* It is scarcely necessary to add that the progress of the pupil will be greatly accelerated by reducing his knowledge, as far as possible,

In acquiring the rudiments of a language, the student ought to be trained to habits of thoroughness and accuracy. Its laws and the principles of interpretation should be fully understood before he is allowed to look into a classic author. He should not only be able to explain all its peculiar constructions by reference to the rules of grammar, but he should be so familiar with them, that he can recognize them as old acquaintances. Then there is some satisfaction in reading a language, and the student can begin in an original author, and advance at once to the higher principles of interpretation and rhetorical criticism. He thus realizes the true design of studying it. But how numerous are the cases where a student rushes forward to Cæsar and Virgil, and assumes the airs of a perfect man in language, before he is prepared to leave off his swaddling clothes, and instead of interpreting upon the principles of construction, and be-

---

to practice. From the necessity of the case, it is evident that much of the pupil's time must be occupied in learning rules. If, however, the teacher is confined to these alone, it becomes intolerably irksome. The mind struggles against it, and is willing quickly to forget what is associated with nothing but pain. It was formerly the practice to carry a boy through the Latin grammar before he began to translate a word; and months were consumed in this dry and repulsive labor. It would be no wonder, if, under such a discipline, he learned to abominate the grammar, the language, and the instructor together.—*Wayland's Intellectual Philosophy*, page 277.

cause he knows it is so, relies implicitly upon the Yankee's prerogative, and guesses it out. Such a course is fatal to scholarship.

But there is not so great a liability to error in acquiring the rudiments of a language as in the subsequent career of the student. Mastering the rudiments is, in a great measure, mechanical. It requires skill on the part of the instructor, simply in introducing things to be learned at the right time, and of repeating the matter accomplished at proper intervals ; and in this the teacher is much relieved if he use a text-book skillfully arranged, and based upon correct principles. But when we come to the interpretation of an original classic author, there is needed the judgment and resources of a scholar ; not merely one who understands the matter himself, but who can initiate others into the mysteries. One great mistake that is made in this part of the work, consists in being content with imparting rudimentary knowledge. Hence all the efforts through the whole course are directed to training in the grammatical structure of the language, and the derivation of words.

Another error of a graver nature, consists in allowing students to translate a classic writer by calling the Latin words in their English order, and giving their vocabulary meanings. This can not properly be called translating, but garbling. That can never be a translation which is not good pure English. There are two requisites for a translation; the first is, that it have the spirit of the original, and still be correct English; and second, that it be as strictly literal as the former condition will allow. By pursuing the method indicated above, the student may give the meanings of the words, and still not realize the beauty and force of the sentence or paragraph which he is attempting to read. His whole attention is taken up with calling the words in two languages, and keeping an eye to the correspondence of construction. It is our object in studying a language, as has been already indicated, to cultivate the habit of making correct English sentences, of using language with ease and accuracy. There are many idioms in every foreign tongue. If, in such phrases, we call the words and give their English meanings, though they may be given in the right case, mood, tense, number, and person, yet it would not convey the true idea, nor would it be good English. The purpose for which we are studying would be subverted; for we should not be learning to use correct English, but a mongrel. Rhetoricians have a term for this; they call it an idiotism. It is from the translation of idiomatic expressions that we derive the greatest advantage. In these phrases we can usually discover the meaning of the author, and our ingenuity is taxed in order to frame the expression which shall properly translate it. This is the kind of discipline we need. Those who have had no lingual culture, often find a difficulty in expressing themselves properly. They have the thought in mind, their opinions are well matured, but they can not use the language which will accurately express them, and they are obliged to appear to a great disadvantage. The proper study of language is designed to remove this defect, and to give power and pointedness of expression. But if the pupil is allowed to make translations as indicated above, it has the tendency to cultivate the habit of looseness and inaccuracy, the habit above all others which we need to correct. A foreign language studied in this way, instead of conferring a good, inflicts upon us a decided injury, and the less time thus spent, the better. The best period of youth is lost in laboring for that which we fail to get. The pupil may seek with diligence, and labor with earnestness, but the apple turns to ashes in his mouth.

After having thoroughly mastered the rudiments, the most efficient way of reaping the largest results from translating, is to take a whole clause or paragraph into the mind at once, and after having selected the meaning of the words with taste, to make the English sentence with the greatest care and nicety, so that when uttered it may appear polished like a gem. It is recorded by Gibbon, in that most delightful fragment of autobiography which he has left us, that in the composition of his History of the Decline and Fall of the Roman Empire, he always made a whole paragraph or section at a single cast, before he had put a word upon paper. This habit is worthy of our consideration, and can in no way be so successfully cultivated as in translating from an ancient language. In adopting, however, this elaborate and comprehensive system of interpretation, there is one error which should be scrupulously avoided. While we make our translations pure English, we should use no words which will convey a shade of idea different from that intended by the author. Our first object should be to ascertain his precise meaning; we have then to use our judgment, and to tax our inventive powers to frame a thought whose language shall correspond to the original. This exercise is very much like looking our own thoughts into shape, and cultivates that power and energy of expression of which we so often feel the need.

In following out the principles indicated in translating a classic author, there is a certain awkward accuracy which should be avoided. The Edinburgh Review for April, 1849, tells us of the case of the Rev. Theophilus Mudge, "who translated Greek

through a brick wall. Imagination and invention, whether in classics or mathematics, were strangers to his soul. He could have walked on his head sooner than have composed a line of Latin or Greek which had a spark of vigor in it. He was familiar with Viger, and knew by heart all the private history of ἵνα and ὅπως, and all the etiquette of the subjunctive and optative moods." It is not enough to be accurate, to be literal, to make good English; but it is requisite that a translation have some of the fire and vigor of the original.

Another advantage which is attainable by the study of the great master-pieces in the foreign languages, is apt to be either wholly overlooked, or greatly underrated; it is the opportunity which is afforded for the study of the qualities of style, or practical rhetoric. We there have, in their perfection, all the elements which rhetoricians so learnedly, and often so abstractly and obscurely talk about. If the student is required carefully to distinguish and analyze the qualities of style of the author which he reads, and to refer each trope and figure to its proper class, he would learn more of the principles of rhetoric, and acquire a greater facility in their use, than the most elaborate study of a text-book upon criticism. He would not only learn how a critic says writing should be done, but he would have continually before him a living model of the manner in which the masters of the art have done it. "I am persuaded," says Burke, "that understanding Homer well, would contribute more towards perfecting taste than all the metaphysical treatises upon the arts that ever have or can be written; because such treatises upon the arts can only tell what true taste is, but Homer everywhere shows it. He shows that the true sublime is always easy and always natural; that it consists more in the manner than in the subject, and is to be found by a good poet and a good painter in almost every part of nature."

Without dwelling at length upon the minor benefits resulting from studying foreign languages, I will, in concluding this part of my subject, sum up what I conceive to be the advantages derived from devoting a liberal amount of time and effort to the mastery of these studies.

I. The principal object, and the one before which all others sink into insignificance, is to cultivate the power of expression, to enable us to use our own language with greater ease and accuracy.

II. Among the subordinate advantages, we may name:

1. The knowledge which we thereby obtain of the derivation of all the words which have been transplanted from those languages into our own, thus giv-

ing a more elementary and comprehensive idea of their meaning.

2. The culture which we attain of the memory, and a habit of concentration of mind, inasmuch as the meaning of all the words of those languages must be learned, and the principles of their construction.

3. The opportunity it affords for the study of the qualities of style, and of obtaining a practical knowledge of the principles of rhetoric.

4. The information which we directly gain of the history, mythology, politics, poetry, and oratory of the ancients, in their original spirit, which we could never gain by means of translations.

Thus far I have said nothing concerning the character of the ancient authors themselves. Are their conceptions worthy of our examination? Is the style of their writings, their acuteness of analysis, and power of disquisition, proper to become the models for our imitation? If we examine with minuteness the works of the great classic writers which are put into the hands of the pupil, we shall find that they challenge our respect and veneration. All that is lofty in thought, or sublime in action, is found upon their pages. Homer, the father of poetry, whose heroes are the gods that tread the golden halls of Olympus, and kings and mighty men clad in celestial armor; Demosthenes, the orator whose "eloquence shook the arsenal, and fulmined over Greece;" Sappho and Pindar, the sweet lyric singers, whose melodious lines are the embodiment of fancy and sentiment; Eschylus, the tragic poet, whose actors are the deep passions of the human heart, and whose messengers are the winged winds; Cicero, the lawyer, the terror of conspirators and the defender of the liberties of his country; Horace, the good easy man, whose odes smack of good cheer and sparkling wine; and Tacitus, the historian, whose sententious periods greatly please while they instruct—such are the men whom the student of classic lore may make his friends. The productions of such men are fitted to inspire the youthful scholar with new ardor in the pursuits of learning. The reading of Homer made Alexander a warrior; and many a youth since the days of Alexander has been enamored of all that is noble and heroic in action, by the verses of that blind old bard. In poetry, in history, in oratory, he has the choicest specimens constantly before him. When we throw aside the classics, we banish from our systems of education the lights of all past ages; we separate from the company of those whose genius and learning have won for them imperishable fame; we reverse the judgment of the learned of every cultivated nation; we dismiss, for other guides, those who, age after age, have furnished models for every species of excellence in thought.

Lord Macaulay, in opening his critique on the Athenian orators, says, "The celebrity of the great classical writers is confined within no limits except those which separate civilized from savage man. Their works are the common property of every polished nation. In the minds of the educated classes throughout Europe, their names are indissolubly associated with the endearing recollections of childhood—the old school-room, the dog-eared grammar, the first prize, the tears so often shed and so quickly dried." And in closing his essay on Mitford's History of Greece, he uses these memorable words: "Of the indifference which Mr. Mitford shows on this subject [that splendid literature] I will not speak, for I can not speak with fairness. It is a subject in which I love to forget the accuracy of a judge, in the veneration of a worshipper and the gratitude of a child. If we consider merely the subtlety of disquisition, the force of imagination, the perfect energy and elegance of expression which characterize the great works of Athenian genius, we must pronounce them intrinsically most valuable. All the triumphs of truth and genius over prejudice and power, in every country and in every age, have been the triumphs of Athens."

Before deciding that the classics shall no longer fill a prominent place in our systems of education, we should consider the necessity which exists of a harmonious development of the faculties of the mind, the importance of that class of powers which the classics are designed to develop, and whether we have any other course of discipline to substitute for them, which will accomplish the work so well. It is idle to talk of substituting the physical sciences in their place, or to advocate such a change on the ground that it is better to study the works of the Creator than the words of man, as though consciousness were not as legitimate a field for the study of the Creator's attributes as the objects about us in the physical world. The fact is, man was made with his face upward, and it is folly for him to spend his days in poking about his feet. Bunyan's muck-rake is a simile in point. Until we have meditated these questions, and decided them understandingly, until we are able to build in its place a more enduring edifice, let us not tear down a structure whose foundations are firm, and whose massive and majestic walls are covered with the moss of centuries.

Whatever means we adopt for its culture, it is the English language that we are to speak. That good old English tongue has been moulding and perfecting itself for many centuries. It had, at the outset, the strongest, yet rudest materials. It has plundered from almost every language that was ever in the mouths of men. It has had the advantage of the highest civilization since the world began.

When we consider that this language which we speak and read, is the language in which Bacon conceived and meditated those thoughts which changed the whole course of metaphysical speculation, and created a new era in philosophical investigation—when we remember that Shakspeare in this language has ranged the whole field of human character, from the monarch on his throne to the peasant in his straw hut, and has touched, with a master's hand, all the passions, and humors, and sentiments of the human heart—when we read the poetry of Milton, and are enabled by means of it to contemplate all those images of beauty which his plastic imagination has created in Eden's garden, and those scenes of grandeur and sublimity where angels, and the Creator himself, speak to us—when we read the clear, the polished, the transparent periods of Hume, the grand and lofty paragraphs of Gibbon, the penetrating and earnest words of Macaulay, the bold and manly eloquence of Webster, and the sweet, graceful words of Clay, and remember that all this is in our own English tongue—is it not worth while to study, and meditate, and perfect our knowledge of it?

A language of such depth, and force, and beauty, is not to be learned in a few short terms of school and college, or with little care. To acquire a thorough knowledge of it is the serious business of a lifetime. By the study of its structure and its grammatical principles, by the attentive reading of the best authors, by the study of foreign languages, that shall throw light upon it, and teach us its derivation, by careful and protracted meditation, and by care in speaking, we should strive to know it in its perfection. Some of the purest pleasure of my life has been derived from the study of language. And although the beginning of the way was difficult, and dusty, and fatiguing, the elevations are easy and pleasant, and the prospects delightful.

LECTURE VI.

THE MEANS AND ENDS OF EDUCATION.

I PURPOSE to speak of the means and ends of a practical education—one that may produce fruit. Education, in its special and restricted sense, is the work of developing the faculties of the mind. It is a process by which the mental energies are furnished with material and put to work. The mind is sometimes compared to a storehouse, where a profusion of articles are indiscriminately stowed away. This is an unfortunate figure. Better liken it to the workshop of the mechanic, or to the hall of the artist, where numerous operatives are engaged in executing forms of beauty and usefulness. The various faculties of the mind, as memory, imagination, taste, are the workmen employed. The material which they are engaged in transforming into beautiful and useful shapes, the marble, the steel, the gold, the silver, are the ideas which we have of the various objects by which we are surrounded. The means by which those workmen have acquired skill in producing specimens of their labor of greater or less excellence, as regards strength, harmony, durability, finish, is, when applied to the energies of mind, what we mean by education.

If this be a true idea, the means employed should be such as to accomplish the end desired. We should not labor so much to accumulate vast stores, as to give the mind clear and vivid conceptions, and to stimulate its energies to long and vigorous exertions. That man is not of necessity best educated, who has read the most books, or spent most time in the schools. Those patents of nobility in the republic of letters, written upon sheepskin, and signed by the president of a college, certifying that the bearer has spent four years of his life within its walls, are, in too many instances, synonymous with those labels we see attached to bottles of patent medicine. Some of them are good for all they call for; but too many are the currency of quacks. This fact does not in the least depreciate the value of a sound collegiate education. The gold coin issued by government always carries with it the value upon its face, although there is abundance of the spurious article in circulation that is not worth the brass of which it is made But there is this difference between the coin and the college degree. Government puts its stamp only upon the genuine article, and we are left to detect the bogus by the want of it; whereas the faculty of a college affix their official seal to the spurious and the good alike, and we are without the means of knowing the value of one A. M. over another, and from frequent deception are inclined to doubt all till we have proven them.

Many men in our midst are possessed of the soundest culture, who have never had the advantage of a liberal education. The newspapers, and contact with the world, have been their tutors. The intercourse of society in the business of real life, where contending passions and counter interests impart a wholesome discipline, is a much better nurse of common sense than the cloistered cell. Careful, keen observation has furnished them with the material of thought from sources in which we are least liable to be deceived. The public journals, which are the only real histories that the world produces, enable them to compare the opinions and reasonings of other men with their own. They thus acquire a discipline of mind at the same time that they obtain an accurate and practical knowledge of the times, and are thereby prepared to act understandingly in any emergency. If we bear in mind the definition of education which we have already given—the furnishing the mind with material and putting it to work—we shall not wonder at their success. The richest classical education, unassisted by any kind of practical knowledge, affords a very uncertain guide in managing present affairs. The student of Grecian lore may be intimately acquainted with the tactics employed in the siege and defense of Thermopylæ; but these would by no means be adapted to the taking of the tower on the Malakoff. He may know all the policy and chicanery which Themistocles employed to deceive the Lacædemonians, and secure the completion of the wall of defense around the city of Athens; and yet he may be a novice in devising a network of plots which shall introduce or exclude slavery in the Territories.

The self-educated man frequently meets with eminent success in the management of affairs, because his school has been the present times; while the adept in classical learning fails, because his school was exclusively among the ancients. If we look into our halls of Congress we shall find that the sword of argument cuts keenest, and is handled right and left most dexterously, when wielded by a man who has learned what he knows from his reading of men, and the present workings of civil society, quite as often as when managed by him who has acquired his knowledge among musty folios, or has with pale and sickly countenance delved deepest in the mysteries of science. We often wonder how it is that the members elected from the Territories and newly settled States, who have enjoyed few educational advantages, can compete with our wisest and ablest men from the old States, where every facility is afforded for the most extensive culture. But it not unfrequently happens that the man transferred from the prairies and stumps of the West, holds his opinions and accomplishes his purposes quite as successfully as his more polished compeer. Everett and Sumner may upon occasion deliver very finished orations; but in originating and perfecting a bill, and in the management of an impromptu debate, they find themselves in an assembly at least their equals. Washington, and Franklin, and Roger Sherman had never received any thing from a college till its degrees of honor were showered upon them; yet their services were quite as important to the country as those of Adams, and Randolph, and Lee, though these had been crowned with the bay of the universities.

I have said that the self-educated man is sometimes more practical and successful in the management of affairs than the professed scholar. I may go farther. We sometimes consider books as the only source of education; but a man may indeed be well educated who knows nothing of books. Material for thought, and the ability of thinking with intensity upon any question at pleasure, may be possessed without their aid. It is possible that a man might possess intellectual faculties of the highest order, and carried to the highest point of cultivation, who could not write his own name. Homer, the father of poetry, the favored of the muses, from whose heroes the poets of all succeeding generations have formed their models, and from whose glowing periods they have drawn their inspiration, lived in an age of the world before letters had been invented. His poems were composed and treasured in the memory, and recited to the people on festive occasions. Wandering minstrels learned them from their author, and they were thus handed down from age to age, through the memory of men, till they were eventually rescued from the weakness and casualties of that treacherous faculty by the preserving power of letters.

It may possibly be inferred, from what has been said, that I do not entertain a very high opinion of our present systems of training, and do not look with favor upon what is termed a liberal education. Such a conclusion, however, would be unwarranted. The remarks which have been made were intended to throw light upon the term education, and to give us a clearer conception of the true idea conveyed by it. An earnest, genuine education is a very different thing from those notions of it which exist in the minds of many. The lad in the district school measures his progress by the rapidity with which he advances in the text-books placed in his hands, rather than by the depth and accuracy of his knowledge of a single principle which he has hurriedly passed over. He judges that to be good reading when the words are called most rapidly, instead of that when the idea is studied, and the proper emphasis, tone, and modulation are employed to convey the thoughts truthfully and vividly. The student in the university oftener prides himself upon having risen to the dignity of a more advanced class, than upon that depth and richness of thought, which accurate scholarship in the elements of knowledge is fitted to impart, or upon that retrospective glance which he is sometimes compelled to take when he is called to give his opinion of questions connected with his earlier studies. He spends the best of his time in cracking the shell of the nut, and rushes on, without stopping to take out the meat, to something else that needs to be cracked, and thus, ever cracking, he scarce enjoys a nibble. He pursues the shadow and misses the substance. Nor is this disposition confined to the lad in the district school or the stripling at college. If we knew the secret thoughts of our fellow-men, we should not unfrequently find the man of mature years, who loves to be classed among literary characters, priding himself more on the number of square feet of books which he has in his library, than upon the number of solid thoughts which he entertains in his head.

We thus perceive that through all the grades of honor, among those who cultivate their minds, from the boy on the lowest form at school up to the counselor and the man of letters by profession, there is manifested a taste for that kind of education which will show, rather than that which accomplishes results, which gives us the power of continuous thought, which nerves the mind to untiring exertion, in which enables us to bring to the examination of every subject, principles that have become settled our minds from previous research and study. The opinions of many men are worth nothing, because they are based upon nothing. They have never taken any pains to accumulate facts, or reflections, and hence, without any capital stock, they issue opinions which are the mere random workings of a vacant brain. Perhaps we have not on record a better example of popular delusion than that which was practiced, a few years ago, by a waggish writer for one of the New York journals. Sir William Herschell was, at the time, at the Cape of Good Hope, making observations upon the heavenly bodies. A column appeared in one of the morning papers, headed, in flaming letters, "Wonderful Developments of the Telescope," in which it was asserted that the great astronomer had succeeded, by introducing a strong pencil of light into the dark chamber of the telescope, upon the image there formed, in observing, with the greatest ease and distinctness, the men and animals living upon the face of the moon. By the representations of the piece, the man in the moon had become our near neighbor. Now a moment's reflection, by any one who knew the first principles of optical science, or who had even advanced so far in knowledge as to have observed his own shadow, would have shown that the image formed in a telescope, which is simply a shadow, would vanish the instant a beam of light is thrown upon it. But so artfully was the piece prepared, and so little discriminating thought did the people bestow upon it, that many of the learned, even, were successfully duped. Men were wild with delight at the triumphs of the discoverer, and some, I have no doubt, were ready to invest small sums in the purchase of wild lands there.

The time has gone by when we are to take the dictum of a man because he pretends to know, and is supposed to have had the opportunity of learning. But we are disposed to try every opinion, and prove it before adopting it. The time was when authority was proof, or at least equal to it in value; but it is so no longer. In these matter-of-fact times we have come to deal with realities and not their semblances. We have learned to judge of the culture of a man's mind, not by the number of years he has been engaged in study, but by what he is able to do—by the fruits his mind is capable of yielding. This is the great lesson that the philosophy of Bacon has taught us—to judge of every thing by its fruits; and indeed a greater than Bacon had, centuries before, declared, "By their fruits ye shall know them." It makes very little difference whether this mental culture, this ability to think accurately, which is the result of a sound education, was obtained by the light of a rush candle, after the toil and sweat of a hard day's labor, or was acquired while reclining at ease, listening to the words of a learned professor, and gazing at him through a gold-bowed quizzing glass. The only question that concerns us is, has the education been acquired? Is it actually possessed? Can we depend upon the genuineness of the pretension? We should be as ready to accord the palm to deserving merit, when won we know not how, as to him who has passed through a course of academic studies.

But lest I may be misunderstood respecting the best course to be pursued in acquiring knowledge, let us examine and compare the means usually employed for the accomplishment of the purpose. I have already referred to a class who have figured extensively in public affairs, and in the domain of letters, who are termed self-educated men. They deserve much credit, as well for their energy as their success. Often they have been obliged to struggle with adverse circumstances, and have accumulated what they possess by dint of untiring application, in the midst of the cares of laborious occupations. But we should not allow them honor and confidence beyond what they deserve. Their education is usually more practical than profound, more special and circumscribed, than general and comprehensive. In common affairs in which they have had experience, their judgment can be relied on. But lacking that breadth and profoundness of view, which thorough training in the elements of knowledge is intended to bestow, they frequently find themselves in the dark, and obliged to act without any settled opinions.

And yet those who have least information, often have the greatest confidence in themselves. Their views are advanced as absolute, and with as much assurance as though they carried the keys of knowledge. Assurance is so characteristic of such, that Inspiration hath declared, "The fool rageth and is confident." There are none so hopelessly foolish, or whose advice is to be taken with so much caution, as those who are over wise in their own conceit.

We not unfrequently meet with demonstrations of the sentiment uttered by Pope,

"A little learning is a dangerous thing."

As the spark which is suddenly struck, in the midst of profound darkness, produces a blinding effect upon the sight, so the mind is sometimes overpowered by being brought from the darkness of ignorance into the light of very common truths. But as the pupil of the eye opens and enlarges before the beaming of intenser light, so the mind is strengthened and expanded by the steady contemplation of new truths.

———"shallow drafts intoxicate the brain,
But drinking deeper sobers us again."

Socrates was indeed pronounced by the Delphic oracle wisest among men. But for what? Because, in his own opinion, he knew nothing. Because he had withstood the first blinding effects of knowledge, and could now look into its serene depths, and see how vain are our greatest acquirements compared with what is possible to be known. The response of the Pythia was in accordance with the declarations of Holy Writ. For we are represented as being truly wise, when we have learned enough to make us meek and humble like little children.

The empiric and the charlatan usually acquire

confidence much beyond what they deserve. Many people manifest a disposition to confide in one who boasts loudly, and who has seized the idea that he has the qualifications for a leader in some art or profession, rather than in one who, by long study and experience, has prepared himself for a responsible position, and puts forth his pretensions with modesty.

The profession of medicine furnishes a good illustration. There seems to be a charm that insensibly draws many people to the quack. Let a man come into a town with a name spelled with a continental combination of letters, and post upon the corners of the streets flaming advertisements that he is some great somebody, from a great city somewhere, and that he has letters from innumerable sick folk, who have been miraculously cured of their leprosy by the use of his all-curing and never-failing medicine, and instantly the afflicted of every kind and degree of disease, without any other knowledge of his character or his acquirements than that which they can learn from the trumpet which he himself blows, rush forward, eager to see which shall trouble the waters first; and, without murmuring, pay any sums which he in his caprice may demand; while the well-read physician at our doors, who has spent money and the best years of his life in a careful study of diseases and remedies, who is acquainted with the hereditary taints and temperaments of our families, who, in sunshine or in storm, by night or by day, is ready with a willing heart to turn out and minister to our sufferings, who has watched by the bedside of the dying mother, or father, or brother, or sister, or child, and has faithfully tried his skill to the last, is passed by, or paid grudgingly for his services.

In the profession of medicine, systematic and thorough culture in the science often comes in competition with skill practically acquired without education. In general, when natural abilities and application to duty are equal, it is always safest to employ that man who has the most thorough medical knowledge. For he certainly can best succeed who, in an emergency, has the most resources at hand. That physician who is content with the knowledge which he was obliged to acquire before he could obtain his degree, who neglects to take and read the leading medical reviews, and who begrudges the purchase of a few new books, from time to time, as the knowledge of the science advances, is not the man in whose hands we should willingly trust our lives.

It will be seen that it is my aim to advocate a thorough, genuine education, and not the mere vague and indefinite pretension. The best means for the attainment of such an education are abundant, and can not be mistaken by the honest seeker.

The first requisite is a spirit of inquiry—a disposition to seek as for hidden treasure—to separate truth from error—to sift opinions and ideas till the true gold has been found. When such a disposition exists, and is united with a resolute purpose, the possessor will make real progress. Real progress: I use the term in distinction from that fictitious progress which prevails in many of our highest institutions, which is measured by studies finished, and terms passed in the college walls. We need a system of training which shall develop a living, breathing, healthy education, and not the mere dry bones of one. Let the boy who enters the common school, be thoroughly drilled in every principle, and be taught the why and the wherefore of every step as he advances, so that he may depend upon his own faculties for a reason, and not trust to the mere arbitrary rule of the book, without knowing or appreciating its bearing. When he enters the high school, the same thoroughness should be insisted on in all that is taught. He should not commence the study of Latin and Greek because he is obliged to have a knowledge of these in order to get to the university. But he should be inspired with a taste for those studies at the outset, and he should be encouraged to pursue them with that enthusiasm which is sure to be rewarded with rich fruits. The attainment of a certain, positive good at each step as we advance, should be the incentive to exertion, and not the prospect of becoming a member of some celebrated institution. The student in the university should aim at the ripest scholarship. He should not feel that any honor is to be conferred upon him for having passed through it, provided he has not got that for which the university was established.

There exists, in the minds of many, a feeling of dislike and opposition to what is termed a liberal education. This feeling is cherished on the part of a certain class of the illiterate, who would in general be opposed to all improvement beyond what is absolutely necessary. It is the class who send their children to the district school to learn just enough that they may not be cheated when they grow up; who value the pieces of hard money which they have laid away in a chest, more than the number of bright ideas which they can store in the mind; and who look upon the life of the thinker, and the professional man, as a life of laziness and rascality, and regard with distrust all he does or says. We do not deny that there are some among the profession of thinkers who can, upon occasion, show some acquaintance with laziness and rascality. There are, indeed, in every rank and grade of society, those who disgrace it. The argument of this class is that the tree of knowledge should be cut down, because we sometimes chance to gather from it bitter fruits. The objection of these is narrow-minded, and goes for nothing.

But there is in a higher class, among our business men, our practical men, an antipathy towards liberal culture. They are not without valid reasons for the feelings which they cherish. There are several causes which combine to produce these sentiments. Many of those who receive a collegiate education are wofully deficient in those branches which they should have learned at the common school, and the college is not a place to mend such deficiencies. Many a young man who is entitled to put the first two letters of the alphabet after his name, is unable to spell correctly a large proportion of the words which he uses, and in the practical business of life he is found a complete novice, even in figures, in geography, and in history. Having proved himself wanting in the most common elements of an education, he is judged to be equally so in all others, and is at once set down as an ignoramus, and his A. B. is at a heavy discount.

Again, many of those who pass through all the grades of a liberal education, know so little about the various branches to which they have been required to give their attention, that they scarcely remember the names of the authors they have read, or the text-books in the sciences which they have studied. Such are held in the estimation they deserve. They have not been true to themselves, and the confidence with which they would challenge the world is forfeited. They not only bring disgrace upon themselves for making pretension to that which they do not possess, but they cast a reproach upon liberal education, and injure the good name of the institution under whose fostering care they have sought protection and support.

There is one fault in the organization and management of the higher institutions, which serves to strengthen this feeling of hostility. The courses of study, in many instances, are not adapted to the purpose of making practical men, but simply scholars. Instead of fitting them for the duties of life, it operates to unfit them for almost any place in society. It is said that one of the most distinguished scholars of the past generation, when asked by the lady where he was spending his college vacation, to harness the horse for her, actually put on the hames first and then the collar, and supposed that this was the way they were intended to be worn. Students, on leaving college,* are often compelled to begin life anew.

* "It is a very common complaint that thrifty, untaught farmers grudge the cost of a thorough education for their sons and daughters

Instead of being fitted to take the lead in society, they frequently find that they have much to learn, and that those whom they left behind them when they departed for its secluded walls, are infinitely their superiors. In the English universities, and in some of the best colleges in this country, changes have been agitated in the courses of study, and methods of discipline. Some wholesome improvements have already been introduced. The demand for the reform is manifested in the public mind, by

---

Hodge, industrious and independent in his ignorance, scorns his educated neighbor, who is but a drone and a beggar with it all. 'I have succeeded well enough,' says he, 'without education; why should n't my children do the same?' Now I regret Hodge's contempt for learning, but I can not pretend to be surprised at it. On the contrary, it seems to me most natural, and not very blameworthy. For do but consider that the *educated* son or daughter too often returns to the paternal home with an ill-disguised contempt for its homely roof, and a positive aversion to its downright labor. Who would expect a sensible, home-bred parent to relish and value such an education?

"That son is not truly educated who can not grow more corn on the acre than his unlearned father, and grow it with less labor. That educated daughter has received a mistaken and superficial training, if she can not excel her mother in making soap, or cheese, or butter. All these are chemical processes, in which her education should render her an adept, far beyond any untaught person. The educated lawyer, doctor, or clergyman, whose garden is not better (I do not say larger), and his fruit trees more thrifty and productive than his illiterate neighbor's, sadly discredits and damages the cause of education."—*Lecture on Education, by Horace Greeley.*

the numerous attempts made for the establishment of People's colleges, and the subject is receiving the attention of some of our wisest educators.

Another reason which operates to produce a feeling against liberally educated men, arises from the fact that they seem to manifest a desire to withdraw themselves as much as possible from mingling in business affairs. They strive to create an aristocracy of letters, and draw a dividing line between themselves and the balance of humanity. Instead of throwing themselves upon the current of every-day life, and braving the struggles manfully, they stand aloof, and talk and act as though they were a different order of beings from their fellow-men; as though to mingle in the common labors of life would detract from their dignity and standing. They look upon business as degrading to the scholar.* They seem to consider it debasing to education to make it subservient to any practical or useful purpose. They are the followers of Aristotle, who taught men that if they would be real philosophers, they must with-

* Sir Walter Scott, whose literary accomplishments have filled the world with admiration, once remarked, "There is no necessary connection between genius and an aversion or contempt for any of the common duties of life. On the contrary, to spend some portion of every day in any matter-of-fact occupation is good for the higher powers themselves in the upshot."—*Lockhart's Memoirs of Scott.*

draw themselves, as completely as possible, from all the real affairs of life that can serve a practical or useful purpose, instead of being the followers of Bacon, who taught that "knowledge is power," and that philosophy is good for nothing unless it enables us to accomplish some useful results, unless it can bring forth fruits.

Such a disposition manifested by those who are educated, is disastrous to progress. The basis of a nation or community is the laboring population; and though it be true that the thinking men shape the affairs of the world, yet they can never accomplish their designs without the aid of the former, and the most splendid triumphs of knowledge must ever be where there is the most cordial coöperation of the two classes. The thinking man and the laboring man must understand each other. They must realize that each is working for the other's good; that they are in a common field, putting forth united exertions to overcome those obstacles which exist to the progress of civil society, and that they are reaching forward to a success equally desired by both. There is perhaps a greater tendency towards this result in this country, than in our sister nations of the globe, owing to our common school education, which is open to every child, and to our free, political institutions, which act as a powerful stimulant in the universal development of mind. My confidence in this assertion has been strengthened by a remark which occurs in the preface to the great work of Mr. Agassiz on the "Natural History of the United States of America." "There is not a class of learned men here," says he, "distinct from the other cultivated members of the community. On the contrary, so general is the desire for knowledge, that I expect to see my book read by operatives, by fishermen, by farmers, quite as extensively as by the students of our colleges, or by the learned professors; and it is but proper that I should make myself understood by all."

The objections which are thus urged against a liberal education, originate either from a narrow-minded view of the subject, or from judgments passed upon weak and imbecile representatives of such culture, or from the fact that those institutions which are established for giving it, are not fully adapted to the purpose. The principal of these objections is not really made against the systems employed, but against the abuse of them. If the results accomplished by these systems be such as they were intended to produce, these objections would have no weight. Faults are charged upon the institutions for which they are not responsible. Not every boy who goes to college is capable, or desirous of receiving that culture which the college is adapted to bestow. It is ungenerous, to say the least, to make the Alma Mater responsible for the ignorance or imbecility of every graceless son. It is impossible, by the nicest skill of the chemist, to make a diamond out of paste, and he should not be censured when he makes the best possible from the materials. One man may lead a horse away to watering, but ten men can not make him drink. Free mental agents have their future intellectual destinies under their own control, and however excellent or efficient the instrument employed for their improvement, a wayward youth may use it for his own disgrace. An awkward fellow may hack his face with the keenest of razors. Indeed, some men have cut their throats with razors. But these facts do not prove that a sharp razor is not a most welcome and blessed implement when a man would pare the beard smoothly from his face.

The systems for the attainment of a liberal education have been adopted from the experience and wisdom of many centuries. They have been modeled and perfected by a long line of illustrious generations. They come to us stamped with the approval of the profoundest scholars of any age. Still they are not perfect. Improvements are yet to be made. This generation has need of a different system of training from that which preceded it. The tide of humanity sweeps onward, and what was good for to-day needs to be remodeled for to-morrow. There are changes now that undoubtedly need to be made. We should probably have more vigorous and profound scholars from our colleges, if there were a less number of studies pursued, with a more generous culture in those which are left. Yet in general they are admirably adapted to accomplish the end designed.

I have thus dwelt at considerable length upon these objections to liberal culture, that they might be set in their proper light, and that its true interest might not be prejudiced on account of them; and have urged the importance of such culture, that every one who has the ability may be induced to acquire it. We have need of more educated men in our midst. I do not say that we have need of more educated ministers, and lawyers, and doctors; for of the latter two we have already enough to last a generation or two without any fear of failure. But we want more educated farmers, and mechanics, and laborers. This class of men should be so educated that our governors and members of Congress can be elected from among them, rather than from a set of political tricksters, who will barter, and buy, and sell the interests of their constituents, and sell themselves, body and soul. If many who occupy the chief places in our political synagogues were this day driven out with a scourge, as were the sinners of old, and their places filled from among the honest yeomanry of our land, I believe our nation would be more wisely governed, more prosperous at home, and more respected abroad.

But there are many young men in our midst who have the ability and the inclination to obtain a thorough education, who have not the means of supporting themselves during the two or three years necessary to prepare for, and the four years in passing through the university, with the numerous demands that are made upon one in an incidental way. But even in the midst of adverse circumstances, courage will do much for a man. If, in the pursuit of knowledge, fortune seems to frown upon your way, take courage, and the shadows will lift before a resolutely formed purpose, and let the light through. Be diligent, and get all that is within your power! Neglect no means of acquiring information, or of securing wholesome discipline of mind! Because you have not all you desire, sit not with folded hands saying you will have nothing! When difficulties irritate and perplex, and discouragements thicken around you, do not retreat, with the excuse that there is a lion in the way! Do not set out in the noble enterprise, and then lay down in your own tracks!

To the youthful aspirant of to-day, who is willing to take so humble a sentiment as labor for his watchword, there are noble examples to cheer him among the great names of the past. Some of the brightest lights that have adorned the generations in which they lived, and have led the way wherever they have appeared, are those who have been obliged to trust to their own hands for maintenance and aid. With strong wills and trusting hearts, their lives have exhibited that majesty which action, steady, noble, successful, alone can give.

James Watt, the inventor of the steam engine, was in early life a toiling mechanic in indigent circumstances. He was employed by the university to repair, and keep in order, the apparatus used in illustrating the principles of natural philosophy and chemistry. Had he been like many mechanics, he would have been content with doing the work assigned, receiving his pay, and then smoking and drinking a portion of it, with such companions as he could induce to join him in the nearest saloon. But his mind, lit up with thought, was busy in inquiring into those laws which the apparatus he was employed to repair was designed to illustrate; and the thinking of that one man has performed more actual labor than all the slaves that have toiled and sweat since creation. The thinking of that man has revolutionized modern society, and unborn generations will rise up to bless his name.

Nathaniel Bowditch was a Boston sailor boy, and spent the greater portion of his years as a practical sailor. He had no instructor, and no opportunities for study, except such as the deck or the cabin of his vessel could afford. On one occasion, it was windbound for a week in Boston harbor. On commencement day at the university, he walked over to Cambridge to hear the performance. At the close the president conferred some honorary titles, and among them he thought he heard the degree of A. M. conferred on Nathaniel Bowditch. He was not mistaken. They indeed gave their degrees to the sailor, and well they might, for he was writing books which scarcely one of the faculty of the university could understand. The Practical Navigator, which was the result of his studies, has carried many a sailor through the storms and darkness of a tempestuous ocean, and has guided him safely over unknown seas. He translated the Méchanique Céleste of La Place, made corrections in the original, and added notes of his own, which caused the author to confess that he was convinced that Bowditch fully comprehended his work. He died lamented as the man, the

Christian, and the first mathematical scholar of his age.

Elihu Burritt, the linguist, antiquary, and philanthropist, was left fatherless when a youth, in company with a numerous family of children, dependent upon their own exertions for support. He apprenticed himself to a blacksmith. But his mind was not satisfied with blowing bellows, turning his iron, and pounding it into shapes desired. He had, previous to this, acquired considerable knowledge of history from the school district library. It would be a consummation devoutly to be wished, I may remark by the way, if the authorities of this State could adopt some means of public policy by which every school district should be provided with a library. He was seized with a desire of learning Latin; and while the iron was heating, with his book secured in the chimney, where the page could meet his eye, he conned the declensions and acquired the rudiments of that great language, and in the evenings of one winter he read Virgil, that masterpiece of Latin poetry. From Latin he passed to Greek, then to the modern languages, and finally back again to the oriental tongues. And thus with no aid but his own right hand, and with no teacher but his untiring mind, he has acquired a knowledge of upwards of fifty of the leading languages of the earth, and has earned a world-wide reputation as the "Learned Blacksmith." I have seen in the Antiquarian Hall in Worcester, Massachusetts, writing done by him in fifty-two languages. When a scholar at the preparatory school, just commencing my classical education, I used frequently to meet him upon the streets of that city, and I never gazed upon that massive front, but with the veneration of a worshiper.

Need I mention in this connection a name which has become a household word, the cherished and honored name of Franklin. Thrown upon the mercies of the world while yet a boy, with no opportunities for school education, it is like listening to a fairy tale, to read the simple narrative of his life as he tells it himself. We are carried along with magic interest, as the panorama of his years passes by. We see him enter the printing office as an apprentice —the wearisome days and sleepless nights at his books. We accompany the youth as he leaves his native city, on that then perilous voyage from Boston to Philadelphia, wandering from his home a stranger, without friends, except such as by his intelligence and kindness he never failed to make. We behold him an awkward boy, wandering up the streets of a strange city, with his three rolls of bread, one under each arm, eating at the third. This was indeed the day of small things, but he did not despise it. He is deluded across the ocean by the false promises of a knavish governor. He teaches the London printers temperance by his example, and philosophy with his tongue. He becomes the proprietor of a printing establishment, and edits a newspaper; nor is he now ashamed of labor, for he carries the paper from the warehouse to the office upon a wheelbarrow, pushing with his own hands. He becomes a master spirit in literature, and penetrates the intricacies of science. He sends his gold-pointed kite into the heavens—with the simplicity and confidence of a child he holds out his hand to receive it, and the forked lightning lays harmless at his feet. Step by step he steadily mounts the heights of fame. It was no flashing meteoric light that dashes athwart the heavens, which he sent forth in the domain of thought, but the warm, steady, genial rays of the summer's sun. When the colonies became involved in trouble with the parent country, and storms and darkness seemed gathering in the political heavens, the intelligence of America pointed to the humble and self-taught Franklin as their safest counselor, and we find him at the bar of the British House of Lords, pleading for the interests of those weak and struggling colonies, the objects of his affection, and advising an infatuated ministry not to proceed to violence against his American brethren. He joins hands with the Father of his Country, and those other patriots, in making and securing the adoption of a constitution for the independent United States. In his age he goes, the venerable man with sage white locks and thoughtful brow, to represent a sovereign nation at the court of France, there to mingle with the wise men and philosophers of that land of letters, and to stand in presence of Louis XVI., the proudest monarch of his age.

Such are the examples which the history of our nation offers for the encouragement and guidance of the present rising generation. If we turn to the account of their lives, we can easily discover what lessons of wisdom they early took. The course was simple, for they were not widely different from other boys, except so far as their energy made them, and their opportunities were less than what most enjoy. They did not despise labor. Labor was the potent spell that transformed their leisure moments into golden thoughts. Labor excited their childish faculties and strengthened the fiber of their minds, as the sapling oak is strengthened by the winds and storms of successive winters. Labor brought them into communion with the great scholars of near and distant ages, and enabled them to think the thoughts that wearied their brains. Labor made the taste of books sweet to them, as the toil of the husbandman makes him relish food. Labor presented them with such rich and golden fruits as encouraged and beckoned them on. She opened before them long vistas of glory and honor, and pointed them to the distant goal. Labor indeed lays grievous burdens upon the back of her devotee; but she nerves him at every step with a vigor and an enthusiasm which makes the burden light, and leads him on through sylvan scenes and lovely lawns, where at every step the senses are regaled with pleasant sounds and delicious odors. She racks the brain and strains the sinews of the mind, but she in turn presents it with a balm which makes it oblivious to every ache; for who does not forget the pains of study, and the weariness of thought, when he knows that he has been a victor in the fields of knowledge? Oh! never will he forget, who has sounded all the depths of science, the ecstatic joy which thrills the soul, as some thought sublime, or beautiful, or profound, breaks in upon the mind. There are the pleasures of sense. The palate may be gratified with the delicacies of the table gathered from many a clime. The ear may be thrilled by the melodies of the minstrel's harp. The zephyrs of evening may cool the moistened brow, or the fragrant breathing morn may gladden the early riser, and the eye may feast on pleasant sights. But these pleasures are small in comparison with those which fill the bosom of him who is an honest worshiper at the shrine of knowledge.

These illustrious examples to which I have referred, are for the encouragement and instruction of us all. But in our admiration of their great acquirements and brilliant success, there is one error respecting them to which some may be liable. It may be hastily concluded, if self-taught men can attain to such preëminence in knowledge, let us be done with schools and colleges. Let us depend upon self-educated men entirely. We need no better. If all were like Franklin, and Bowditch, and Watt, such reasoning might be accepted. We say that these men had no teachers. This is not true. They had teachers, and those of the very best kind. They were their own teachers. And who would not have rejoiced to have been a pupil under such instructors? Who would not have delighted in learning philosophy of Franklin, or mathematics of Bowditch, or languages of Burritt? Our academies and colleges were not good enough for them. They were in advance of the universities. The wisest professors could not teach them. But if the mass of mankind were to depend upon such instruction as each could give himself, education would meet with a signal defeat.

It is true that Elihu Burritt possessed a mind and

a will sufficiently strong to enable him to conquer the dry and intricate details of the dead languages, during the leisure moments snatched from incessant toil, and to become a finished classical scholar while working eight hours a day at the anvil. But if we were to search the whole earth, we could not probably find in his generation an example of so much energy and self-sacrificing zeal. It is doubtful whether he would himself have become such an eminent scholar, had he not observed the respect which is paid to the great minds of every age, and been incited to exertion by knowing the results, the fruits, which education produces. So that it is probable that liberal culture was the means indirectly of making him a scholar. But if we were to depend upon such means for universal education, the great mass of mankind would soon lapse into a state of intellectual night, worse than that which brooded over the dark ages.

Perhaps no man is oftener quoted as a leading example of a self-taught man than Franklin; and yet he was one of the strongest advocates of common school and collegiate education. In a plan which he drew up for the establishment of a State university, he speaks in the strongest language of the importance of a classical and scientific education. "When youth are told," says he, "that the great men whose lives and actions they read in history, spoke two of the best languages that ever were, the most expressive, copious, beautiful, and that the finest writings, the most correct compositions, the most perfect productions of human wit and wisdom, are in those languages, which have endured for ages and will endure while there are men; that no translation can do them justice or give the pleasure found in reading the originals; that those languages contain all sciences; that one of them is become almost universal, being the language of learned men in all countries; and that to understand them is a distinguished ornament—they may be thereby made desirous of learning those languages, and their industry sharpened in the acquisition of them. All intended for divinity should be taught the Latin and Greek; for physic, Latin, Greek, and French; merchants, the French, German, and Spanish; and though all should not be compelled to learn Latin, Greek, or the modern foreign languages, yet none that have an ardent desire to learn them should be refused; their English, arithmetic, and other studies absolutely necessary, being at the same time not neglected." Such was the language of the self-taught Franklin upon the subject of liberal education; and much of the latter part of his life was spent in devising plans for the systematic and thorough training of the young.

In conclusion, we may remark that a cultivated mind will always command respect. It is the thinking man that takes the lead in society, whether he hail from college, from work-shop, or from tented field. Intelligence everywhere challenges our reverence. It has been somewhere remarked, that we should honor Columbus not so much because he discovered America, as for having thought through the problem that there was in existence a continent heretofore undiscovered which he could go in search of. We honor Leverrier and Adams because they figured out, by means of mathematical principles, that place in the heavens where a new planet could be found, more than Dr. Gall, who actually turned his telescope to the spangled vault and discovered the wandering world. Our reverence and gratitude are due to James Watt, not because he actually made a steam engine and put it in operation, but because he thought out a plan by which a steam engine could be made. We should ever be ready to give credit to him whose thoughts are most valuable, and who thinks most successfully. The day is past when men are held in honor for what they are presumed to know, and are only accredited with the amount of available stock.

It is when such principles as these prevail that real merit receives that encouragement and credit which it deserves; when thought is unfettered and is free from embarrassing restraint, whether imposed by arbitrary rule, or the forms and usages of an aristocracy in letters, that the mass of intelligence in a nation will produce its greatest results. It is then that every means adopted for mental development will meet with the greatest success. No step has ever been taken by any nation, which is calculated to accomplish this result so successfully, as that for the founding and putting in operation a system of common schools,—one of the distinguishing characteristics of our civil polity. Here all the children of the State are put on a common level. Every form of aristocracy is broken down, and the utmost freedom is given to every child to make the greatest progress possible. Around our common schools all good and true men should rally, and every means which can improve and perfect the system, should be freely lavished upon it. It is only when made worthy the confidence of all interested that it will accomplish the greatest good. In general, the means that have been adopted, are, as systems, well adapted to the ends they are designed to accomplish. But the chief trouble is, they have not been put into effective operation. Our plans are good upon the statute book and in the laws of the corporation, but we fail in the skill necessary to make them work well.

It is only when our combined organizations in all their parts, from the primary department up through the academy and college, to the university with its professional schools, are made thorough and effective, that they can produce satisfactory results, and that the scholar who shares their benefits can become truly learned. At every step of the progress ripe scholarship should be the motto. Then should we behold the lovely sight of education bearing rich fruits, and the votary of learning would become the disciple of Bacon indeed.

LECTURE VII.

POPULAR EDUCATION.

IT is with feelings of sincere pleasure that I come to meet with an association of teachers, and with citizens and friends anxious to promote the cause of education. You are engaged in a noble enterprise, one which can not fail to enlist the sympathies of every generous bosom; and although your Institute is in its infancy, you will be certain of producing good; for if you fail to impart to those around you that spirit which you possess, you will at least strengthen your own aspirations, and nourish in your bosoms a yearning for improvement and excellence, which is one of the fundamental conditions of success. It is a source of consolation to feel that one is aiding in the improvement of the race; that he is doing something to dispel the darkness of ignorance, even if he holds up but a feeble taper.

One of the means of pleasure and pastime among the ancient Greeks was the Bacchanalia. These were feasts in honor of Bacchus, the god of wine, and were extremely popular throughout all Greece.

Men and women joined in his festivals, with their heads wreathed with vine and ivy, with fawn skins flung about their shoulders, and blunt spears, twined with vines, in their hands. Dressed in these grotesque habiliments they gave way to riotous revelry. They sometimes wore the most indecent emblems, they beat upon drums and sang lewd songs, and thus they sought amid these frantic revels for pleasure and enjoyment.

In our own times, we have Bacchanalia, though with less of poetry and æsthetic emblems than the ancient. We have not the vine leaves, nor the fawn skins, nor the thyrsi. The scenes of our Bacchanalia are the breweries, the groceries, the country taverns; and instead of the juice of the vine we have the juice of the barley, the corn, and the old rye. Many of the rising generation among us,—young men at that period of life which is the bloom of manhood, when the character is becoming established, and those opinions formed which are to give them influence among men, and by which an estimate of their abilities is made,—seek for the highest pleasure and gratification which they are capable of feeling, in some dingy saloon, on the floor of which has been splashed from year to year the juice of that filthy weed, ground and soaked in filthier mouths, whose vapors mingle with the thick volumes of smoke that curl about their heads, and with the breath of human beings from lungs steeped in the fiery poison of copperas and logwood, and nameless drugs,—more resembling in its conglomerate qualities the deadly airs that arose from the fabled lake Mæotis, the Stygian wave, or the fumes of hell fire, than that sweet and pleasant atmosphere which mortals ought to breathe,—surrounded by companions whose foul-mouthed conversation is in keeping with the filthiness by which they are encircled, who are satisfied with this enjoyment, and are waiting to renew it during the long winter evenings of the season. And this is pleasure! Without one ray of intellectual light, without one generous aspiration for improvement, they are willing to give themselves up a prey to the passions and the appetites, and degrade themselves to a condition worse than that of the brutes.

I rejoice that I am permitted to meet here with those who have a higher notion of pleasure, who are actuated by a nobler purpose, who are stimulated to the attainment of a more exalted end. I rejoice that I am brought into sympathy with those who can find pleasure in intellectual pursuits. How noble! how generous! how philanthropic the purpose for which you associate. It is not sensual gratification that has called you here, but you have come to mingle in earnest inquiry for the elevation and improvement of our common schools. You have come to impart each to the other the fruits of your own experience, to detail the plans which have proved successful in arousing and energizing the faculties of the youth under your charge, to speak words of cheer and encouragement to those whose faith is weak, and who are ready to falter by the way.

We pour out lavishly the meed of sympathy and praise to the philanthropist, who directly alleviates human suffering and woe, who goes forth in a crusade against misery and crime. Such a purpose is indeed noble and generous. But he deals only with our physical natures. He labors to relieve us of the wants and distresses of the body, this mortal frame which will soon crumble into dust. You have to do with the mind, the intellect. You are laboring to relieve the wants, and poverty, and nakedness of the immortal spirit, to awaken within it new energies, to prepare it to battle successfully with ignorance and folly.

It is this business of education, of Popular Education, upon which I propose to speak. Education, the development of the faculties, the acquirement of knowledge, must always depend upon two facts: First, that all our perceptions either come directly or are suggested by the operation of external objects upon the five senses; and, second, it must depend upon the mind itself whether the impressions are converted into permanent knowledge. There are these two stand-points from which education should be viewed. There is the process of reception and assimilation. The basis of all learning is upon these two conditions. We may force the elements of knowledge upon the mind as long as we please, but if there is not the power or the disposition to assimilate that knowledge, and make it a part of the mental energy and being, its presentation is useless and our efforts are vain. Nay, more, it is like the crude and indigestible food which is taken into the stomach, which not only fails to nourish, and is not used by the vital energies, but throws us into pain and convulsions.

Hence, in adopting a system of education, we should study not only the best means of presenting the elements of knowledge, but also the most successful methods of arousing the mind, of giving it energy and vivifying power, of leading it forth to seek for itself. There is no high-pressure system by which knowledge can be forced upon the mind if the mind is not prepared to receive it. You may supply the child with the most skillful teachers, you may put into his hands the best prepared text-books, but unless the faculties are alive, unless there is something of intellectual hunger your efforts will be vain.

We often see, where the faculties are crowded beyond what their age or capacity will bear, that they become surfeited, and that quickness and readiness which was observed at an earlier period is gone and can never be reproduced. We observe in childhood that "Mother Goose Melodies" and stories told in a very simple style, or united to rhythm and melody are most attractive and can be most easily learned. At a later period the elements of the sciences are understood. At a later period still, when arrived at the age of reflection and reason, of abstraction and generalization, the more complicate principles of the higher mathematics are grappled with and mastered, and the taste for philosophical investigation is developed. If, therefore, the mind at one period is put upon knowledge which is the appropriate object of another period, instead of conquering it, the mind may itself be conquered by it, and its power and elasticity for ever lost.

When we consider these two facts which I have named chronologically, we observe that the process of reception must precede that of assimilation. But when we examine them in their logical order we see that the reverse is true; that the mental energy, the disposition to learn must exist anterior to the reception of ideas. I therefore propose to treat the subject in its logical order.

Let us then first consider this fundamental requisite of knowledge, the disposition. When we look abroad upon mankind and observe the various forms of popular ignorance, we can not but be filled with feelings of sadness in view of the general degraded condition of the race. What a vast proportion of all who are created are content to go through life ignorant of almost every thing, except the few notions which pertain to us as animal beings! How large a number, especially in the old world, are compelled by the constitution of society to toil on day after day, till the grave closes over them and relieves their strained and aching sinews, for the morsel they eat and the rags they wear! And yet, when we consider ignorance even in its worst forms, when we think of this dark veil which envelops the greater portion of the race, are we not arrested with the thought that there is in man the ability, if there were the disposition, to know more and rise higher; that there is a spark now buried that might be fanned into a flame to give life and vivacity to the energies? How many are there who have absolutely no thoughts above the dead level of the animal nature, in whom, if some elements of knowledge, some facts concerning the simplest phenomena we meet could be divulged in youth, it would awaken inquiry and set the mind in motion; and those facts recurring, even during the periods of incessant toil, would be the means of suggesting other and original knowledge, the product of the naked intellect itself; and thus step by step would they ascend in the scale of intelligence.

How many do we meet whose minds have been aroused and who have a purpose, but who have been aroused by the word or deed of some base companion, and are sinking lower in ignorance instead of advancing higher; who are intent only upon revelry and dissipation; who, by passion and appetite unrestrained, are blotting out the human shape divine; but who, if there had been awakened early, when the mind was fresh and pure as the opening blossom, some aspiration for mental development which should act as an impetus, might have made commendable progress in knowledge. We do not know how slight a circumstance may set in motion a train of events which shall decide the career of the man. Like the rivulet upon the top of the mountain, a twig, or bush, or the footprint of an animal may turn it on the one hand where it will descend gently through fresh pastures, bright sunny plots, and rich meadows, irrigating and gladdening as it goes; or on the other, will divert it where rocks and barrenness hurl it in devious ways, until it is finally lost deep down amid the caverns and darkness of the mountain. How many there are about us who actually squander the time and opportunities in their possession, and permit the faculties given them to rust out in absolute idleness and inanity; who sleep and loll upon sofas one half of their time at least, and spend the remainder in small talk and belittleing thoughts; who by a judicious direction of youthful energy, might, instead of being dwarfs and pigmies, advance to the proportions of generous and thinking manhood.

In considering that part of our subject which relates to the disposition of mind, we perceive that the spirit of man can never make progress in any direction until there is a desire. One does not become a libertine or a debauchee until he begins to satisfy his tastes for those things which make one; until he sees something in that course of life that gratifies his wishes, and is ready to put forth effort to satisfy them. On the contrary, a man can never become eminent for virtue until he loves the character of those who practice it; until his imagination is excited in admiration of goodness, and he has enkindled in his bosom a desire to possess it. At the foundation of every successful system of education there must be created a thirst for knowledge; there must be a taste for intellectual pursuits, a sense of the dignity and influence of mental culture.

Many years ago, a rustic lad, in a remote town in Scotland, was sent to the metropolis with a message to a man of letters. He had been bred in obscurity, had rarely visited the village, and had never seen a city, with its mansions, and stately edifices, and public grounds with walks and fountains. His lot had been one of want and poverty, his clothes homespun, his fare coarse. He had known nothing of intellectual improvement, for he had been blessed with no intellectual advantages, and had heard only the coarse and vulgar talk of unlettered and ill-bred husbandmen. He was ushered into the study of the nobleman. He saw rare paintings and marble sculptures of renowned men, his papers and manuscripts, his books and charts. The scenes were novel; his heart heaved with new-born emotions; he secretly vowed that the splendid equipage of the scholar should one day be his.

The boy returned to his obscure habitation, but the beautiful vision went with him. His mind had received an impulse,—a new desire was in his heart. With irrepressible energy of soul he toils on, anxiously waiting for that day to come when he shall be free from parental obligations, shall have the command of his own resources, and be at liberty to direct them to what end he pleases. During the long and weary day the bright vision is before him. His faculties are all awake, and he reasons out many a process before he reads it in any book. The youth grows to be a man,—he obtains public consideration,—he sits in Parliament,—he becomes a peer of the realm,—he possesses a mansion and pleasure grounds,—he collects a library and paintings finer than he had dreamed in his most sanguine hour. His vision was realized, his youthful desire was satisfied.

From an incident like this we learn a principle of human nature. The life of a single individual is in some sort an index of a propensity of the race; and we may derive therefrom truthful lessons which are of universal application, and which may save us much speculation and theorizing, and tedious experiment. It is not our first purpose to impose tasks, and to insist upon a rigid and exact verbal performance of them, as we would teach a brute governed by instinct; but it is our primary object to create a desire, so that the youth may approach the task with a true idea of its utility, with a manly resolution, and

> "——not like the quarry-slave at night
> Scourged to his dungeon."

If this desire for improvement be united with a resolute purpose that will not be daunted or repressed, it will necessarily result in progress, in noble attainments. Without this latter element, the richest powers of mind are useless. Many a youth has formed the desire, and has looked with a wishful eye towards that eminence where stand the good and great of all ages and climes, but has not possessed resolution enough to take the first step toward reaching it. There have probably been many good poems planned, and a few lines of the first cantos written. Visions as grand and lofty as ever filled the poet's eye have flitted in the fancy, but the poet's pen has never turned them to shapes, and he dies, leaving Milton still in the clear upper sky. The plea of the eloquent advocate, in a cause that cries for justice, has perhaps awakened in him a desire and a resolutely formed purpose to promote its ends with transcendant abilities. But he has formed a thousand purposes with equal resolution, and not one of them has ever been carried to its completion, and this one likewise shares their fate. Many have desired to be like Moses, leaders of the people. They think very favorably of their own fitness for such a position, and of their own superior skill to manage and direct, but they neglect to do any deed which will manifest their ability. The friends of a certain

French officer besought Napoleon to confer on him the marshal's bâton. Napoleon asked them what he had ever done. They replied that he had never yet done any thing, but that he had great ability, and they thought that he would one day do some noble deed. "Well," said Napoleon, "wait till he does."

The mind of youth is not easily brought under control. It has a disposition to wander. Until strict habits are formed, he finds a feeling of indolence preying upon all his plans for improvement. Having the desire to press forward and having given his time to the work, he feels ashamed to squander it, even if he is held accountable to no one. But how ready he is to abandon his tasks on the slightest pretext, and for the most trivial excuse that will acquit him before the tribunal of self. Thus he fritters away the precious hours. He is very exact about the performance of minor duties. He is kind and obsequious to friends, but he leaves undone the great duties of life, and he dies and "makes no sign."

We have thus far considered the temper of mind which must exist in the learner, in order that what has been taught him may become permanent knowledge. We come now to treat the second division of our subject, which embraces the various methods of presenting knowledge to the pupil. The means which have been adopted in this country, for the general diffusion of knowledge, whether from public provision, or from private munificence, have in general been crowned with flattering success. We have the advantage of the experience of all other nations. We are trying the latest experiment in civilization, with a new model of government. To those ideas which we gain from abroad, we add our own reflections and digest our systems. To some of those means of communicating knowledge which have been adopted among us, I shall now allude.

Of the first importance are our common schools. To these, the populace as well as the higher classes, are deeply indebted for whatever of education they possess. When the Pilgrim Fathers landed on Plymouth Rock, they raised their voices in thanksgiving to God for their deliverance from persecution and the dangers of the ocean, and erected a church in which they might worship Him. But, hard by the village church they built the school-house and established the village school. Their primary devotion was to the worship of God, their secondary to the education of their children. To our Pilgrim Fathers belongs the honor of first having established by the laws of the State these two principles,—that each man should worship how, when, and whom he pleased, without compulsion or restraint, and pay no taxes to support a ministry except such as he should impose upon himself; and, second, that all the children of the State should be educated at the public expense. For the former of these we are indebted to Roger Williams and the State of Rhode Island; for the latter to the early settlers of Massachusetts. Never before had these two principles been promulgated by any nation upon earth.

There were indeed schools and systems of education in the States of antiquity. There were men in those times, who possessed as much mental culture, and as great scope of thought and political sagacity, as any in our own time. Pericles was as fine an orator and consummate a statesman as was Burke or the younger Pitt. Cicero was as able a lawyer and as accomplished a rhetorician as our own Webster. But while there were a few who possessed the means of prosecuting their studies in the celebrated schools of those days, of becoming finished scholars, and who uttered thoughts that have withstood the shock of upwards of twenty centuries, and that are now studied and admired as the choicest productions of the human mind, there was a vast populace who lived and died in ignorance, fit instruments of universal slavery and vassalage. The pupils of Socrates and Plato could loiter in the groves of the Academy, and about the porches of the temples; but a great majority of the nation must sweat and labor on during the long day, blessing the night which relieved them of toil; and little cared the philosopher and statesman how helots lived, or how helots died.

But when the Pilgrim Fathers came to these shores, they brought with them an overwhelming sense of religious obligation. They took the Bible as their counsel and guide, and in accordance with that gospel which Jesus Christ came upon earth to promulgate, they looked upon every human being as of inestimable worth. Actuated by those principles and motives which are there displayed, they held fellowship with every human soul* as an image of the divine being, freighted with immortal hopes, and destined to endless existence like themselves. The idea that the child of the rich man was better than that of the poor found no place in their code. Hence they enacted, among their first laws, that every child should be educated at the public expense, in a common school, where the rich and the poor, the high and the low, should share in common privileges, and where the only insignia of rank should be worn by

* "Therefore respect humanity in all its members, for in all its members is the divine ray of intelligence, and there is an essential confraternity in the unity of the fundamental ideas which the most immediate development of reason produces."—*History of Modern Philosophy*, *Cousin*, vol. i., page 134.

him who, by devotion to learning, should aspire to the noble qualities of the scholar.

It is the glory of that system that it draws all classes together and places them upon a common level. It brings the whole collection of minds into collision, and says to them, he alone shall conquer who most nobly strives. There have been objections raised to the system of common schools by those who by wealth or birth feel something of the aristocratic notion. Their children will be contaminated by contact, and will imbibe the notions of the ignoble throng. It would be equally reasonable to shut a boy up in a tight, warm room, for fear that the damp and cold of the out-door weather would injure his constitution, when everybody knows that if you wish him to be healthy and robust you must let him take the rough and tumble of life, and inhale copious draughts of the fresh, free air, damp and cold though it may be. If children are allowed to imbibe into their mental constitutions the idea that they are better than other children, if they are taught to draw lines and marks of distinction based upon wealth or birth, they may, in mature years, be convinced by some luckless urchin whom they were encouraged to despise, that they have missed their calculations; that he is the nobleman, and they are the base and ignoble slaves, the slaves to pride and arrogance.

The youth may be kept for a while from mingling with those of his own age, and be educated in the family. But a time will come when parental restraint must fail. He will go forth and find associates, and he then will be at that age when imagination is strongest and the passions most impetuous, and when he will have the least power to withstand temptation. He will then be a fit subject for the tempter. Flattered by the attentions of the genteel but wily villain, he falls an easy prey to his deceitful charms. Having been taught to hold in contempt those beneath him in rank, and never having engaged in tussles of physical and intellectual strength, he has no experience for estimating his powers, and is by no means so well prepared to act manfully his part in life as one, who, from infancy has joined in friendly strife with those with whom he will necessarily mingle in after years, either as his equals in ability and influence, or as the objects of his regard and charity.

The common school acquaints us with human nature. He who has passed through the several grades knows something of what he is to expect of mankind when he enters upon the active duties of life. In general, the motives which actuate boys will actuate men, and he shapes his course in his dealings with the latter, according to his experience with the former. It has a tendency also to break up those artificial lines and distinctions* in society which are its bane; lines and distinctions which may exist in other countries, and be permanent when upheld by despotic power and the force of custom, but which, in our country, can last only for a generation or two at most, and which have no value founded upon right.

The common school is the offspring of this nation and of our fathers. The wisdom of the institution may be seen in the general diffusion of knowledge among us, in the success which has attended our elective form of government, and the progress which is seen in every branch of art and industry. Why do we so often hear it remarked that France and Spain, and those other nations of Europe, are not prepared

* "One invaluable merit of out-door sports is to be found in this, that they afford the best cement for childish friendship. Their associations outlive all others. There is many a man, now perchance hard and worldly, whom we love to pass in the street simply because in meeting him we meet spring flowers and autumn chestnuts, skates and cricket balls, cherry-birds and pickerel. There is an indescribable fascination in the gradual transference of these childish companionships into maturer relations. We love to encounter, in the contests of manhood, those whom we first met at football, and to follow the profound thoughts of those who always dived deeper, even in the river, than our efforts could attain."—*Atlantic Monthly*, March, 1858, page 589.

for civil liberty? It is because the masses of the people are not educated. The systems of education which prevail there, even to the books and newspapers, are under the control of priest-craft and king-craft, and these well know that the best means of effecting their security is to keep the people in ignorance, or to instruct them in those dogmas which are alike false in theory and damning in practice. Our security and prosperity as a nation must depend upon the excellence of our common schools. If the influence of these is weakened or destroyed we undermine the very foundation of the republic. They are to the body politic what the arteries are to the human system, which convey nourishment to every part, and were these cut off, the heart of the nation would cease to beat.

Within a few years there have been vast improvements made in our common schools. Reports of the secretaries of the boards of education and the superintendents of public schools in the several States have been printed and circulated, in which are embodied the statistics, the experience and progress of the year, reflections upon the failure or success of the various methods adopted, with recommendations for the guidance of future efforts, plans for school-houses and cuts of furniture, the best methods of heating and ventilation · and by means of these a vast amount of reliable information has been circulated among the people. Normal schools have been established, in which teachers have been thoroughly instructed in the theory and practice of teaching, and prepared expressly for their profession. Teachers' conventions and institutes have been held, in which the most eminent teachers and professors have been employed to instruct, and to impart to their brethren the elements of their own success, in some instances being paid by the State for their services, and in others freely giving their time and energies for the promotion of so noble an object. As a consequence school-houses have been vastly improved and furnished for the health and comfort of the students. Apparatus and libraries have been provided, and all the means of advancement have been lavished upon the system.

It is only by a combination of such means, and by such exertions, that we can derive from it full and legitimate results. We can not look after the interests and well-being of our common schools with too much solicitude. Each man should feel that he has a personal interest in them. His dearest affections should cling about them as being the nurseries of the thoughts and feelings of his children. He should look upon the teacher as his friend, laboring for his interests, and should inculcate into the minds of his children confidence and respect for him. He should never countenance in them a spirit of disobedience, and insubordination to wholesome restraint, but be ready to stand by the right, crush out the disposition to rebellion, and never see the teacher misused by those whom he is laboring to improve.

The teacher on his part should feel that he can not be a drone in a common school. He should not feel that he has come into a neighborhood where he is to assemble with the youth and be a master over them for six hours a day, and then receive a certain sum of money for his authority. But he ought to realize that the parents of the district are placing confidence in his capacity and virtue, that they are entrusting to his care their children, their dearest and most cherished earthly possessions. They are expecting that he will be to those children a father, and will guide them in the ways of knowledge and truth, that he will carefully unfold their youthful faculties, that he will judiciously train and conscientiously correct. He ought to feel that he has a company of human souls from the hand of the Creator entrusted to his care, whose character he is to mould and fashion, and that he is not only responsible to those who employ him, but that he will one day be held to an account by the Judge of all the earth for the good or evil which he may have done, as well as for the opportunities for doing good which he has neglected. He ought to feel that the day is not long enough for the accomplishment of the great work entrusted to him, and be willing to make any sacrifice of ease and comfort for their benefit. If such feelings could mutually exist between patrons and scholars, and teachers, we need never despair of the prosperity and ultimate success of the common school.

The second means for the diffusion of knowledge to which I shall allude, is that of books and printed matter. Since the invention of the art of printing, this method of communication has been regularly increasing in power. At no period has that power been so great as at the present, especially in this country. Previous to the invention of the art, there were few books, and those were in the hands of only a few learned men, their possession being a matter of little consequence to the great mass of the people, who had never learned to read. The price of a book was very great, as each copy had to be transcribed with the pen.

It is with difficulty that we can imagine the condition of a great and enlightened nation existing without newspapers. The people of Athens were accustomed to meet in the market-place, where, if any thing had happened out of the ordinary course of events, it flew from mouth to mouth until the whole city knew of it. Their own historians tell us that the first question of an Athenian was, "What is the news?" It was no doubt from this anxiety to learn the earliest intelligence of what was passing, and the scene presented by the populace gathering in crowds and knots to learn the particulars of some great event, that Rumor is personified by the Grecian poets, and is represented as a sleepless divinity moving amid crowds of people, arousing and exciting their minds. There were some advantages in this method of learning the news over that which we have. Those interested would be likely to hear from all sides of the question; all the circumstances would be brought out and discussed, and the opinions of leading men would be known.

By our own method we hear in effect but from one mind, with such coloring and bias as he may see fit to give it, unless we take several papers. Knowledge is however more wisely diffused by ours than we could hope to have it by any other. When a speech is made in Parliament at night, the mails of the morning scatter it over the whole kingdom. Not unfrequently is the first portion of a speech delivered in Congress being read by the people of New York and Boston, while the member is making the concluding portion of it. Not a circumstance of note happens, but the newspaper carries intelligence of it to every part of the world.

The question has been frequently raised, whether our increased facilities for diffusing knowledge, and the consequent increase in printed matter, have made us really more learned than those of ancient nations. If the question be whether we have as many very eminent thinkers, it is an open one, for the best original thinkers of our time are men of limited general information. Many a boarding-school miss has read more volumes than the best intellectual philosopher in the country. Of course much new knowledge has been added from generation to generation, to our accumulating store, and hence our educated men have a broader and truer basis upon which to found their reasonings and investigations, and may consequently arrive at a greater amount of positive knowledge. Whether this increase of printed matter has augmented the mental energy—the intellectual *vim*—may be a matter of doubt. But if we consider the aggregate of knowledge, we must decide vastly in favor of our time. Many a school-boy might have instructed Plato or even Locke.

It is almost needless to observe in this connection, that there is much printed that ought never to meet the eye of youth. To say nothing of that class of books which is positively evil in its tendency, which is debasing and demoralizing to the heart, the taste, and the intellect; many a man would have died better satisfied with himself, and his heirs infinitely better pleased, had he committed his manuscripts to the flames instead of the hands of the printer.

It has been wisely said by Mr. Carlyle, that "the true university of these days is a library of good books." The responsibility which rests upon parents of furnishing suitable books for the family is not generally realized. Many men think the purchase of a book a needless expenditure of money; believing either that it will not be read, or if it is, that it is thenceforth good for nothing, nay worse than nothing, for it occupies space which might be devoted to some other purpose.

The history of many a youth, if carefully traced, would teach parents a duty they owe to their children in providing intellectual food suited to the several stages of mental development. There is manifested in every youth, at some period, an inclination to read. If the right kind of matter is not furnished when this disposition is developed, that kind may be procured which will act as a poison or a loathsome drug. How many a culprit and degraded villain has dated the beginning of his evil days to the reading of some obscene book, borrowed from a companion and read stealthily. From its degrading thoughts and pictures, his fancy, full of the impetuous vigor of youth, has been fired with lust and passion that has only ceased to burn with his ruin.

Every parent, every farmer, every mechanic and laboring man, ought to provide a few choicely selected books, that shall be accessible to the members of his family. If they are not read at one time, they may be at another. If he does not feel capable of selecting them himself, let him apply to some judicious friend for aid. Do not buy a book for its fine binding, or because it is recommended by some itinerant peddler. Better have no books than those which are bad, or even indifferent. The biographies of good and noble men, and histories of interesting periods in human affairs, are the species which will be most attractive and most useful to the young. The first book that I ever read in course was the life of Benjamin Franklin. I read it and re-read it, until I knew it by heart; and the reading of that one book created within me a thirst for knowledge which I hope will never be quenched.

It is also necessary that there be provided in every family the means of acquiring accurate knowledge of current events. For this purpose a newspaper, which keeps a faithful record of what is passing in this and foreign countries, should be obtained. If the newspapers of the county fail to furnish such record, if they pander to a depraved taste—if, instead of supplying matter which shall encourage a desire for elevated literature and morality, they contain tales of passion improbable as untrue, throw them aside and send to the city for one that shall meet your wants. No journal or periodical is worthy of patronage, that does not commend itself to reason and sober thought, to candid and virtuous intelligence. We can never have a high-toned morality and a purified intellectual taste, until the common people, the laboring classes, better understand their duties, and have the inclination, yea, the resolution to perform them.

I come now to consider the third means for the diffusion of knowledge—that of public lectures. This method of imparting instruction has, within a few years past, grown to importance with surpassing rapidity. There is scarcely a city or a village of any spirit in the land, that has not during the winter one or more courses of public lectures from eminent men. Lecturing has become a profession. There are many men who make it their business to prepare in the summer a number of well-digested lectures, which they are employed to deliver during the winter.

There is one advantage in this manner of instruction not possessed by any other. The thinker himself comes into the immediate presence of those whom he would instruct. To the thoughts themselves are added the effects of the tones of the voice, and the accompanying look and gesture which constitute a natural language of emotion. The influence which one carefully-prepared lecture, pronounced by a bold, fearless orator may produce, is incalculable. It may set in motion a train of thoughts which will modify or change the tone of life, not only of a single individual, but of a whole audience. An accomplished public speaker has the power of taking captive the minds of his auditory, and swaying them at will by the force of his inspiration.

There is one error of lecturers to which I must refer; it is that of framing the speech so that it may create sensation, to the sacrifice of some leading thought. Pleased with the applause which one stroke of wit has called forth, he determines on the next occasion to out-Richard Richard. He therefore prepares a plum-pudding, and puts nothing in but plums. He reasons like the Irishman, who took a pill on retiring at night for some indisposition, and in the morning, finding himself better, concluded that if one pill had helped him, a whole box would make him well, and died under the operation. The experiment is a dangerous one, and he who makes it is liable to share the fate of poor Pat. It should be the object of the lecturer to instruct as well as to please. He should endeavor to create a sound and healthful public taste, rather than stoop to a depraved one which already exists. He should lead in the right way, rather than be led in the wrong.

I have thus briefly alluded to a few of the means of education. As you perceive, I have treated only of those which are employed for training the mental faculties. I hope it will not be inferred that this is all that is embraced in the term education. There are the moral sensibilities, the manners, the habits, and all those qualities which unite to form the character of a well-bred person, which are of equal importance with the training of the intellectual faculties, and which must form a constituent part of every successful system. But this part of my subject I must leave undisturbed.

These systems of education which were adopted by the fathers of the republic, and which have been developed and improved during subsequent time, have been fruitful of wonders. Under the influence and stimulus of these institutions, our nation has prospered beyond any other on the face of the earth. If the spirit of the sainted Washington could now descend and visit us, could behold the improvement and progress which has been made, and could look through the length and breadth of our land, now grown to a giant nation stretching from ocean to ocean, he would hardly believe that this is the development of those thirteen little colonies whose independence he fought to establish, and whose integrity he prayed for and labored to maintain. And who can say that this prosperity and growth would ever have been attained without our educational systems? It is then the part of wisdom to uphold these institutions. It is our duty to cherish them, and build them up as the instruments of our success. Where is it that we find most misery and degradation, and fewest of the comforts of life? It is where there is most ignorance. Where, on the other hand, do we find the greatest prosperity,—where do we find those communities that stand in the very first rank, and take the lead in civilization? It is in those nooks and corners of the earth where the spirit of education and improvement has taken up her abode, where she is permitted to dwell in peace and honor, and where she is cherished and loved.

During the year 1854, one hundred and sixty five men were hung in the United States for murder. Of this number only seven could read and write! What a lesson! And will you, parents, neglect to educate your children? Will you allow any opportunities to pass unimproved, to draw out and expand their youthful faculties, to lift them up into a higher and nobler life, to raise them above the dead level of the beast that creeps, and enable them to know something of the godlike and the divine? The parent sometimes thinks that if he can lay up a little hard silver, which his sons and daughters can use after he is gone, he is conferring upon them the greatest earthly blessing.

There is a fable in a French school-book which reads thus:—A miser being dead and decently buried, arrived upon the borders of the river Styx in order to pass over with the other spirits, the companions of his voyage. The boatman, Charon, demanded of him the price of the passage, but was surprised to see that, instead of paying it, he threw himself into the black river and swam to the shore, in spite of all the entreaties that could be made. This action put all hell in a tumult, and each judge endeavored to find a punishment proportioned to a crime, the consequences of which would be so disastrous to the revenues of the infernal regions. "Let us chain him to the rock with Prometheus, where the birds may perpetually tear his vitals," said one. "Let us associate him with the torments of Tantalus," said another. "Or, what is better, let us send him to aid Sysiphus in rolling his rock up the hill, which rolls back as often as he rolls it up." "No, no," said

Minos, the supreme judge, "let us invent a punishment more terrible; let us send him back to earth, to see what use his prodigal heirs make of his riches."

Ignorance, when put in possession of wealth, is often the instrument of evil. But knowledge will make its possessor an honor to his race, and will enable him to obtain wealth if he desire it. Active intelligence is a safe investment. It needs no insurance, for it is beyond the reach of fire and flood. Intelligence guides the business of the world. Who is it that in your town-meetings takes the lead in managing business, suggests the best plans, and advocates the soundest policy? Who is it that represents you in Congress, sits upon the judges' bench, and fills the various offices of honor and trust? It is the man of intelligence. Who on the contrary fill your alms-houses and jails and penitentiaries? The men who are debased by ignorance and crime. Intelligence is the first element of prosperity. Intelligence builds our factories, and invents the machinery with which to fill them. It constructs our railroads, and places upon them models of beauty and monuments of the skill of man. It stretches the wire of the telegraph and teaches us to talk with the lightning. It enables the farmer to make two spears of grass grow where but one grew before.

It puts a better plow in his ground, better implements in all his labors, and thereby saves a vast amount of the wear of muscle and weariness of nerve of both man and beast. It gives to the possessor that confidence in his abilities, and that respect for self, which raises us in the scale of being. It makes the earth seem brighter, the foliage richer, the bird's song sweeter, its plumage more gaudy, the colors of the flower more brilliant. It is the result of that improvement of the talents entrusted to us for which we shall be accountable. It yields us that satisfaction which prosperity may heighten but which adversity can never take away. It enables us to interpret the purposes and designs of the Creator, and to approximate nearer to his character. It soothes sorrow, tempers the asperities of disposition, mends the broken threads of life, smoothes the rough places in the mind and heart, and softens the pathway to the tomb.

LECTURE VIII.

THE EDUCATION OF THE MORAL SENSIBILITIES.

DELIVERED AT THE DEDICATION OF THE NEW SCHOOL EDIFICE AT TITUSVILLE, 1859.

IT is a custom hallowed by long usage, to dedicate our churches to the purposes of religious service. On this account we regard the church with different feelings from those entertained towards any other place. It is sacred in our minds as the house of God, the gate to heaven. It is here that the voice of inspiration speaks to us. Here the father assembles with his family, where they join their voices in songs of praise, and learn that wisdom which cometh from above, which will make us wise indeed. There is a sacred feeling which comes over us when we enter the place thus consecrated, and we are filled with better thoughts. Not that the service of dedication has rendered the church more holy than any other place. But the thoughts we there think, and the desires and aspirations we there cherish are more holy. The place is united to us by sacred associations, and the spirit of devotion fills it in proportion as that spirit fills our own hearts. The custom of dedicating our school edifices to the purposes of education is not so common. But the propriety can be established upon the same principles, and will apply with equal force. The school-house should be held in veneration, because our minds are there occupied with the truths of science. It is the place devoted to the culture of the mental faculties, the spiritual nature, that part of us which is imperishable. Here we discipline those faculties so noble in power, so expansive in design, which the Creator has beneficently bestowed upon us. Here are developed and strengthened those gifts which at birth are so weak and feeble. Here we become acquainted with all those laws which have been established for the government of the world of matter and of mind. It is here that we acquaint ourselves with every species of knowledge which can lift man above the brute, and advance him towards those perfections which characterize the angels and God himself. If such be the purpose of the school-house, and such the thoughts which there fill our minds, we ought to honor the place. It should be linked in our hearts with sunny memories. Our fondest affections should linger about it, and it should be set apart by exercises of learning and wisdom to these noble purposes.

The youth often looks upon the school-house with feelings of aversion and contempt. He regards it as public property, and a fit object for the spoiler. The marks of his ruthless hand prove his utter disregard of its honor and sanctity. Its broken windows attest his disposition to pelt it with stones, and his skill with charcoal is displayed upon its weather-beaten sides. The seats and desks set up for his accommodation, while preparing to fill some exalted station, as every fond mother hopes, and to erect

——"monumentum ære perennius,
Regalique situ pyramidium altius;"

display evident marks of his jack-knife, where he has by persevering efforts wrought shapes which do infinite honor to his skill with that useful instrument, and rival in artistic merit Græcian frieze and architrave; but alas! his brain-work is far less imposing, and the memory of his school-days soon sinks into oblivion, or is only perpetuated by the stripes on his back.

The indifference which is manifested towards the school-house is, in too many instances, founded upon sufficient reasons. Formerly it was a poor hut, often built of logs, cold, cheerless and dark, situated upon the verge of a road trodden into a quagmire during a greater portion of the year, with no grounds, or shade-trees, or out-buildings, destitute of every kind of convenient furniture or apparatus within, and presenting a dare-devil and repulsive air without. It would be difficult to attach any reverence to the place, even if the disposition existed. The very thought of it makes one shake the dust from his feet. The picture of the long rough board slanting from the wall, and the slab seat supported by four ugly-looking legs, sets the pains and agonies capering up the spinal cord; and the remembrance of the cold frosty mornings spent there, puts the teeth chattering on a summer day.

The school was often very much after the pattern of the house. It was thought economy to employ the services of a man who was cheap, rather than one who was competent. His capacity was measured by his ability to twist the locks and wring the ears of his pupils, rather than by his power to twist difficult problems into intelligible shapes and ring the changes upon the truths of science. His authority in preserving order was estimated more by the thickness of the soles of his boots, than by the sensibilities of the soul that filled his bosom. Tasks were imposed and forced upon unwilling minds. In place of that interest which the skillful teacher imparts to every study, came the harsh complaint of the pupil that the lessons were hard and dry. There was no throbbing of the heart at a triumph achieved over doubt and difficulty, for the pupil was not encouraged to master a difficulty, and never knew when he had triumphed. There was no beaming of the eye which follows when those sublime truths are presented that make the breast of him who appreciates them to throb with enkindling emotions, for the teacher himself had little such knowledge to impart, and with such emotions his own bosom never heaved.

It is a consoling reflection to the patriot and the Christian, that a great change has taken place in the spirit of the people, and in the intelligence and zeal of the teachers. The latter now spends freely his time and his substance in preparing himself to discharge with fidelity the arduous, the responsible, and the perplexing duties which are to devolve upon him. He seeks a thorough acquaintance with the branches of a liberal course of training. He searches out the most ingenious methods of explaining the difficult questions that arise, and plans the most attractive style of presenting his knowledge to pupils who have never known what it is to be interested in study. He devises expedients for bringing the wayward to a sense of shame, and wins him by gentle and persuasive means to a course of rectitude and honor. He is fired with a noble enthusiasm in his labor, which he regards as a most delightful employment of his faculties, rather than a task and a drudgery. He loves most of all to be surrounded by his pupils, to see them interested in his instructions, and be satisfied that they appreciate as he does their force and bearing. He enjoys the pleasing work of leading them forth to taste the delights of learning, and to realize that he is enstamping his own character upon theirs, that he is fixing in their young and tender minds his thoughts and opinions, his tastes and habits, and that he is creating in them an influence and a motive power that shall outlive him—that shall widen and deepen to the end of time.

As a result of this improvement in spirit and capacity on the part of the teacher, there is a corresponding change in the feelings and desires of the scholar. He finds his tasks easy because they interest him, and he is eager to feel all that satisfaction in his studies which he sees beaming in the countenance of his teacher, as often as he explains or touches upon them. He loves to encounter the difficulties of science, for there is the field of his triumphs, from which he bears away proud trophies. Instead of being hard and dry, he finds his labors most pleasing and delightful, and his path strewn with flowers instead of thorns.

The people are not behind in the spirit of improvement. They have learned to honor the school-house themselves, that they may with propriety impose it as a duty upon their children. In the recent structures a commendable taste has been exercised. A pleasant site has been selected, elevated, commodious and attractive. They have secured a generous piece of ground, in most cases not less than an acre. They have planted it with shade-trees, and, nicely grading, have sown it with a carpet of green. The structure itself, a model of taste and beauty, light and airy, graceful in proportion, and of approved architecture, stands as a monument of the liberality and public spirit of the neighborhood. Maps adorn its walls, and books and charts and apparatus are furnished the teacher with which to render his work successful. Thus they provide, that the sacrifices they are making may return in blessings upon the heads of their children.

As a proof of the spirit which prevails, we can point with pride and satisfaction to this edifice which we have now met to dedicate to the pursuits of learning. Central in location, convenient in arrangement and division, simple but attractive in architecture, substantially built and tastefully finished, it commands the respect alike of citizen and stranger. Its taper spire, pointing heavenward, first greets the eye of the traveler as he approaches this beautiful valley, and is the last object that lingers in the vision as he leaves it. The lawn, which you have provided, will be the scene of artless and playful sport, and generations of children will be happy because of it. The trees which you have planted may not grow to shelter you, but your children and your children's children shall sport beneath their shade, and when grown venerable with age

> "Will mind them of departed joys,
> Departed never to return."

You plant and build for the future. There is a pleasure and a satisfaction in the thought. You furnish for posterity a better chance for education than you had yourselves. You labor to leave the world better than you found it. The time will come when your work shall perish, and this noble edifice shall moulder into dust; but the record of your efforts will be secure. It will be chronicled upon immortal spirits which shall here be educated, upon a material that knows no decay.

Education, in the common acceptation of the term, has reference to that knowledge and discipline which is acquired by pursuing certain branches of study in a text-book at school. And when we speak of a common school education we usually intend the expression to comprehend a course of instruction in those branches which the law provides shall be taught. Although this is a correct signification of the term in the restricted sense, it is far from embracing all that we ought to expect from a course of training that is to prepare one for that higher life, which, in manhood and in a future state of existence, we should be prepared to live. The boy may be very good at arithmetic, but as he grows up he may make a very bad citizen and an unprofitable member of society. He may be an elegant grammarian, and still become a wretched husband and father. He may be an accomplished scholar in the Greek and Latin, and yet be dead to every noble sentiment that should fire the bosom of the patriot and the Christian.

That will prove a very unprofitable school for fitting children to be men and women, in which there is nothing learned but what is provided for by legal enactments. The teacher who can give no other instruction than this, is unworthy of a place in a profession whose office is to develop and train our spiritual natures with all their complication of desires and energies. Under the soubriquet of Pedagogue such an one is everywhere the butt for merriment and ridicule, and the sweet bard of the Deserted Village has made him the object of his playful satire:

"The village all declared how much he knew:
'Twas certain he could write, and cipher too;
Lands he could measure, times and tides presage,
And e'en the story ran that he could guage.
And still they gazed, and still the wonder grew,
That one small head could carry all he knew."

Education, in its more liberal sense, or if you choose to call it school-day culture, embraces a wider scope. It includes in the means employed, all those influences which can be brought to bear upon the mental and moral improvement of the pupil. Its excellence must depend upon its adaptation to accomplish this result. In our haste to make our children wise, we are often blind to their real interests. We give them a great deal of book knowledge to a very little plain common sense. A routine of tasks monopolizes the time for practical thinking. The mind is jaded with words and rules and problems, in place of being energized and warmed by those thoughts and feelings which have inspired the benevolent and good in all times. It is quite as much a matter of education to learn a nice sense of honor in keeping one's word, as the most elaborate and complete explanation for extracting the cube root that has ever been discovered. That piece of knowledge which prompts us to forgive him who has done us an injury, is not less valuable than the precise whereabouts of Kamtschatka or the South Sea. The spirit of brotherly love and generosity, that, spurning all mean and selfish motives, will sacrifice its own advantage for the happiness of another, or will dare even to peril life for the general weal, will be quite as servicable to a man as the ability to dispose of some knotty point in grammar. To love God and to keep his commandments is a lesson that we need thoroughly to learn and constantly to practice, more than all the sciences which human ingenuity has reduced to form.

Leaving therefore those studies that are commonly taught at school, I purpose during the remainder of the passing hour to speak of THE EDUCATION OF THE MORAL SENSIBILITIES. We are possessed of a moral nature as well as mental powers, and the former need care and culture equally with the latter. In the exercise of the common duties of life, the moral powers are far more frequently brought into action than the mental. As often as man comes in contact with his fellow-man, he has occasion to display some of the motives by which he is governed. There are no text-books especially adapted to giving instruction in this department of culture, though the works of Mrs. Willard, and of Messrs. Cowdry and Hall, have of late supplied teachers with what has been felt to be a great want, and may with much propriety and profit be used. But, though the teacher has no text-books to guide him in his instructions, there are abundant opportunities for impressing upon the young a sense of their duties and responsibilities, and of making virtue and honor respectable, yea, lovely in their eyes. In the affairs of a school there is something that is constantly going wrong and needs to be righted. A company of youth whose habits are all unfixed, vacillating in purpose, and weak in judgment, many of whom have had little or no correct training at home, and some even destitute of civil breeding, may be considered of all others the most fruitful of improprieties and errors, demanding the most frequent counsel and correction, and the most severely testing the virtue and faithfulness of him who is its leading spirit.

There is no person from whom a word of advice, a caution against the violation of a moral duty, an appeal to the sensibilities, will be received and be impressed upon the pupil with such force, as from the lips of the faithful, conscientious, virtuous school-teacher. He will get his ears and reach his heart when no other man can. There is no other person who stands in a position in which the opportunities of giving such instruction are so abundant, and which must be considered by the teacher not merely as opportunities which he may improve or neglect, but as occasions imperatively demanding his guiding hand. When I think of the vast and responsible duties which properly devolve upon the teacher, and which so much need to be performed in addition to the regular routine of lessons, and remember the indifference and unconcern with which they are viewed by many who eagerly and unhesitatingly assume them, I tremble for the interests of the rising generation, and for the reckoning those teachers will finally make with the Judge of all the earth. For no man can assume a position of trust, without becoming amenable to justice for a neglect of its most important duties.

The first and highest of the moral ideas which should be instilled into the minds of children is that of love to God. The propriety of this is so obvious that it does not need to be urged. And yet there are many teachers who never utter a word of counsel or entreaty to enforce the duty. His pupils may violate the Sabbath and hear no word of disapproval from him, and perchance he is guilty of the same offence himself. They may show a disregard, and positive contempt for their Maker by cursing his name, and he has not moral courage, or moral sensibility enough to admonish them of their open defiance and blasphemy, and perchance, in moments of passion, or of folly, such language is not an unknown tongue to him. It may not be expedient for him to make a law that his pupils should not violate the Sabbath, or that they should not use profane language. I believe that it is not wise for him to make many arbitrary laws. But he can, by an appeal to their better feelings, make those vices appear mean and despicable, and particularly odious in the character of the youth. He can, if his heart is alive to sensibility and these moral virtues, carry them along with the zeal and enthusiasm by which he is actuated, and make them think and feel with him.

A portion of Scripture, without note or comment, should be daily read in school. The Bible is the great source of spiritual life and light. It contains every thing respecting our moral relations that we need to know. There is in many parts of our country, a strong opposition to the use of this book in the common school. But there can be no valid objection to its continuance, unless some considerable portion of the scholars would be excluded on account of it. No man can be injured by reading its truths; and if he is disposed to receive he may realize from it inestimable treasures. If God has made a revelation of his will to us, he undoubtly intended that we should read it. How can we make our lives conform to the teaching of his word, if we do not read it? Is not the opening of school a proper place and time for attending to it? It is objected that we have not a true translation, but this does not affect the principle that God's word ought to be read in school. If we have not the true translation, then let us have one that is. He has given us his word in an exact and definite language, and there is no doubt but that it can be made truly into our language. If those in present use are wrong, then let the errors be pointed out and righted. It is God's word, not this bible or that bible, that we claim should be read to the young. We are not yet too wise to do without it, and the youthful mind has need of its purifying influences. It is objected that we can not understand it. "Do unto others as ye would that they should do unto you." Who can not understand that? The bible is full of truths just as plain. There is enough truth on almost any page, that can be understood by the child even in tender years, to give us correct moral principles in all the relations of life. Every child in the State has the opportunity of becoming sufficiently well educated to read and understand for himself the spirit and meaning of the great moral lessons which the bible contains. I would unhesitatingly condemn any disposition on the part of the teacher to inculcate narrow or sectarian dogmas. But against the simple reading of the Scriptures, either by the teacher or by his pupils, there can be no reason assigned that can have weight in a rational mind.

If we regard the Bible merely as a literary production, where shall we seek one among the works of the greatest masters, that for elaborate finish, for figures of speech, for majesty and sublimity of thought can be compared to it. Where in the whole range of literature, ancient or modern, can we find such a description of spring as that portrayed by Solomon. "For, lo, the winter is past, the rain is over and gone; the flowers appear on the earth; the time of the singing of birds is come, and the voice of the turtle is heard in our land. The fig tree putteth forth her green figs, and the vines with the tender grapes give a good smell; arise, my love, my fair, and come away." It is but a few words that the inspired penman employs. But in those few words is brought to mind a combination of the most delightful and pleasing objects that nature, prodigal of beauty, presents. The senses each in turn are regaled with an object appropriate to please.

Where among the books of the sages do we find such sentiments as these: "Love your enemies; do good to them which hate you; bless them that curse you; and unto him that smiteth on the one cheek offer also the other; and him that taketh away thy cloak, forbid not to take thy coat also; and as ye would that men should do to you do ye even so to them." What mind is not made better by the contemplation of such truths as these? Are not these the sentiments which, of all others, need most to be impressed upon the mind of the child? Is it not by nature selfish and revengeful, and envious and grasping? Does it not need an antidote to all these evil desires and passions? When our Lord was hanging upon the cross, and his enemies were spitting upon him, and in his agony giving him vinegar to drink, and thrusting their spears into his side, those divine sentiments which had marked all his teachings did not forsake him, and he prayed, "Father, forgive them, for they know not what they do."

The second of the moral sensibilities which the scholar should sedulously cultivate is love of country or patriotism. After the allegiance due to our Maker, we owe our warmest devotion to the country in which we live. It is from civil government that we derive the right and privilege of enjoying every other blessing. The state is the kind mother who dispenses the means for using, unmolested and untrammeled, every social and virtuous principle; or, if she fails to do this, it is because her children have not been instructed in the lessons of patriotism. For, if the rising generation as they grow up to assume the rank of citizenship, are fully imbued with the love of civil liberty and civil rights, they will never permit any other form of government to dictate to them, inasmuch as they are in their sovereign capacity the primal source of all civil power. The pupil at school should be reminded of these truths, and be taught to feel and fully appreciate the spirit of independent thought and action, subject only to the law of love and virtue. The study of history, which should be one of the branches taught in every school, will furnish abundant opportunity for practically carrying into operation the spirit of the principle which has been stated.

But even if history is not a study in school, and there is no text-book in civil science used, there are numerous occasions constantly presented, in the occurrences of the school-room, in the allusions of reading lessons, and in the facts connected with geographical science, which may naturally form the basis for such instruction. The sensibilities of youth are usually alive to feelings of patriotism, and to deeds of noble daring. The interest is easily enlisted in allusions to those adventures which characterized the opening scenes of our revolution. Where is the scholar whose heart does not kindle with emotion at a recital of the heaven-inspired patriotism of Washington? Where is the scholar whose heart does not beat quick in contemplating the self-sacrificing spirit of the hero who, in the flower of manhood, left home and the wife of his bosom, subjected himself to the varying chances of war, and freely devoted life and energy to the future good of his country? What youth is not elevated in spirit as he beholds, in all its breadth and loveliness, the sublime virtue which was displayed in every event in the life of the Father of his Country? But the feelings which inspired the chief were shared by every rank and grade of the army to the lowest subaltern in the camp. There is something marvelous and sublime in the spectacle of a poor people, just established in their homes in the wilderness, with no hope of profit or reward beyond the inestimable treasures of civil liberty, embarking in a cause so arduous, seeing in prospect their property pillaged, their homes burned, submitting to a sacrifice of all they held dear, periling even life itself, and, in a spirit of unexampled patriotism, gathering about their trusty leader and pledging "their lives, their fortunes and their sacred honor."

"Patriots have toiled and in their country's cause
Bled nobly, and their deeds, as they deserve,
Receive proud recompense. We give in charge
Their names to the sweet lyre. The historic muse,
Proud of her treasure, marches with it down
To latest times, and sculpture in her turn
Gives bond in stone and ever-during brass,
To guard them and immortalize her trust."

I have always been struck with the spirit of that Athenian youth, who declared that the trophies of Miltiades would not let him sleep. So thoroughly imbued was he with the spirit of patriotism and the love for glorious action, that his young heart yearned for labors fitting to the hero. The sight of the enemies of his country, bearing down upon and ready to crush her, enkindled within him the desire to drive back the impending foe, and vindicate her honor and her glory. He envied the renown of that skillful leader who was achieving those honors in the field which he longed to win. And those sleepless nights gave presage of that future brilliant career of glory that lay open before him.

It should be the care of the teacher to impress upon his pupils on all suitable occasions, the necessity of virtuous principle in the conduct of affairs. He should strive to implant in their youthful minds a love for honesty and integrity of purpose, that may serve as their guide in transacting all the duties which are incident to citizenship. They should be made acquainted with the examples of those sainted patriots and martyrs in all ages of the world, who have sacrificed their lives to the living principles of liberty and truth, and whose names, surviving the wreck of thrones and dynasties, will be remembered to the end of time. The struggles between privilege and despotism from which they have been made to suffer should be recounted, that the pupil may understand the full value of their virtue and at how dear a price the present condition of society has been purchased. He should be taught by a comparison of the most striking lessons to appreciate the difference between good and bad government, and to love those institutions which we, as Americans, prize so much. In a word, the youth of our common schools should treasure up the principles of the most enlightened patriotism.

The third of the moral virtues which should receive attention, is love to man. It is comprehended in that golden rule, "Do unto others as ye would that they should do unto you," and embraces the principles of reciprocity and philanthropy. The school is eminently the place where the evil passions and propensities are most signally developed. Here they are brought plainly to view. Families of children are thrown together. Perhaps the parents of those children have had difficulties and cause for quarrel, and cherish bitter feelings of enmity which are shared by them. Pride of family and of birth is brought into collision with the born plebeian. The aristocracy of wealth brushes against the tattered garments of poverty. It is the task of the teacher to reconcile all these conflicting elements, to bring peace out of contention, and form and beauty out of chaos. The law of love and kindness is to be established, and the universal brotherhood of man to be vindicated in the face of pride and the dubious claims to ancestral honors. He is to tax his ingenuity to see how mean, and cowardly, and sinful he can make every species of vice appear,

"And virtue in her shape how lovely."

It was a part of the education of the Spartan youth to learn to steal, and he who could take that which did not belong to him, and avoid detection, carried off the palm. We sometimes see a similar disposition manifested in our time. There are those who look upon a man who can, by misrepresentation and deceit, overreach another in a bargain, as shrewd and smart. That species of vice which, in common parlance, passes under the name of cheating, is, in some circles of society, considered as a fundamental element of success in business, and the boy who manifests acuteness in the practice of it as possessing flattering prospects ahead. It is evident that every such propensity is directly antagonistic to the divine precept, and that if one be right, the other must be wrong. The teacher ought to labor assiduously to eradicate from the mind any such impression, for it is not only dishonest and sinful in itself, but it may be the fruitful source of other crimes of a darker dye. That "honesty is the best policy" is not only a trite maxim that is glibly spoken, but it is a sublime truth that every man would do well to profit by. Duplicity may succeed for a time, but ill-gotten gains yield little satisfaction to the possessor, and they leave a stain upon the soul which neither time nor circumstance can remove. There is no feeling that so warms a man's heart as a consciousness of rectitude. Firm in his reliance upon his innocence, he does not fear the face of any man.

"What stronger breast-plate than a heart untainted?"

Hence honesty, in its broadest sense, becomes not merely a moral duty, but a duty which he owes most of all to himself, to his success and his happiness.

The minds of children are, in general, keenly sensitive to wrong and insult, and the disposition to retaliation and revenge is quick. Buoyant and ingenuous in spirit, they have not yet learned to brook delay and disappointment in the righting of wrongs, and the impulse is to take justice in their own hands. When cuffed and abused, the propriety of turning the other cheek is not quite so apparent. The North American Indians believed that revenge was a duty and a virtue. Revenge was sweet to them. If a dispute arose between two, and an encounter ensued in which one was killed, it was the duty of the nearest relative to take up the quarrel, and thus eventually whole tribes and nations would become involved from a personal altercation, trifling and unimportant. As a consequence, they were kept constantly in warfare, and whole countries were thereby depopulated. How contrary to this were the mild and gentle teachings of our Saviour. Love your enemies. Forgive as ye hope to be forgiven. The teacher will often be under the necessity of reproving and correcting the spirit of revenge in his pupils, and if he would make his corrections effectual and vital, he must labor earnestly to incorporate into their mental constitutions the principles of a perfect morality.

It is vain to attempt to point out all the varied forms which a transgression of this golden rule may assume. Nor is it necessary always to take notice of all the violations of it that may come to his knowledge, or to warn his pupils of all the sins which they are liable to commit. It is sufficient if he imbue them with the spirit of the precept, and, by frequently reminding them, seek to establish it as a ruling principle in their character. The great design should be to make it appear lovely in their eyes, for a youth will never be induced voluntarily to adopt a principle and to enter upon a course of conduct which has not first been made to appear desirable. Virtuous action ever carries with it its own great reward, and he who in youth becomes enamored of it, is likely to enter upon that bright shining way that shines more and more unto the perfect day, and is surely fortified against the allurements to vice and folly. The invitation of the attendant spirit in the Mask of Comus is seasonable, and happy is he who accepts it:

"Mortals that would follow me,
Love virtue; she alone is free.
She can teach ye how to climb
Higher than the sphery chime;
Or if virtue feeble were,
Heaven itself would stoop to her."

The moral sensibilities comprehended in love to God, love to country, and love to man, are the leading ones that pertain to our conduct in the affairs of life. From the manner in which these are trained and developed results that character which we are to sustain. During our school days, our thoughts and dispositions are pliant and peculiarly susceptible. The character is then easily moulded. It is especially desirable that wholesome instruction should then be given. A neglect of proper training or a wrong impression may be the source of incalculable evils. Scratch the rind of a sapling, and the crooked and disfigured tree will bear testimony for ages to the work of your ruthless hand. It is important that the teacher should have a thorough acquaintance with the branches he is to teach, be able to explain what is difficult in an interesting and intelligible manner, and have the desire and the ability to excite in his pupils a zealous ardor in the preparation and recitation of their lessons; but it is even more important that he should be capable and intent upon giving the highest and best instruction to the moral sensibilities.

To this end it is absolutely essential that he be a man of irreproachable character, nay, that his life be a noble exemplification of the moral virtues. He should be a pattern after which his pupils may profitably copy. The child is naturally imitative, and the teacher is placed in a position in which he is constantly the noticed and the observed, and if his character be not exemplary, evil consequences may result to his precious charge. It is desirable that the pupil should be instructed and encouraged in the adoption of correct habits. Neatness, cleanliness, proper care of property, order, respect to superiors and to the aged, politeness in personal intercourse, kind and respectful salutations and adieus, courtesy to strangers, a becoming modesty and reserve at all times—to inculcate and enforce these upon his pupils should be the object of his constant care. But alas! for the pupils and the best interests of the school, if the teacher be not himself instructed in these habits.

We hear much said about the importance of an education, and we talk about the inestimable treasures of knowledge; but learning and knowledge, and all the fruits of study and discipline, are of little worth if not under the guidance of correct moral principles.

> ——"Talents angel-bright,
> If wanting worth, are shining instruments
> In false ambition's hand to finish faults
> Illustrious, and give infamy renown."

A cracked bell gives forth discordant sounds, and the more it clatters the more we are disgusted. Knowledge without virtue gives to its possessor the ability to perpetrate untold evil upon society and upon himself, and is immeasurably a worse condition than ignorance. Aaron Burr was a scholar of eminence and one of the most accomplished lawyers of his age, but he used his great abilities and his fine learning for the overthrow of the most cherished institutions of his country, and died despised and abhorred as a traitor and a villain. Byron, with all his talents and fine poetic sentiment, was a shameless rake, and with the might and power of his genius, which every one of judgment and taste must admire, he inflicted a wound upon society that ages of pious teaching and example will not cure. That education may be important, and possess the value of inestimable treasures, it must be under the control of goodness. The records of vice and crime which every week's paper brings to us, and the disgusting and heart-sickening details of the execution of miserable wretches even in boyhood, declare with commanding emphasis that our systems of education are deficient in the culture of the moral sensibilities.

Every person who has been eminent in a career of crime, has, upon reflection, been constrained to attribute his unfortunate course to the guidance of his own evil passions. Indeed, the passions when fired with sinful purposes make a man a very devil. But there are no passions of which we are possessed that are in themselves evil or unholy. They are merely the instruments which we may use for a good or a bad purpose. Our Saviour was possessed of all the passions which fire the bosom of the most weak and sinful, but under the control of fervent piety they served to make his life sublime. The passions are necessary to the highest attainment of virtue. Without them to inspire us with fervor, our mental faculties would be powerless. There would be no high purpose and firm resolve, no heroic valor and noble daring, no martyrdom for truth, no self-sacrificing philanthropy. Our passions are our best having when under proper control, and are the means of that high life which commands respect and love.

The teacher occupies a position of great responsibility. The importance of the trust must be apparent to every reflecting mind. It is a profession requiring qualifications the most varied, demanding a combination of rare talents and elaborate culture. The demands which an enlightened discharge of his duty will make upon him, require that he should go forth to his labor fully panoplied with knowledge and virtue. He needs liberal mental culture, but he needs most of all a double portion of God's Holy Spirit to enlighten his understanding and warm his heart, to support and strengthen him in times of trouble, to make him firm and resolute in the correction of the wrong and the vindication of the right, to guard him in the hour of temptation, and to refine and purify every holy enjoyment. The teacher, in view of the responsibleness of his position and the qualifications needed, may despond, and say, these requirements are too great for a station commanding so small remuneration and so little esteem and honor. But you are the one to make the profession honorable, to inspire people with respect for it and you, and thus merit better remuneration. It is weakness for you to falter in this cause and fall back in presence of such weak foes. He who would win victories in a field like this, must not shrink from the arduous tasks it imposes, or be daunted by the apparent difficulties that he may fancy he sees staring him in the way.

> "Then stand ye up,
> Shielded, and helmed, and weaponed with the truth,
> And drive before you into uttermost shame
> Those recreant caitiffs."

The inhabitants of this village have sacrificed their means, and weary hands have builded this house, and teachers will be employed to give the best of instruction, but vain will be sacrifice, and labor, and instruction, if the knowledge acquired is not sanctified by the spirit of truth. It is better that this noble edifice should at once crumble into ruins, than that these pupils should be taught the truths of science without a corresponding cultivation of the moral sensibilities. But we will not despond. A noble work has been begun. The erection of this house is an era in the history of this town. It is a mark of the intelligence and public spirit which prevails. The first means of prosperity to any community is an educated and enlightened people. That nation, or city, or hamlet has been prospered most that has possessed the most intelligence. The erection of this house will give a new impetus to the desire for obtaining it. You now have in your midst a building suitable for a school of a high grade. You can now command the means for the most liberal culture. May children and parents and teachers and school-officers be faithful to their trusts, and by their united efforts make this the place where the rising generation may come up as to a fountain of living waters, and take copious draughts of the pure limpid stream. And when the people of other towns shall boast of their public halls, and magnificent blocks, you may point with pride and satisfaction to this place, and say, the best public building of our village is devoted to the education of our children.

LECTURE IX.

EDUCATION AND DEMOCRACY THE TRUE BASIS OF LIBERTY.

DELIVERED AT TOWNVILLE, JULY 4TH, 1857.

FELLOW-CITIZENS:—It is a mark of enlightened policy that we have a national holiday, and I know no time in the year more appropriate for the purpose than the fourth of July. The dreary winter has given way to the jocund spring. The husbandman has drained the damp earth of the liquid frosts. The weary ox, bearing meekly the yoke, has mellowed up the cold heavy acres. The seeds have been scattered, and the vines planted in deep trenches. The pruning knife and the implements of labor have been applied with tireless hand. And now, as the dusty garb of husbandry is to give place to the clean habiliments of summer, and the grain and fruits are beginning to mature for the sickle, what time can be more appropriate for a day of national recreation than this point of transition between seed time and harvest.

The time is appropriate. But were this all, it

might become dull and meaningless. There would be no living motive for its observance. It would become a day of debauchery for the immoral, and, consequently dreaded and hated by the intelligent and virtuous. But it comes to us with happy memories and endearing associations, because it marks the day of the nation's birth. The youth, the man of affairs and hoary age annually look forward to this day with buoyant and exhilarated feelings. Those who are bending beneath the weight of years are carried back to the time

"When their hearts were stout and brave."

The celebrations of other days are brought back vividly to mind, and they are again aroused by that soul-stirring eloquence hurled from the lips of orators and poets now mute in death. The man who is in the prime of life, whose heart is eaten with care, and whose head begins to blossom, is glad to turn aside from the toilsome and dusty walks of life and breathe the inspiring breath of patriotism, review the origin and workings of civil liberty, tremble for its perils, weep for its persecutions and rejoice over its triumphs. And the child leaps for joy, he knows not why, for his heart is lit up with hope and anticipation, and his affections have not yet been chilled by the disappointments with which life's journey is thronged,

The grave and the gay, the matron and the maid, all reckon its approach in eager anticipation, and on the morning of this day a nation wakes like the child to the enjoyment of a new toy. Cannon herald its approach, and bells ring out their merriest peals. Music lends her spirit-stirring tones. The blast of the trumpet, and the mellow strains from the bugle and the horn of the well-regulated band which leads on the gay procession, the chorus chanted by hundreds of living voices, down to the tin whistle and jews-harp of the boy who is obliged to stay at home, and who gets up a celebration on his own account, decorated with, wooden sword and a paper hat surmounted with cockade and feather, and who delivers his own oration by crawling up into a tree or the back end of a hay cart—all unite to swell the fountains of enthusiasm. The old patriot uttered truth when he looked forth with prophetic eye and said, "We shall make this a glorious and immortal day. When we are in our graves our children will honor it. They will celebrate it with thanksgiving, with festivity, with bonfires and illuminations. On its annual return they will shed tears—copious, gushing tears, not of subjection and slavery, not of agony and distress, but of exultation, of gratitude and joy."

The celebration of this day is not to excite the feelings of hatred and exultation over those who formerly believed that they could with propriety pursue a line of policy which was degrading to us; but of joy and gratitude that the fruits of its labors have proved so glorious, that the era which this day has heralded in, has been so fortunate and happy to our youthful nation, that the fondest hopes and anticipations of those who took part in its deliberations have been more than realized, that a combination of such fortunate circumstances has centered in this, the latest experiment in civilization, and that we can this day rejoice together in the goodly inheritance bequeathed to us by the fathers of the republic. Indeed, we scarcely remember that England ever attempted to force us to subjection at the point of the bayonet, and hardly realize but that, in the intimacy of her relations with us, she has her fourth of July, and celebrates with us the triumphs of liberty. That feeling of animosity which originally existed between the generations which were parties to the contest, and that was kept alive and annually fed by spirited Philippics on our boasted greatness and the defeat of the British arms, was buried in the graves of the actors in the scene.

As the birthday of our nation, we celebrate it. On its annual return, our thoughts are naturally directed to the history of civil liberty, to its progress among the nations, and the struggles it has met. We are reminded that we have a country whose welfare and safety should be near our hearts. On this day the rising generation may learn something of the history of the past. They may imbibe the spirit of that incorruptible virtue which animated the bosoms of our fathers, may understand the dangers they encountered, the hardships with which they struggled, the sufferings they meekly endured in establishing a form of government which has secured the blessings of liberty and prosperity through the successive generations, and, as we may fondly hope, to the end of time. That portion of our fellow-citizens who come among us from foreign countries, and who have received their earliest impressions of civil rights from experience under government exercised by arbitrary power and a system of police, may learn the basis upon which our government is established and the essence and true spirit of our national origin by listening to that Declaration of Independence which has just been read, and which is so dear to us all. The foreigner who comes here ignorant of our laws and customs may, from the song that is sung and the words that are spoken, catch a truer notion, a more genuine inspiration of American liberty and American law than from the reading of all the volumes of her legal codes.

But the question which most concerns us, and

which should on this day be the object of inquiry, is how we may preserve the institutions which have been bequeathed to us. If the government under which we live is a good one, and has made us prosperous and happy beyond that of any other nation whose history has been recorded, we ought to labor to preserve it in its purity. If the liberty we enjoy is precious to us, and we are privileged to move and act in its sunshine and genial warmth, we should guard it as a precious treasure, a priceless gem. There is need of watchfulness. The casket that contains the jewel is always in danger of being rifled. Secure in the enjoyment of our boasted favors, and flattered by the prosperity which they secure to us, we may, in some unguarded moment, be deprived of them; our national temple may be rifled, and we be despoiled of our dearest inheritance. The enemies of popular government will ever be ready to lend a helping hand to compass its ruin. Heartless villains in our midst would sell its liberties for the gratification of their own ambition and reckless lust for power. To study the means for preventing so lamentable a result, should be the care of every good citizen, and shall form the topic of the remainder of this discourse.

To preserve a system intact we should first understand the principles upon which it is based. What is the basis of civil liberty? The answer to this question will point out the interests which we are to foster and protect in order to preserve it in health and vigor.

EDUCATION unrestricted is the first element of national liberty. The history of every civilized nation has shown that the rights of the citizen, his property, his person, are insecure in the midst of an ignorant and brutish populace. The nations of antiquity invariably built strong walls of defense around their great cities, in which the intelligent and educated could assemble with their treasures, where they could outnumber and manage the servile class in their midst, whose labor they needed, and, from its ramparts, could govern and tyrannize over the ignorant and barbarous who dwelt beyond its limits. During the best period of the most polished nations of antiquity the great body of the people were never enlightened. The cities in which letters triumphed and art most signally excelled, in which Plato discoursed upon the principles of his philosophy, and where Tully plead, were surrounded by an uneducated populace. Civil liberty was never enjoyed in any of the boasted republics of antiquity by any except the inhabitants of the cities; and even the rights and privileges of these were only possessed so long as protected by the strong arm of a great central power. Their governments were never secure, because not founded on the true basis of that liberty which they professed.

Attempts have often been made to establish liberty for a people uneducated, and the efforts have always failed. The wise and virtuous, with clear vision, who have distinctly seen that liberty was best for a nation, and have realized in fancy the blessings which ought to flow from it, have labored and sacrificed to give it to the masses; but the ignorant and besotted have only trodden it under their feet and turned to rend their benefactors. Republican principles have again and again been established in France, but they have never lasted a score of years. The efforts of her patriots have been unreservedly given to the cause, and it has been sealed with the blood of her best citizens; but even at this price it has not been secured. And why is it? Why may not one of the most polished and gallant nations of the earth enjoy liberty? Why may not the nation which reckons among its sons the first scholars of the age, in every walk of learning, enjoy this inestimable gift? Figures will tell. The report of the chief of the statistical bureau shows that twelve millions! (12,000,000) of her population can neither read nor write. When we read these figures we no longer wonder why this unhappy country has so often failed in establishing a republican government, nor why it is so often rent by turbulent and treacherous factions. Until France* shall learn to educate her masses she may never reasonably hope for the full enjoyment of civil liberty.

A people to be free must have intelligence. The walls with which ancient nations surrounded their cities would not have been needed if the common people had been educated. If the money which is

---

* An eloquent writer in a late French journal says, "Twelve millions of our fellow-citizens, entitled to vote and to decide the common destiny, are still ignorant of the first rudiments of reading and writing." No wonder that he follows this astounding statement with the inquiry, "How can France be free so long as you have to drag this dead weight, to apprehend the explosion of these embittered and discontented classes?" Never, of course. A free State including "twelve millions" of citizens who can't read or write! The thing is impossible. Freedom requires thought, knowledge, scrutiny into the claims and measures of magistrates and law makers. The man who is "ignorant of the first rudiments of reading and writing" is destitute of the first elements and incapable of the first duties of freemen. . . . . M. Montalembert says, that, though he is not an old man he has lived to see ten revolutions in his native country. No wonder: he may live to see ten more, if he reaches a good old age, with "twelve millions of voters in France who can neither read nor write."

Yet we may shed a tear over the unhappy condition of one of the bravest, most generous and highly gifted of races. It is not their fault that they can not read or write. No man learns quicker or is more anxious to learn than a Frenchman. Ages of despotism have made them incapable of freedom. It is to no purpose that the same journalist affirms, "Our superior culture, our special schools, are the admiration of Europe." It is not superior schools nor special culture that can make a free people.—*New York Ledger*, 1859.

expended in building lofty walls of defense, and maintaining a large standing army, with scarcely a less body of police for enforcing laws upon an unwilling people, were used in supporting a system of common school instruction in which every child of the State could be educated,

"Thick wall or moated gate"

would be a useless appendage, and battalions of soldiers, with a detective at every corner and by-way, would be a needless exhaustion of its life.

The man who can neither read nor write is not a fit person to exercise the elective franchise. Some of the States of our confederacy have enacted that he who can not read or write shall not vote at an election. "A man," says President Wayland, "who can not read, is a being not contemplated by the genius of our Constitution. When the right of suffrage is extended to all, he is certainly a dangerous member of the community, who has not qualified himself to exercise it." Knowledge is the first means of safety and security to a nation. A body of uneducated citizens, each with as loud a voice at the ballot box as he who is educated, are fit tools for the artful and designing. It has always been the province of knowledge to dictate to ignorance, and so long as there are those who will take advantage of the latter whenever the opportunity presents, there can be no safety for civil rights till the people, the δῆμος, are able to understand opinions and the tendencies of measures which they are urged to support, and can judge for themselves of their truth or falsity. The first element of security to civil liberty is education. If then we would erect a bulwark which shall be a substantial means of safety, if we would guard against the assaults of open foes, and the more dangerous attacks of the false-hearted and intriguing, we should labor for the efficiency of our common schools.

That form of government which is most favorable to the success of civil liberty is that in which the decisions upon its great vital questions are kept nearest to the voice of the people, so that abuses may be speedily corrected when felt. This form is a DEMOCRACY. The fundamental principles of this are embraced in our Declaration of Independence. Its simple statements are founded in truth—truth which has been developed by the struggles of civilization during many ages. It is the natural expression of the rights and relations of humanity, drawn from the experience of every nation that has played any important part upon the earth. No man who is thoroughly imbued with the principles of Christianity can deny its truthfulness or justly resist its binding force.

There has always existed a struggle between prerogative and power, between the class governed and that exercising dominion. This struggle originated either from the ignorance of the people in not being content to submit to wholesome restraint, or from an attempt on the part of those who hold the power to assume to themselves arbitrary authority. An equality in rights and privileges of every member must exist, or the class deprived will contend with those who withhold from them what they can justly claim. Hence, whenever in any nation there is a class under the authority of law which is deprived of its political rights and can not have a voice in the government, then the institutions of that nation are not stable. Submission to power without a voice in managing it, among a civilized people, will never be endured, and, sooner or later, the contest will come.

We have already referred to the States of antiquity. Many of these possessed forms of government applicable to the noble families of a single city, commendable for the extent of political freedom which they insured. The democratic republics of Greece have long been celebrated as models. The philosopher has dwelt upon the excellence of those systems till, in his heated imagination, he has formed his conception of the model republic. The historian has portrayed in his brightest colors their splendid triumphs in cabinet and field. He has presented to the dazzled eye the tramp of armies clad in buckler and helmet and vizored in steel. He has pictured the brazen-beaked galleys and fleets covering the ocean and meeting hostile fleets—the triumphs of a handful of republican forces over myriads of barbarian soldiery. He has preserved with care the speeches of their orators, powerful and persuasive like the words of Jove, and the policy of her statesmen planned from the profoundest views of political philosophy, and fruitful of wonders. The poet has sung in his loftiest strains of their triumphs in arms, in athletic sports, in letters, in art.

But while we gaze delighted at this picture of renown secured under the protection of democratic forms of government, we are filled with far different feelings as we look beneath this semblance of liberty and see that while the inhabitants of a single city, who are enrolled as citizens, enjoy the privileges of freemen, and have an equal voice in making the laws, the great majority of the people, who cultivate the earth, who bear the heavy armor in war, and help fight the stern battles, are in a condition of abject slavery and vassalage; who live trampled in the dust, forsaken and despised, and die unwept, unhonored and unsung. Sparta may boast in pompous terms of the freedom of her city, of her heraldry in arms, of the vastness of her power, and her glory in literature and art. But the tears, and groans and blood of her serfs are unnumbered and forgotten.

When we are admitted to a nearer view of this boasted free republic, and see the real condition of that portion of her State on which she must of necessity depend for her daily bread, we must conclude, according to the proposition which we have already advanced, that her institutions are not stable, and can not long endure. From the facts in the organization of her society we may truly figure her concluding scenes. Those who were enrolled as citizens, and who alone had power in the government, were soldiers and gentlemen. They bought and sold, heard the news, discussed politics, made laws in the assembly, managed the affairs of state, and lived at their ease, while the helots performed the drudgery. The clear-sighted of the Spartan statesmen plainly perceived that so long as these relations subsisted between the two classes the ruling party would never be secure. They knew that idleness and luxury would waste the energies of the one, while fresh struggles and hardships would fill the other with new vigor. Knowing that danger was lurking in the future, and anxious to perpetuate institutions under which the helots had to do the work while they enjoyed leisure and the fruits of this labor, they placed the helots under the surveillance of the most vigilant police, and atrocious violence was used to reduce their strength and break their spirit. In addition to this, a law was enacted called the Cryptia, according to the provisions of which* "a commission was given every year to a select number of young Spartans to range the country secretly, armed with daggers, for the purpose of assassinating those helots, wherever they might be found, who, by eminent qualities of body or mind, had excited the fear or jealousy of the government. * * * On one occasion, when the weakness of Sparta gave reason to dread an insurrection of the helots, all those whose past services seemed to entitle them to claim their emancipation were publicly invited to come forward and receive their reward. The bravest and most deserving presented themselves, and two thousand were selected as the worthiest. They joyfully crowned themselves, and went around the temples to offer their thanks to the gods; they were then secretly dispatched, so that the historian could not learn the exact manner in which the horrible crime was committed."

No government can long be upheld by such

* Schmitz's History of Greece, pages 95, 96.

revolting means as these, and it is a mockery to call such a State a free republic. We can as surely predict its downfall from its early history as the rising of the sun. A halo of glory may surround its rise and progress, and its meridian splendor may dazzle with its brightness far away in the midst of those barbarous ages, but the damp shades of night must ere long envelop it, and we hear

> ———"its tuneful echoes languish
> Mute but to the voice of anguish."

No class of people in an enlightened nation can long remain stationary. If there is an order which is rich and powerful, and which has exalted itself in influence above the rank which they leave beneath them, and hold the government in their hands, they may perhaps be successful for a few generations to rule and domineer. But there will be members of that class who will become degraded by folly and crime, and will deserve to fall beneath their companions. No despotic system can keep them in their place. No law or force of family renown can exalt a man and make him respected or hold a rank which his ancestors held before him. He who has pursued a deliberate course of evil, has brought dishonor on himself and forfeited the confidence of his fellow-men, deserves no longer their friendship. On the other hand, however much a class may be ground down and oppressed, or however menial its labor, it will not be long before the spark of true manhood which has been implanted in the bosom of us all will show itself. There will be a desire to rise higher and know more, to imitate deeds of heroism, to labor meekly in a true philanthropy, and work out a higher destiny. If government has drawn arbitrarily the lines between them, and will allow none of the former to fall to their true level, and none of the latter to rise, then that government is not firm, and will soon become the subject of contention, and will eventually be overwhelmed amidst the ruins of the temple in which it seeks to enshrine itself.

There must always be two classes among every people. There are those who, by weakness of temper or inactivity of body will be imbecile to think or act; and there will be those who, with imperious disposition and constitutional strength, will push on to eminence, whether in the field, the cabinet, in trade, in philanthropy, or in letters. But because the father was weak it is no sign that the son will be so, and the son of the wise may be a simpleton. Hence the sons may not be fit to assume the places and join the ranks which their fathers filled. If in society there is not a free passage between the two extremes, the progress of civilization is cramped, and the safety of the government is endangered. For the man who is held in a position above his talents or morals, because he has gentle blood in his veins, becomes an object of disgust, and impairs our confidence in the law which keeps him there. And he who is prevented from rising to that position for which he is eminently fitted, and which he would fill with honor and ability, nurtures a hatred of the oppression that keeps him down, which, like a smouldering fire, is fed by that which is heaped up to extinguish it. A large proportion of the active meritorious business men of the city of New York were once poor boys, the sons of farmers and mechanics scattered over New England and the adjoining States, who annually visit the old homestead in the country. While a majority of the sons of those who were most successful in business in a former generation, are the bloated inmates of brothel and groggery, or figure as dandies on Broadway, and mankind are none the wiser or better for their living.

It is only when there is a free pass from one extreme of society to the other, with no restraints except virtue and her eloquent persuadings that a nation can be said to be truly free—when merit is crowned with its deserts. It is then that the mechanic arts best flourish. Then nature is most encouraged to perfect her work. Then literature accomplishes its greatest results, and rises to its highest perfection, because all have the assurance of a fair opportunity.

The contentions which have been constantly going on between prerogative and power, and which have occupied almost exclusively the pen of the historian in every nation of any note, have originated in a departure from the principle just enunciated. The Roman republic was founded upon the principle that the governing was a distinct order from the governed, that an aristocracy and menials were the foundation of power. But that haughty spirit which is the characteristic of human nature everywhere when placed in a position to domineer, and which was so marked a characteristic of the old Roman, soon began to manifest itself. The relations which originally subsisted between the Patricians and the Plebeians were such that the two classes were mutually dependent upon each other, and were of consequence naturally drawn together. But at the basis of this organization there was established this barrier which effectually prevented the worthy Plebeian from rising to the rank of a Patrician, and that retained among the Patricians, all whether good or bad.

The opportunity of being unjust begot recklessness in power. The Plebeian became the object of tyranny and insupportable bondage. He was dragged to the field and compelled to fight the battles of the nation. When he returned to his home and found it pillaged or burned, and his stock driven away, and to replace it was forced to borrow money from the Patricians at so exorbitant a rate of interest that he could never pay it, he was then sold, thrown into durance vile, and compelled to submit to stripes and torture. Such is the tendency of power unrestrained. It runs into the wildest excesses when not amenable to any higher authority. But there was a point beyond which it could not advance.

An old man who had been despoiled of his property and had fallen into the power of his debtors, appeared among his associates covered with blood and wounds which were still fresh, and told his sad story. This was a signal for universal rising. The Plebeians stepped forward in their might, seceded from the city, and demanded a restitution of their rights which they could claim by virtue of their manhood. Their power was too great to be resisted, and their wills too stubborn to be tamed. New political rights were granted to them, their debts were abolished, tribunes, who should defend and represent them, were allowed, and that political standing was established which enabled them to cope successfully with the Patricians, and to maintain those celebrated struggles which lend to Roman history and to Roman character their peculiar charms.

We have witnessed the same struggles from time to time in England. Encroachments upon the rights of the people have aroused the indignation of the masses. Sanguinary contests have ensued, and although at times the friends of constitutional liberty have seemed to be stricken down, yet it has finally appeared that the cause of humanity has steadily improved; that in every contention its course has been onward. The happy fruits of a constitutional monarchy, one of the most fortunate forms of government, which the English people now enjoy, has been secured at a costly sacrifice. The lovers of liberty have poured out their life's blood like water in its defense. The world does not recognize its benefactors till it has crucified them. Algernon Sydney, on the night before his execution, said that for himself he did not care a chip; but the law which condemned him to the block would condemn every one of his associates. "He marched," says Smyth, "to the scaffold as to a victory, displaying at his execution as at his trial, all the bold and sublime traits of the republican character; the untroubled pulse, the unabated resolve, the unconquerable mind, and freedom's holy flame; the memory that still lingered with delight on the good old cause, as he termed it, for which he was to shed his blood; the imagination that even in death, disdainful alike, of the government, its judges, its indictments, and its executioners soared away to some loftier code of justice and of right, and hung enamored on its own more splendid visions of equality and freedom."

The struggles of the champions of liberty during eighteen centuries could not secure to our fathers the inestimable boon without a long and fearful contest. The colonists brought with them to these shores the experience of all the past. The infant nation was far removed from the jealousy and intrigues of the old continental powers. But the spirit of arbitrary rule followed them even here, in the wilderness, and placed its yoke upon their necks. The freedom which they sought and for which they had periled the dangers of the ocean, had endured privation, and would meet even death itself, was crushed to earth.

It seems that Providence has so ordered that no signal blessing shall be enjoyed without passing through tribulation to attain it. Power commenced his encroachments, and prerogative must again to the onset. It was fortunate in our Revolution that men were found equal to the emergency, determined to embark in the enterprise and pursue it to the last. With firm hearts, and unwavering purpose, in the spirit of unexampled patriotism, they stood around each other and pledged "their lives, their fortunes and their sacred honor." In deed and in word they stood faithfully together, and mocked alike at promises or threats. The fortitude of those has been rarely equaled, who, amidst the greatest indignities and bodily sufferings, spurned with contempt the offers of reconciliation. Colonel Ethan Allen was taken prisoner and carried in irons to England. The emissaries of the king offered him a township in the new world when the war should be closed if he would lend his aid to the royal cause. The answer of the bold colonel was characteristic: "Gentlemen, your proposition reminds me of the devil's when he took Jesus up into an exceeding high mountain and showed him all the kingdoms of the earth, and promised that they should be his if he would fall down and worship him, when the poor devil had not a foot of land on earth." When an unlimited price was offered Samuel Adams by an agent of the king, he replied, in a determined manner, "I have long since made my peace with the King of kings. No consideration would induce me to abandon the righteous cause of my country. Tell Governor Gage it is the advice of Samuel Adams to him, to insult no longer the feelings of an exasperated people." It was such men as these, that filled the vision of Alcæus when he fashioned in poetic fancy the ideal of a perfect State:

"What constitutes a State?
Not high-raised battlements or labored mounds,
Thick walls or moated gate;
Not cities proud, with spires and turrets crowned;
Not bays and broad-armed ports
Where, laughing at the storm, rich navies ride.
Not starred and spangled courts,
Where low-browed baseness wafts perfume to pride.
No! Men—high-minded men,
With powers as far above dull brutes endued,
In forest, brake or den,
As beasts excel cold rocks and brambles rude.
Men who their duties know,
But know their rights, and knowing, dare maintain;
Prevent the long-aimed blow,
And crush the tyrant while they rend the chain.
These constitute a State;
And sovereign law, that State's collected will,
O'er thrones and globes elate
Sits empress, crowning good—repressing ill."

To education and democracy must be ascribed all the triumphs of civil liberty, and to the want of these must we ascribe its failures. Wherever the people are enlightened and educated, there a democratic form of government is possible, and the fullest enjoyment of rights is secured. It is the duty of every lover of his country to labor assiduously for the permanence of these two principles, for they are the basis of liberty. Where liberty is, there is prosperity and life. Civil and religious liberty are the chief of our blessings. For these have martyrs laid down their lives upon the scaffold and at the stake, and myriads of men fought to establish or defend them. Take away these, and we are degraded to the rank of slaves, of brutes, and life becomes not worth the living. Give these, and every faculty is exalted, the work of our hands is blessed, the gifts of nature smile upon us, and brighter hopes beam upon us from the future.

METHOD

OF

TEACHERS' INSTITUTES,

AND THE

THEORY OF EDUCATION.

BY

SAMUEL P. BATES, A.M.,

DEPUTY SUPERINTENDENT OF COMMON SCHOOLS OF PENNSYLVANIA, AND
AUTHOR OF "INSTITUTE LECTURES."

I too am a Teacher.

A. S. BARNES & COMPANY,
NEW YORK AND CHICAGO.

Entered according to Act of Congress, in the year 1862,
By A. S. BARNES & BURR,
In the Clerk's Office of the District Court of the United States for the
Southern District of New York.

PREFATORY NOTE TO THE SECOND EDITION.

The following brief Treatise on Institutes, intended as an introduction to the Lectures, was prepared nearly a year ago; but, on account of the troubled times, has been withheld from publication till the present. The author takes this occasion to acknowledge his obligations to numerous educators throughout the country, who favored him with valuable suggestions, and to return them his sincere thanks. It is hoped that the work he now presents will meet their approbation.

School Department, Harrisburg, *Dec.* 6, 1861.

PREFACE.

THE numerous inquiries which the author has received since the publication of his "INSTITUTE LECTURES," respecting the best method of conducting an Institute, suggested the idea that a detailed account of the object, organization, plan of instruction, and the true theory of education upon which that instruction should be based, would do good. Availing himself of all the information on the subject at command, and guided by the light of his own somewhat extended experience, he has wrought the materials into a form that will, as he trusts, be found a tolerably complete treatise.

The Institute, which is capable of being made the instrument to impart the highest order of professional training, was in many cases, for want of proper organization and management, degenerating from that high vantage-ground. Its novelty having worn away, and the difficulty of securing the services of competent educators to conduct it being seriously felt, it was exposed to the dangers of feeble support and popular distrust.

To guard it, therefore, against the dangers of failure, to impress upon teachers the value of professional training and professional skill, to direct attention to those scientific principles upon which education is based, and to make the organization and instruction of the Institute of that high grade which shall render it ever attractive and secure of confidence—this work was undertaken. Bearing directly upon the vital questions of Education, it is presented for the candid consideration of the members of the profession.

The author takes this occasion to acknowledge his obligation to numerous educators throughout the country, who favored him with valuable suggestions, and to return them his sincere thanks. It is hoped the work he now presents will meet their approbation.

School Department, Harrisburg, *Jan.* 6, 1862.

CONTENTS.

VALUE OF INSTITUTE INSTRUCTION.

"TEACHERS' INSTITUTES" have inaugurated a new era in the science of teaching. The impetus which they have given to inquiry and earnest thought is very generally felt in the sphere of public instruction. They occupy a place which can not be supplied by any other agency; and though they do not furnish the solid nutriment, yet they supply the teacher the vital air which is equally indispensable to him. Wherever they have been most regularly and systematically supported, there have the abundant fruits demonstrated their necessity.

Previous to their establishment, the methods of instruction were in many respects arbitrary and unphilosophic, and were very much allied to those which prevailed in the dark ages.* A reason fit to

* The scholars of Abelard, as he himself tells us in his *Introduction to Theology*, requested him to give them "some philosophical arguments such as were fit to satisfy their minds; begged that he would instruct them, not merely to repeat what he taught them, but to understand it; for no one can believe what he can not comprehend, and it is absurd to set out to preach to others concerning

satisfy a rational mind was rarely required. *Ipse dixit* was an ample explanation for that which was intricate. The Teachers' Institute has provoked inquiry. It has taken methods of instruction and examined them by the light of philosophy, and, rejecting the worthless, has shown the practical value of the good. It has discovered new methods of proof and illustration, and entirely revolutionized the practice of primary teaching.

The plan of instruction adopted in the Institute is suited to the wants of every grade of schools. The superiority of the training which it has inaugurated is beginning to be realized, and the professors in our colleges must adopt the methods and the spirit which it imparts, or the defects of their systems of instruction will detract materially from their usefulness and their prestige; for already a comparison is beginning to be instituted in the public mind, between the value of Normal and Collegiate culture.

The professor who sits at his desk and *hears* class-

---

things which neither those who teach nor those who learn can understand."—*Guizot's History of Civilization*, vol. i., p. 147.

When Pestalozzi first propounded his principles, the education of the poorer classes, everywhere, was essentially defective. In *method* it was purely mechanical, without any basis of sound science. The head was but little improved, and the heart remained wholly untouched. Among the higher classes, the only aim was the acquisition of knowledge. The faculties of simple apprehension and verbal memory, especially the latter, were called into action. Other faculties were neglected.—*M. E. M. Jones, of the School of the Home and Colonial Society, London.*

es, keeping tally the while with his pencil, and preserves the same indifference toward the dunce and the brilliant scholar, is contrasted with him who studies the mental peculiarities of his pupils, who classifies them according to the power of thought which they have attained, and who puts his instruction in such a light that it can not fail to elicit reflection, and induce a healthy and vigorous development. The difference between the two systems is very marked; it is that between mechanically *hearing* pupils recite the words of a text-book, and that of intelligently instructing them in correct processes of thought. The advantage to the pupil of normal instruction over the stereotyped methods pursued in many of our colleges is worthy of note. Even if a person is never intending to teach, but simply desires to obtain a thorough education, he can not fail to perceive the superiority of the former. He learns every thing from a new stand-point, more elevated and independent. He not only learns a lesson so as to be accountable for it in the class-room, but he must have it so digested and matured as to be able to teach it to others. This additional culture gives permanence and definiteness to his conceptions, and ripens his judgment.

The importance which Institutes have assumed within a few years past, has rendered it necessary that the most efficient and well-digested plans for conducting them should be studied. The objections which have been urged against them, and the prejudice which exists in some minds, has commonly resulted from mismanagement. The time during which an Institute usually remains in session is very limited, and in order that the best results be attained and the time be employed to the best advantage, it is necessary that the exercises be reduced to strict system. There must be a plan, and the proceedings must be made to conform to it. Before we can know what plan is best, it is necessary to know what the ends are that it is to subserve.

OBJECT OF A TEACHERS' INSTITUTE.

THERE are two main purposes designed to be accomplished by the Institute. The first consists in imparting to the teacher a knowledge of the Philosophy of his Profession. The second is the establishment of a common sympathy between teacher and people. There are several minor results connected with these which the Institute properly contributes; but they should ever be held subordinate to these.

A system of instruction will meet with success in proportion to its conformity to the laws of psychological development. To be fruitful in good results, it must be founded upon principles which govern our spiritual natures. If a teacher proceeds upon a theory contrary to this, he either gives an erroneous development, or he endeavors to force upon the minds of his pupils instruction which they do not appreciate, and which can never be of any practical value. To discover the philosophical principles which underlie every department of instruction, and to properly apply these to the natural order of mental development, should be the first and leading object of attention.

Teachers are too apt in practice to follow on in the beaten track, and adopt the plans pursued by those who taught them. If these plans were erroneous, the teacher is to be convinced of their falsity, and that others are preferable, because, when tried by reason, they are found to be in harmony with the constitution and growth of the mental faculties. Teaching is not an imitative art, but a science based upon immutable principles. If we make it an imitative process, and devote the time of the Institute to a detail of the plan for teaching each branch, we may present a plan which one man can imitate but another can not. But if we develop the elements of the science, we put into the hands of every one the means for independent action, and each can develop his methods in accordance with his own subjectivity.

Unfortunately, many of our text-books are written not by teachers who understand the true theory of teaching, and are fully imbued with its spirit, but they are "made" by men who have facilities for publishing and forcing them into use, and are desirous of having a full "series." The teacher, therefore, needs to be so familiar with the fundamental principles of the branches he is to teach, that he shall be above text-books,—that he shall himself be the text-book in every branch; and where books are at fault, by proper instruction to set them right. The day is past when the teacher is to be pinned down to a superstitious adherence to authority, and go hobbling upon crutches into such a noble work. The general principles upon which every branch rests should be thoroughly discussed and understood, so that his views shall be correct and clear; and he who intends to keep up with the times and be a reliable practitioner in the profession, must come up to the Institute, once or twice a year, at least, to get his opinions adjusted, as the navigator comes to have his chronometer corrected before departing on his perilous voyage over restless seas.

The Institute is not the place to give instruction in the elements of the sciences. These are to be learned in the schools, where there is opportunity for thorough drill. It is useless to waste the time of an Institute in this kind of labor, since, in the limited period for which it is convened, every moment is needed for higher purposes. If a person is not versed in the rudiments, he is not fit to be admitted as a member, much less a member of the profession. What could be accomplished for a person in an Institute of a week's continuance in such a branch as geometry, for instance, if he had not previously familiarized himself with that science?

Musical conventions, conducted by able composers, have a similar purpose to that of the Institute. No one ever proposes to become a member of a convention for the purpose of learning the rudiments of music, but to acquire power of expression, to be apprised of the effect which different styles of execution have upon the sensibilities, and, in short, to learn the philosophy of the art. A week's drill under a skillful master will bring out powers which had never been reached by the ordinary course of instruction, and give the pupil new views of music that will be of more value to him than all he ever knew before. Yet it is necessary that he should have all his previous instruction, in order to be prepared to appreciate and be profited by that kind which is now imparted.

In the township or district Institute, class-drills in forms of solution and methods of explanation are in place. It is the purpose there to have teachers instructed upon those subjects which are demanding their immediate attention. If difficulties are met with in their daily class-room duties, it is proper to present them here for solution. The number is not so large, nor the time so limited, but that instruction in their class-studies is practicable and proper. But in the County or State Institute, where instructors are usually present who are capable of developing those principles which will enable the teacher to understand the true relations of his elementary knowledge, it is a waste of time and rare opportunity to engage in that kind of labor which legitimately belongs to the preparatory schools.

The second purpose of the Institute is to create and maintain a sympathy, a common bond of interest between teachers and people. In order that the instruction which the teacher imparts in his school may produce the best results, it is highly important that he have the confidence of the parents. A teacher who fails to command the respect of the people is robbed of much of that power for good which he could otherwise exercise, however skillful and efficient he may be.

It is, therefore, the sphere of the Institute to demonstrate that the teacher is alive to the interests of his calling; that he is making sacrifices to be the better fitted to discharge his duty; that he is worthy of the confidence of his patrons; that his knowledge is superior to that possessed by the teachers of a by-gone age, from which their judgment of teaching capacity was formed; that his ability is such as to challenge their respect; that he is really mastering the theory of his profession, and by a thorough knowledge of the discoveries which have been made, is able to practice with skill, in one of the most delicate and arduous positions in which the members of any profession are called upon to act.*

---

* It is a fact which can not be denied, that comparatively few school-officers really know what sort of an education they are providing; whether it is well or ill adapted to the purpose intended; whether it is founded upon the unchanging principles of mental progress, or upon crude theories, half-digested schemes, and superficial views of the philosophy of mind. Few, comparatively, are aware that there are any well-settled maxims upon which, as an immutable basis, the whole superstructure of all round culture must rest. And hence, men who can "keep the children still," six hours a day, and hear them "say their lessons," are deemed fit to

It is a hopeful feature in the history of popular education, that the people generally are accustomed to attend these gatherings, and are thus enabled to see and judge for themselves of the spirit which prevails, and of the practical utility which must result from them. It is one of the most effectual means of disarming prejudice, of awakening among parents an interest in their schools, of enabling them to sympathize with the teacher in the success of his plans; for they are thus enabled to understand what those plans are upon which he is depending for success in instructing their children, and in nourishing their spiritual natures. There is no interest so dear to a man as that which pertains to the welfare of his children. If there is no other way of reaching his pride, it is sure to be enkindled when he is conscious that his children display aptness for learning. When parents are made to realize that the teacher is acting upon enlightened views, and that he is imparting the most valuable kind of instruction, they are encouraged, and incited to pursue a liberal policy in the maintenance of their schools, and their warm-hearted co-operation is secured. The teacher's task is half accomplished, when the hearts that guide the home circles of his pupils, are throbbing for his success.

There are some minor purposes to be subserved

---

be teachers. At the Institute the fallacy of these views is exposed, and their mischievous results pointed out.—*Hon. Newton Bateman's Report, for Illinois*, 1860.

by the Institute which may properly be mentioned.

The teacher is brought into direct intercourse with his professional brethren, and is enabled to measure himself intellectually and professionally with others. Were he to remain isolated, knowing little of any one beyond his own neighborhood, he would naturally contract narrow and selfish views, and be filled with his own sufficiency. He has, perhaps, regarded himself as possessing superior attainments, and his own methods of teaching as infallible, while they may at the same time be very unphilosophic and injurious to the mental habits of his pupils. But when he comes to the Institute, and is brought into contact with those of equal and of superior ability, he is enabled to make a more sober estimate of his capacity, and to suspect that there may be

> "—— some things in heaven and earth
> Not dreamed of in his philosophy."

He is brought into connection and close communion with earnest-minded, thinking teachers, who are accustomed to criticise the soundness of every view, and only satisfied with that which bears the genuine impress of truth. He catches their spirit, and thus a new life and new modes of thinking are infused into the whole mass of teachers.

Nor is this intellectual acquaintance the only advantage of their coming together. They become acquainted socially. They are enabled to sympathize with each other, and to form intimate and lasting attachments. Refinement and culture exert their elevating influence upon the rough and the uncouth, the different classes of society are brought nearer to each other, the barriers which separated them are thrown down, and, while none are degraded by contact, all are elevated in feelings, in manners, in sentiments.

Growing out of the relations which we have named above, is one which the French term *esprit de corps*, a professional pride, a feeling which is an element of success in every calling. The eyes of the teacher are opened to the real nobility of his work, and he is relieved from that embarrassment which causes him to go about with head bowed down because he is only an humble schoolmaster. In thus opening to his view the true position he occupies, he is enabled to realize the responsibilities that rest upon him, and is nerved to more earnest exertions in the performance of his whole duty.

The Institute is an excellent school for young teachers to learn to express their thoughts in public. It is the fault of many of them that they can not "think upon their legs," and hence can not be successful in teaching what they know well enough, because they have not the power of talking it into their pupils, and making the thought appear to others as it is felt by themselves. The extemporaneous debates, which call out the opinions of the members at the close of each lesson, form a good preparatory exercise for the practical business of teaching.

The habit, which should be insisted on, of taking notes of every important fact or opinion that is expressed, and of reserving for future consideration what can not be duly pondered at the time, is one of vast importance to the young teacher, and, if persevered in, will in a few years be fruitful of surprising results. It will serve to establish the principle of never passing upon any thing hastily, and of noting for future reflection and use, whatever may be met with in a course of reading or observation that is worthy of preservation. No lesson can be learned that will more conduce to accuracy of scholarship, or more effectually contribute to richness of thought.

Another prominent object subserved by Institutes is the opportunity they furnish of readily introducing into the practice of the profession such new improvements as are made in the science and art of teaching. Were it not for these general gatherings, it would require a long time for a new method to work its way into use among the isolated members of a profession so numerous as this. But through the agency of the Institute, a happy invention in proof, in illustration, or a discovery of a new application of education, quickly spreads from rank to rank, and scarcely has it assumed form in the inventor's brain before it is heralded from Maine to Minnesota, and is being practiced in the little log school-house upon the frontier of civilization. In this respect it is a means of improvement more thoroughly organized and more practically effective than is possessed by the members of any other profession.

The whole body of teachers are brought into contact, at the Institute, with distinguished scholars, and can learn something of their manners and course of thinking. Teachers thus become imbued with their spirit, and absorb the cast of scholarship which they display. There is an opportunity afforded for not only the teachers, but also the citizens of the vicinity, to hear a course of lectures on literary and scientific subjects, and in addition to the information which is imparted and the enthusiasm which they inspire, teachers are enabled to learn something of the manners and modes of delivery of the Lecturers.

The talents of superior teachers are made public, and their services are thus brought into requisition in parts of the country where they are needed, and where they will accomplish the greatest good. No teacher need remain buried in neglect and obscurity whose abilities fit him for a higher sphere. The Institute thus becomes a means of bringing forward the meritorious, and rewarding them with deserved promotion.

A familiarity is acquired with the usages of a deliberative assembly, and the rules that should prevail in it. The officers should take a pride in having all their proceedings in conformity with parliamentary rules. These rules have been deduced from the experience of deliberative bodies for ages, and of course embody the most systematic plan for transacting business. To have the business of an Institute promptly and systematically done, is not only instructive to those members who are ignorant of the usages of such bodies, but it is a great saving of time, and produces a favorable impression upon those who witness it.

Having thus set forth in a general manner the purposes which the Institute is designed to accomplish, we now propose to detail the best methods of conducting it to secure these results.

ORGANIZATION OF AN INSTITUTE.

Time for holding the Institute.—The most ap propriate time for an Institute is that immediately preceding the opening of the schools for the season, or in the early part of the school-term. The teachers, at this time, will display greater anxiety to learn, and will be enabled immediately to make a practical use of what they have gained. In cities and villages, where the schools are kept open during a greater portion of the year, the time of holding it is immaterial, provided it is convenient for the people, and will be favorable for a general attendance. Election and holidays should be avoided. It is the teacher's week of jubilee in itself, and should not be interfered with by festivals or public days. In sections where the traveling is bad, a time should be preferred when the roads will be settled, and that time in the month when there are moonlight evenings.

Notice of Meeting.—Notice should be given of the time and place of meeting through the newspapers, and, so far as practicable, should include a schedule of the exercises, and the names of Instructors and Lecturers. It ought to be inserted in the papers as an editorial, where it will attract attention; and there are few publishers in the country who will refuse to give it such a position. When notice can not be efficiently given through the newspapers, it should be done by hand-bills and circulars. A full notice should be secured at all hazards, and every facility for a full attendance should be extended. The precise hour in the day at which the Institute will be organized, and the exercises will commence, should be distinctly stated, so that the members may be punctually present, and not, as is too often the case, be a day or two in getting together. Not a moment of time or a single remark should be lost.

How LONG CONTINUE.—An Institute should not convene for a less time than one week, when suitable Instructors can be secured for conducting it; nor is it advisable to have it continue longer than a week or ten days. Experience has taught, that an Institute of a week's continuance has met with far better success than those of either longer or shorter duration. It is hardly worth while for a general assembling of teachers, from all parts of a county, for a less time than a week; and it is often not convenient for them to stay longer, and in some instances might become burdensome for the people to furnish entertainment longer, especially in places where hotel accommodations are limited. Besides, the exercises sometimes become dull and monotonous, when continued; and Instructors may, if the matter of their discourses is properly digested, present it with more vigor and effect in one, than in two weeks, and may succeed in creating more enthusiasm, and do greater good, than if more extended and diffuse. When it is kept in session two, four, or six weeks, the nature of the instruction must necessarily be similar to that adopted in normal classes, and is hence changed to a normal school, and should be known by that name.

PLACE OF MEETING.—This should *not* always be where it is sure of the most cordial reception, and the largest and most enthusiastic audiences. The Institute should sometimes perform the offices of a missionary. A section where there is indifference, will never fail to be aroused and warmed by the presence of a good Institute in its midst. It is not judicious, however, to select such a place, unless there is some good active teacher or citizen in it who desires it held there, will labor for it, and will form a connecting link between people and Institute. Some enterprising village will often do more than the large towns and cities. It ought not to be confined to any one locality. Its influence should be given to each section in turn, always selecting that place where the best prospect of success and the greatest need seem to be most strongly united. A joint Institute between two counties, at some convenient point, is attended with many good results. The teachers in the outskirts of the counties are thus accommodated. The sympathies of a portion of people are enlisted, who would not otherwise be reached, and the leading teachers of the two counties, with their Superintendents, can thus render each other mutual assistance.

COMMITTEE OF ARRANGEMENTS.—When the time and place of holding the Institute have been fixed, it is desirable that citizens or school-officers of the locality chosen, should designate some persons to act as a committee of arrangements. It is proper for this committee to secure a place for meeting, and to extend an invitation to such citizens as are disposed to entertain teachers coming from a distance. They should make a list of such families, and the number each can accommodate, for use at the opening of the session. It may seem like a burden, at first, for families to furnish such entertainment; but if the deportment of teachers is judicious, the hearts of such are always opened, and a feeling of satisfaction and pride is felt in the end. Aside from the aid and encouragement which is thus afforded teachers, the interest which is thereby excited in the feelings of the people, and the personal responsibility and co-operation which is engendered, furnishes the strongest motive for encouraging it. It should not be forgotten, that one of the objects of the Institute is the formation of such a bond of sympathy, and this is one of the means to be employed for establishing it.

EXECUTIVE COMMITTEE.—The executive committee are charged with making provision, some time previous to the meeting, for all the literary exercises.

The chairman of this committee should be the County Superintendent, or some person who is well acquainted with the teachers of the county, and who will make it his business, in conjunction with his associates, to secure the Lecturers,* make arrangements for their coming and going, fix the time on which each is to speak, and attend to their reception—engage Instructors who shall give daily lessons in each of the branches to be taught—correspond with teachers to have essays written and ready to be delivered —and to have vocal and instrumental music prepared. All these arrangements should be made a sufficient time previous to the meeting to allow of all necessary preparations.

Organization.—Too much time is frequently squandered in organizing. If the Institute has had a previous existence, and is provided with a constitution, the only detention from the regular order is the choice of officers. But if an original organization is to be made, it is best to choose a temporary chairman, and appoint a committee on permanent organization, and another on the formation of a constitution. Then let the instructors commence immediately upon their regular business, and the constitution and list of permanent officers can be reported and

* The term *Lecturer*, when used in these pages, is employed to designate the man who delivers the formal lecture for the evening session; the term *Instructor*, to indicate the person who gives the regular daily lessons in one of the school branches; and *Teacher*, to refer to the members of the Institute.

adopted as soon as the committees have had time to complete their labors. Constitutions and regulations should always be thoroughly discussed in committee, and so perfected that their adoption need take but little time. Institutes where the relations of all concerned have been most pleasant and satisfactory, have been presided over by some prominent citizen of the place where held.

REGULAR OFFICERS.—The regular officers of an Institute are similar in name to those of other public bodies; yet the manner of discharging their duties is in many respects peculiar, and corresponds to the special objects which they are constituted to subserve. It is different in its objects and in its operations from any other deliberative body, and its management and regulations must consequently be special.

PRESIDENT.—The duties of the President in the maintenance of due decorum, in the decision of points of order, in putting motions, in allowing or stopping debate, are similar to those of presiding officers of other deliberative assemblies. But in managing the exercises, and guiding the Instructors, he has new and delicate duties to perform. He should, in the first place, have placed in his hands an exact programme of exercises, detailing the time which each is to occupy, and a limitation upon that which is allowed to each person in debate. When the time has arrived for an exercise to close, it is his duty to give prompt notice of the fact, and announce and be ready to enter immediately upon that which is to follow. Much of the interest and profit depend upon the promptness and dispatch with which the presiding officer brings on and closes the exercises as marked down in the programme. If the members are disposed to interrupt the Instructor with questions designed to perplex him, or consume his allotted time with trivial or irrelevant debate, it is the duty of the presiding officer to interfere, and request that he have the exclusive management of his subject, and that all questions for information or statement of differences of opinion be deferred till the proper time for debate, which should follow each lecture or essay. Promptness and decision in the presiding officer are of the utmost importance to the success of an Institute, and can not be too highly prized.

Business Committee.—This committee consults with the lecturers, instructors, and leaders of singing, and makes out for each session the programme which is to govern it, stating what subjects are to be attended to, how much time is devoted to each, and the persons who are to conduct them. The chairman of this committee should be the same as the chairman of the executive committee, and is very properly the County Superintendent, when there is one, and if not, the chairman of the board of examiners, or some leading member of the association.

It is also the business of this committee to furnish blackboards, maps, charts, and apparatus, so far as they are able, and see that some person is engaged to attend to fires and lights, and to sweeping and dusting the room. The following form of programme will answer as an illustration for an Institute composed of teachers of our common district-schools, and as it embraces quite a full range of topics, need not be essentially varied during the week. If, however, the body of teachers demand it, a higher range of topics may be substituted, so that any grade of teachers can be suited, even to the professors in colleges.

Programme for Monday, Jan. 13, 1862.

MORNING.

	MINUTES.
Calling roll of members	5
Devotional Exercises, conducted by Rev. Mr. A——	15
Reading and correcting minutes of preceding day	10
Instruction in Arithmetic, by Mr. B——	20
Discussion on do.	20
Instruction in Physical Training	20
RECESS.	
Instrumental or Vocal Music	5
Mathematical Geography, by Mr. C——	20
Discussion on do.	20
Discussion. Question — Resolved, that punishment should not be inflicted in presence of the school nor in school-hours	25
Report of critics	5
Music	5

AFTERNOON.

	MINUTES.
Singing	5
Primary Instruction and Elocution, by Mr. D——	20
Discussion on do.	20
Exercise in Penmanship, by Mr. E——	20
Instruction upon Moral Training	20

RECESS.

How to Teach the Elements of Music, by Mr. F——	10
Language, by Mr. G——	20
Discussion on do.	20
Sub-lecture on Object Lessons, by Mr. H——	10
Essay, by Miss I——	10
Report of critics	5
Music	5

EVENING.

Music	5
Select reading, by Miss J——	10
Discussion. Question — Should females be excluded from our colleges?	30
Music	5
Essay, by Mr. K——	10
Lecture, by Mr. L——	50
Music	5

The business committee should also prepare and present, at the opening of the Institute, resolutions of the following purport:

Resolved, that the sessions of this Institute be from 9 to 12 o'clock in the morning; from $1\frac{1}{2}$ to $4\frac{1}{2}$ o'clock in the afternoon; and from 7 to 9 o'clock in the evening; and that the presiding officer call to order and adjourn this body, according to the provisions of this resolution.

Resolved, that in all discussions no person be allowed to speak longer than 10 minutes, except by permission from the Institute; nor to speak a second time, till all who desire have had an opportunity.

SECRETARIES.—The Secretary's book should present a faithful daguerreotype of what is done and said. The substance of the lectures, instructions, debates, and business should be briefly and succinctly reported, so that from it can be made out a summary of interesting matter for publication, and a true record be preserved for future reference. In order that the records may be thus fully kept, there should be, in addition to the regular Secretary, one or two assistants; so that as the exercises change, each can take his turn, and while one is reporting, the others can be correcting their notes and copying them into the record-book. Much care should be taken to report faithfully what is said; but no opinion of the Secretary, respecting the merit or demerit of the performance, should be given. By having the labor thus divided, excessive fatigue is avoided, and opportunity for revision and careful copying is given. Besides, the minutes should be written out immediately, while the whole subject is fresh in the memory, and any unavoidable omissions in the notes can be easily supplied in the engrossed minutes. The records should be read and revised each morning, so that if the Secretaries have misapprehended or omitted any thing they may be corrected.

Treasurer.—It is the business of the Treasurer to keep an itemized account with the Institute, in a book provided for the purpose, of all moneys received and paid out; to pay from whatever moneys are deposited with him all orders on the Treasurer properly authenticated; and to settle his accounts with the Auditor at the expiration of his term of office. His accounts should be neatly and systematically kept; and his book should present that business-like ap pearance which is expected to characterize the work of a teacher of a common-school,—that institution in which the majority of our people receive all the education they ever get in preparation for the business of life.

Financial Committee.—In case the State furnishes means for the support of County Institutes, there would be little business for this committee to transact, unless such committee is designated by law to superintend its expenditure. But if money is needed for meeting the ordinary expenses, it is the business of this committee to devise the ways and means for raising it. In some cases the regulations require an initiation fee, or an annual tax on all its members. In others, to encourage a larger membership, no fee or tax is imposed, and all necessary expenses are met by voluntary contributions of its members, or by an assessment about equal to the expense. When this latter policy is pursued, the committee should ascertain, as early in the session as possible, the probable expense, and have the collection made in time for the Treasurer to pay all bills before the final adjournment. It is, however, the best policy, as there is always considerable expense attending the operations of an Institute, to have an annual tax on all alike, whether old or new members. The committee should attend to the collection of this tax, and should issue certificates which will constitute a receipt for its payment, and will be evidence to school-officers of membership and attendance. A neat phraseology, with an appropriate device printed upon card-paper, is a very convenient form. Each certificate should be signed by the President, and countersigned by the Secretary. This certificate will also be convenient in case railroad companies grant reduction of fare to members, as a means of identifying them.

Auditor.—The Auditor has to examine and decide upon the accounts of the Financial Committee and the Treasurer, and make his report to the Institute. When this report has been accepted and passed, it should be entered upon the Secretary's book.

Committee on Resolutions.—It is usual for an Institute to pass, before adjournment, a series of resolutions expressive of its feelings and sentiments. As these resolutions are usually published, it becomes a very convenient means of directing public attention to any needed improvements, and of leading the sentiment of the community in the right direction. These resolutions should be thoroughly meditated and carefully drawn, avoiding all matters calculated to excite odium, unless needed to correct existing abuses, or to inaugurate needed reforms. This committee should hold a meeting early in the session, and take the proper steps to have the resolutions perfected and adopted in committee, without being compelled to resort to unusual haste.

Committee of Reception.—The members of this committee should attend to the arrangement and seating of members of the Institute and spectators, should give all information desired to new members, and look after the general interests. It is also the business of this committee to furnish the Secretary with lists of the names and residences of the teachers, and should keep them revised from day to day as new members arrive.

TOWNSHIP OR DISTRICT INSTITUTES.

Township or District Institutes. — These are formed by the teachers of a single township, or by a union of the teachers of two or three contiguous townships. They are held weekly or semi-weekly, and are designed for the mutual improvement of the members in the studies which they are teaching, for comparing their methods of instruction and government, and for their advancement in general information.

The place of meeting is in some cases permanent, at some central point; in others it is changed from week to week, so as to visit all parts of the section embraced. It is doubtless the better policy to have a regular place of meeting. The time of meeting is either in the evening or on Saturday. A plan which is sometimes adopted, and which, if judiciously conducted, will result in much good, is for all the schools to be closed on Saturday except the one where the Institute is to meet, and that is kept open during the forenoon of that day. The teachers all assemble there in the morning and witness the operations of that school for a half day, and in the afternoon attend to the business of the Institute. By circulating in this way through the different schools, opportunity is afforded for observing the practical ability displayed by each teacher, and much valuable information is thereby gained.

For cities and villages a permanent organization can be made, similar to that adopted in the County Institutes; but for the rural districts, where the school-term is short and there is frequent change of teachers, a temporary organization from one meeting to another may be adopted, selecting some one of the citizens to act as chairman. Care should always be exercised, however, to have the order of exercises reported before adjournment for the next succeeding meeting, so that those who are appointed for special duty may have opportunity to prepare themselves upon the subjects assigned. The following order of exercises will suggest the course to be pursued:

Programme for Friday evening, Jan. 31, 1862.

		MINUTES.
1.	Calling roll of members, and responding by sentiments	5
2.	Singing	5
3.	Class-drill, conducted by Mr. A——	30
4.	Select reading by Miss B——	10
5.	Singing	5
6.	Sub-lecture on Map-drawing by Mr. C——	10
7.	Essay by Miss E——	10
8.	Singing	5
9.	Lecture or Discussion	35
10.	Answering questions from the "Query-box"	20

It is expected that the older scholars of the several schools and the parents will attend these Institutes. The exercises will not only afford entertainment and instruction to spectators, but will demonstrate the utility of such associations, and show the progress which is being made in the science of teaching.

Care should be exercised by every member to cultivate a friendly feeling, and to foster the spirit of forbearance and courtesy. He should aim to be prompt and regular in attendance, and always be prepared to perform the part assigned him. As it is a purely voluntary association, it must have the hearty support of all, to be eminently prospered.

METHOD OF CONDUCTING THE EXERCISES.

Calling Roll.—The first business, after coming together in the morning, should be calling the roll of the members. This should be done as a means of securing punctuality; and the Secretary, after finishing it, and checking the names of those present, should read off the names of absentees,—a practice that may be imitated to advantage in school. The regulation of requiring each member at the morning roll-call to respond by rising and repeating a clause or verse of Scripture, is advisable. This need not be made obligatory, as those who do not choose to do so can simply respond, "present." To have the mind fixed upon some passage of divine truth, serves to bring it into a proper frame, preparatory to the devotional exercises; and the rising to repeat it, gives each one some degree of confidence, engenders a feeling of personal interest, and makes him realize that he is truly a member. Every effort should be made at the outset to impress upon the teachers the necessity of being punctual and regular in attendance. The exercises should be conducted with as much order and discipline as in a school, and the idea never be allowed to gain credence, that an Institute is a sort of holiday that may be turned to amusement or recreation.

Devotional Exercises.—These should be conducted by the clergymen of the place, who usually take sufficient interest in public education to be present without special invitation. But lest they may fail to understand the nature of an Institute, or may not feel that they are personally identified with it, an invitation should be sent at the opening of the session to each one to be present. Every cause prospers best when it has the moral force of the representatives of religion on its side. Besides, the interests of Education and Religion are identical. These exercises should consist of reading a portion of Scripture, singing a hymn or psalm, and prayer. No undertaking can be successful without the Divine blessing. It is to be feared that, in our schemes of education, we have labored to divorce it too much from religion. One of the objections urged against our free-schools is, that they are *godless* schools; and if there is any one thing from which we should pray to be delivered, it is from being a godless nation. It is fitting, therefore, that the teachers should be reminded of the claims of religion, and that each session should be opened by solemn devotions.

Instruction.—As indicated by the order of exercises given above, it is intended that each of the several branches shall be in charge of an Instructor, who shall give a connected series of discourses upon that branch. The Instructor should be apprised of the part he is to perform in time for him to make careful preparation, and be able to present well-digested views. In order to discharge his duty profitably, he ought to be able to answer in a clear manner the following questions: For what purpose do scholars pursue this branch? Are the methods of instruction, which have heretofore been practiced, such as are calculated to secure the best and the largest results? If not, what changes can be made to improve them? Can I develop and elaborate the plan which I would adopt in teaching this branch, so as to secure the results for which the study is pursued, and at the same time secure the interest and enthusiasm of my pupils? Until an Instructor can answer these questions intelligently, he is not prepared to stand up before a company of teachers and demand their attention. The person assigned to a particular branch ought to continue his instructions in that branch through the whole Institute, so that he can have a fair chance to develop his plan; but there is no objection to his giving instruction in several branches, if he is capable of carrying them along satisfactorily.

The Instructor should be provided with a black-board, and all needed apparatus for illustrating and presenting his ideas in the neatest and clearest manner; for his teaching is intended as a kind of pattern for the members to follow. He should aim to avoid all display in manner and language, and simply strive to do the most possible to inspire his hearers with his idea, to imbue them with his spirit, and to enable them, when they go to their school-rooms, to achieve success. He should not be interrupted during the time which has been allowed him, but when that time has expired he should promptly close; for if he has not completed the treatment of the topic under consideration, he can resume at the point where he leaves it in his next lesson. Then the matter thus treated should be thrown open for a general discussion. It may be that some one has a better plan than the Instructor, or that during his remarks a question has been suggested upon which information is desired. This is the proper time for answering questions, solving doubts, and offering suggestions.

Lecturers.—It is usually expected, that at the evening session, which the citizens commonly attend, a lecture will be delivered, in which the speaker will, in a measure, ignore the specialties of the teacher, and will treat such a subject, and in such a manner, as will be interesting and attractive to all who may hear. Such a topic should, however, be considered as will contribute to the progress of popular education, and will edify thinking men. It is not necessary that the lecture be written. Indeed, one who is accustomed to extemporaneous discourse will generally make a better use of the same material in extempore speech than if written, and produce a more marked effect upon his hearers. But it is necessary that the subject be well digested, and every position carefully considered; as one is liable, if he trusts too much to the inspiration of the moment, to say things that his calmer judgment would condemn.

If the subject is one that is susceptible of being illustrated by diagrams, or by the use of apparatus, no pains should be spared to procure them, as it adds much to the interest, and also to the permanence of the conceptions, if they are conveyed to the mind of the hearer through two of the senses. Objection is sometimes made to employing men from other professions, as the Law and Divinity, to deliver these lectures, because, as is alleged, teaching as a profession is thereby degraded. In answer it may be said, that the best talent at command should be secured; and if the profession of teaching can not furnish so good material as the other professions, it will necessarily be put in a subordinate position, and no propping can prevent it. But as these are promiscuous assemblies, it seems not only proper, but advisable, that men from other professions should be called for these occasions, when the services of such are needed. It is at least a means of enlisting their sympathies and their mental energies in the success of the Institute.

Discussions.—It is customary to discuss one or two

questions each day. These discussions should be managed with a view solely to elicit truth. In this respect they differ very widely from debates in a village lyceum, where the leaders take sides, and choose their positions like military chieftains, marshaling their hosts for the conflict,—judges being chosen to decide upon the result, and the only object being to win. This is not the spirit in which a question before a Teachers' Institute should be discussed. Indeed, it is not necessary that the matter to be considered should be presented in the form of a question. Some of the most interesting and valuable discussions are often based upon points informally presented. The object is simply to have some topic that is suggestive, and fruitful in its applications to the practical business of the educator. One which relates to the responsibilities of citizens, or which involves the mutual interest of teachers and parents, and which can be appropriately discussed by all, should be preferred, especially for the evening sessions.

Subjects calculated to excite the prejudices of the people, and to set them against the teachers, should be avoided, as there is an abundance of topics of vital importance which will command the devotion of all. It should be the aim in these discussions to pursue a high-minded course, and endeavor to develop the most valuable thoughts in the strongest light and most attractive style,—thoughts which will lead public sentiment, and will tell most favorably upon the progress of broad and liberal views. A number of questions are proposed at the close of this chapter, as specimens of those which may properly be discussed.

CLASS-DRILLS.—These exercises are intended to draw out the methods pursued by teachers in conducting classes and in governing their schools. It is the custom, where the number of teachers is very large, to divide them into two or three classes. This plan is advisable when rooms can be secured, or accommodations afforded for the classes, without interrupting each other; but in ordinary-sized Institutes there is no necessity for any division. The method of conducting a class-drill is to have some one appointed to lead, who states the subject for consideration, as for example the methods of teaching spelling, and then calls upon each one in turn, or first upon a lady and then upon a gentleman, to state the methods practiced, and the success attending the employment of each. In this way the experience of a large number of teachers, and the comparative success of different methods, is obtained in a little time. A similar purpose is subserved by what are called informal meetings, where the teachers meet an hour before the regular time of opening the daily session, and the exercise is conducted as detailed above.

ESSAYS.—It adds much to the life and literary elevation of an Institute to have some good essays read every day. These should be previously prepared, and should consist of clear, well-arranged views upon some subject with which the writer is thoroughly conversant. The success of new methods of teaching, the beauties and poetic relations of each study, or any of the reforms in education that are being agitated, are very proper subjects. It should not be longer than can be read in ten minutes. Essayists should remember that the value of their pieces is to be estimated by the number of good thoughts they contain, more than by high-sounding phraseology; and that ideas drawn from one's experience will be more likely to attract attention than an imitation of the style and opinions of another.

SUB-LECTURES.—This is a practical and very useful species of instruction. It consists of a short extemporaneous exposition of some school-room topic, and is given by some one of the most experienced teachers. It should not exceed ten minutes in length, and should be as practical and pointed as possible. The teacher selected to give it should have a day's notice for preparation, and may be chosen by the Institute, or selected by the business committee.

MUSIC.—It is expected that music will be regarded as a regular school-branch, and that it will be treated by an Instructor just as thoroughly and systematically as any other branch. But aside from that, it is customary to have instrumental or vocal music between the other exercises, for rest and entertainment. Sometimes the services of a string-band, with the addition of some wind-instruments, can be secured, which will add much to the pleasure of the occasion. It is not unusual that members of the Institute can organize and furnish this music. Martial music is not desirable. A quartette of voices, with all the parts represented, forms very agreeable entertainment. Several such clubs can be organized by the teachers, and can practice some pieces in preparation for the occasion, and each club can furnish the entertainment for the day. The music of a piano or melodeon is also desirable, where it can be had.

The best music, however, for an Institute, where all will cordially unite in it, is for the whole assembly to arise and unite in singing some familiar air every half-hour, or at the end of each general exercise. The school song-book in common use in the county can be used, and the teachers will thereby be acquiring facility of execution, and cultivating a habit which will be of great service to them in leading their schools in this exercise. The airs usually set down in this class of books are simple, are easily mastered, and, if sung with a hearty good-will by the whole assembly, will cause an exhilaration of feeling and a satisfaction that no other kind of music can afford. It is recommended that the teachers adopt some good school song-book for uniform use in the schools of the county, and that this book be regularly used at the meeting of the Institute. When this plan can be carried out successfully, no other music is desired.

RECESS.—Every opportunity for improvement should be embraced at an Institute, and the recess may be made to contribute largely to this end. Teachers, of all other persons, need to cultivate their social habits.* The recess is a favorable opportunity to form acquaintances and improve the conversational powers. Those who are well acquainted with the members, should be attentive in introducing those who are not. Each one should endeavor to guard

---

* *Extract of a letter from Alexander Clark, Editor of "School Visitor."*—One thing, however, does occur to me as a point much neglected, and it is of great value in the management and utility of Teachers' Institutes—viz., Sociality.

I attended an Institute not long since, where about one hundred teachers were assembled. Very few had ever met before in the same relations. The several lectures were able, and somewhat practical. The teachers seemed to be interested. Yet, when the hour for adjournment came, at noon or night, each one would course his lonely way silently to his room. The lectures were long, and the faces were long. There was no genial spirit abroad to happify and to bless. Theories and technicalities took the place of smiles and song. And the time began to grow weary, until a teacher with a heart proposed to substitute a half-hour in social intercourse instead of a lecture. He struck the right key. The idea was new, but it was reasonable and right, and it was agreed to unanimously. Such another shaking of hands and general acquaintance-making I never saw. It was the most profitable half-hour of the whole week. There seemed to be more life and love and earnestness in every subsequent exercise. I think, sir, if you should suggest the propriety of such an exercise, as the cultivation of our social faculties at Teachers' Institutes, you would be faithfully remembered.

Yours, ALEX. CLARK.

against a stiff and awkward reserve on the one hand, or being too loud and familiar on the other. The movements should be graceful, the tones of the voice pleasant, the countenance open, and the heart full of the desire to make everybody agreeable and happy.

MISCELLANEOUS.—It is sometimes the practice to have the roll called at the close of the evening session, and to have each member respond by rising and offering a sentiment. This usually creates considerable interest, and if all would seek good and noble sentiments, or even true wit, it might be advisable. But the tendency to give those which will create merriment is so great, that it frequently descends to buffoonery, and its propriety is questionable, unless under very skillful guidance.

The query-box is another means of exciting interest. A box is provided, into which queries upon some useful and interesting topics are dropped, and at a stated time each day it is opened, and a half-hour devoted to reading and answering them. It should always be under the charge of the executive committee, who should exercise a strict censorship over its contents, and allow no irrelevant or improper queries to be read.

The "old and new school" is another means of entertainment combined with instruction. Some teacher who understands human nature pretty well, calls out a class of scholars, and proceeds to *hear* their lessons on the old stereotype method, and maintains order on the autocratic plan. Then he is followed by one who teaches a class by the "better way," maintaining authority without seeming to do so. Reading and spelling are very good subjects to treat in this way. It is a means of exciting much merriment, and of impressing a useful lesson upon the minds of those who are ignorant of the improvements being made in methods of instruction. A half-hour in the early part of the evening may be thus employed very profitably.

FORM OF CONSTITUTION.

The following brief form of Constitution is presented as a guide in organizing an Institute. Several provisions have been omitted, which might very properly find a place in such an instrument, but which are not absolutely necessary to the efficient working of such an organization. The greater the simplicity in laws and ceremonies, in an Institute as in a school, the better.

Art. I. This Institute shall be known as the ——— Teachers' Institute.

Art. II. The object of this Institute shall be, the improvement of its members in the science of teaching, and in the most approved practice; the diffusing of information upon the system of Common School Education among the people, and promoting harmony of feeling; and the greatest possible advancement in scientific and general information.

Art. III. Any teacher or friend of education may become a member of this Institute by subscribing to the Constitution, and paying an annual fee of ——.

Art. IV. The regular meetings of this Institute

shall be held ——— in each year, at such times and places as shall be fixed by the Executive Committee.

Art. V. The regular officers of this Institute shall be a President, three Vice-Presidents, a Secretary and Assistant Secretary, a Treasurer, an Auditor, and an Executive Committee, and shall be elected annually, on the first day of the first session in each year.

Art. VI. It shall be the duty of the President, and in his absence, a Vice-President, to preside at all meetings of the Institute, decide points of order, preserve due decorum, and regulate the exercises according to a programme furnished him by the Institute.

Art. VII. It shall be the duty of the Secretaries to keep a faithful record of the proceedings of the Institute, take down an abstract of the instruction, debates, essays, and lectures, record the report of the Auditor, and prepare certificates of membership.

Art. VIII. It shall be the duty of the Treasurer to keep an account with the Institute of all moneys received and paid out, and to settle his accounts with the Auditor at the expiration of his term of office.

Art. IX. It shall be the duty of the Auditor to examine the accounts of the Treasurer, and report to the Institute the condition of the treasury on the last day of the last session of the year.

Art. X. It shall be the duty of the Executive

Committee to fix the time and place for holding the Institute,—give at least three weeks' previous notice of the same through the county papers or by hand-bill,—and secure the services of competent lecturers, instructors, essayists, and singers for conducting the exercises.

Art. XI. All regular officers shall be elected by ballot, and a majority shall elect.

Art. XII. Any of the provisions of this Constitution may be amended, and new articles added thereto, at any regular meeting, by giving two days' previous notice of the proposed amendment or addition, provided two-thirds of the members present vote in favor of such amendment or addition.

SUBJECTS FOR DISCUSSION AT AN INSTITUTE.

Is it necessary that the laboring class in a nation should be educated?

Should a military spirit be encouraged among the pupils of our common-schools?

In what way can a teacher most successfully impart moral instruction in school?

Should moral instruction be a stated exercise, or be only incidentally introduced?

Should physical culture be made one of the regular branches of instruction in our common-schools?

How can pupils best be taught good manners?

Should singing be one of the regular branches taught in school?

Are our courses of study and methods of teaching sufficiently practical?

What disposition should a teacher make of his time out of school-hours?

What is the true philosophy of school-government?

What motives and incentives to study ought to be appealed to?

Are public school examinations and exhibitions advisable?

What is the true philosophy of illustration?

What methods of instruction will most successfully lead pupils to original investigation?

What are the proper spheres of the inductive and the deductive methods of instruction?

What is the best method of teaching by the use of object lessons?

Should a text-book be prepared in the form of question and answer?

By what plan can a teacher best succeed in keeping his pupils employed?

Should prizes and rewards be offered for superiority of scholarship?

What rules ought a teacher to make at the opening of his school?

What are the prominent causes of failure in teaching?

What kind of physical education is best adapted for introduction in the school-room?

What are the causes of the declining health of pupils, and the remedies?

Can music be combined to advantage with physical education in our common-schools?

How can the cordial co-operation of parents be best secured?

What are the prominent defects of text-books?

What is the best order of time for arranging the classes for recitation?

What is the natural order of mental development?

Can teaching be reduced to a science?

What are the comparative merits of mixed and graded schools?

Does the pecuniary prosperity of a nation depend upon its intelligence?

Does the stability of a nation depend upon the universal diffusion of intelligence?

Do the good morals of a community depend upon its intelligence?

THE THEORY OF INTELLECTUAL EDUCATION.

Having sketched the object of a Teachers' Institute, the method of conducting it, and the plan of instruction, it seems proper in concluding to present, as a base of operations, some views upon the Theory of Education.

Much has been said of late about "Object Lessons," the "Pestalozzian System," the "True Order of Studies," the "Hierarchy of Knowledge," and the "Science of Pedagogy." The minds of scholars seem to be deeply agitated upon these subjects,—the inquiry is being earnestly made whether teaching is really a science,—and from this movement in the educational forces, we may confidently anticipate some substantial progress.

The plan of making Object Lessons a part of the course of instruction for primary schools, is a great improvement over former methods. It consists in presenting to a class of children some object, as a book, and suggesting an inquiry into its constituents —paper, leather, thread, paste, ink—how each of these is made—how printing is done—how the pictures are made—the art of engraving. Get the children themselves to search in dictionaries, encyclopedias, inquire of parents, visit printing-offices, book-binderies; and induce them to find out and tell every thing that it is possible for them to know upon the subject. The next lesson may be a knife, involving the raw materials of which it is made, and the method of transmuting them into the finished implement.

Object Lessons are an off-shoot of the plan of Pestalozzi, the chief merit of whose system consisted in seeking out the most ingenious method of presenting a subject so as to catch and rivet the attention of the pupil, so as to enable him to think about it for himself, and induce him to present inquiries of his own. It was the system of feeding the mind sparingly, with only such material as it was capable of digesting, and for which a healthy and regular appetite was thus created. Hence, the pupils of Pestalozzi were noted for their vivacity, the clearness of their conceptions, for their animation and interest in all their duties.

Disquisitions upon the True Order of Studies, are based upon an inquiry into the order in which the several faculties of the mind are developed, and an arrangement of the studies which each faculty is capable of investigating in a corresponding order. And by the Hierarchy of Knowledge is meant an exhaustive analysis of the whole field of spiritual inquiry, embracing in their broadest signification, Mathematics, Physics, History, Psychology, and

Theology. Each branch in the domain of science, by this theory, is assigned to that period in the mental life of the pupil, when that faculty is supposed to be developed which is fitted for its investigation.

The Science of Pedagogy, though not systematized, is supposed to rest upon a thorough knowledge of the human faculties, and of adapting the training of each to its needs and capabilities. It is maintained, that, as the mathematician can calculate with unerring certainty on the results of his reasoning, and the chemist can combine his elements with an unfailing confidence in the product which will come from them, so the teacher, when he has examined and knows the mental condition of a pupil, can, without difficulty, prescribe the course necessary to be pursued with him to secure the wished-for results.

Such is in brief a statement of the progress which speculative inquiry has thus far made upon the Theory of Education.

It is indeed gratifying to know that the minds of the present generation of educators are aroused, and that the whole subject is undergoing investigation. But in making our generalizations, and in establishing our theories, we should be careful to proceed upon correct principles, and not push the application of a system beyond its legitimate bounds. It is one thing to set up an arbitrary theory, and bend all the facts and reasonings to the support of that theory: but it is quite a different process to begin in the opposite direction, and, from a diligent search of the facts and their relations, accept such a theory as an unbiased mind would naturally draw from them. In our attempts at theory we must not forget those rules of investigation bequeathed to us by Bacon and Descartes.

The first inquiry to be made in prosecuting our researches should be, What is the character of this human soul that we propose to educate, and what results is it desirable to attain as the end of our labors? Whether the mind of the child is a kind of vacant receptacle, that it is the business of education to fill, or whether it is really an independent living intelligence, susceptible of growth and capable of originating thought, does not seem to be definitely settled in the minds of our educational theorists: nor do they seem clearly to understand how much the pupil ought to have done for him, and how much he ought to be made to do for himself.

If we rely too much upon the system of object lessons, we may succeed in accumulating vast stores of knowledge, all very useful, but we may fail in strengthening the mental fiber, in securing acuteness of conception, and the power of original thought. By this course the senses may be nicely developed, and the objective powers receive thorough culture, while the faculties of reflection and generalization are dwarfed, and the subjective elements are submerged beneath miscellaneous accumulations.

Any attempt to arrange the order in which the faculties are developed, and to draw up a corresponding order of studies, is attended with much perplexity. The study of geometry, for instance, which calls into exercise the perceptive faculties, the earliest of the mental powers developed, requires for many of its most elementary demonstrations a nicety of conception, and a power of combination, which is rarely attained till the period of maturity. The study of language, on the other hand, which involves in its investigation the exercise of powers among the last developed, is among the earliest gifts brought into requisition, is retained in most constant use through life, and should be cultivated with the greatest care from infancy. Imagination and taste, too, those faculties which are the last to be philosophically developed, are seen in active operation in earliest childhood. Observe the little girl, all alone in her rude play-house, and listen to her as she entertains company, and waits on her table, or "keeps school" and chastises her refractory pupils. Observe, too, how readily she recognizes taste in dress, and designates this as ugly, and that as beautiful.

From these considerations, it would seem that we can not safely follow any arbitrary analysis in making a true order of studies; though such analysis may be of use to us in pursuing our investigations.

Let us come then directly to the inquiry, What is the true Theory of Intellectual Education?

There seem to be two periods in the development of the mind which are sufficiently distinct to be marked, but which are not capable of being entirely separated from each other. The first and the earliest period is that during which the objective elements are in the ascendency, and the knowledge acquired is, in the main, of the concrete. The second and later period is that during which the subjective elements are in the ascendency, and the knowledge acquired is, in much the larger proportion, of the abstract.

The perceptive faculties and consciousness first set the mind into operation, and by them we acquire a knowledge of the qualities of matter and the energies of mind, the only kinds of knowledge which these two faculties reveal. But intimately associated with these, and apparently stimulated into action by them, are suggested ideas of space, time, cause and effect, and the results of reason, reflection, and generalization. But every one who is acquainted with the minds of children, knows that these latter knowledges are not grappled with, and mastered, till the mind has attained a considerable degree of maturity, and that it must acquire extended experience of the world around, and the realm within, preparatory to entering upon the investigation of these ideas.

During the first period of development, the perceptive faculties and consciousness are much more active and acute than at a subsequent stage, indicating that nature designed this to be the period during which these faculties should be most carefully educated. It is doubtless true that during the first five or six years of life, by far the greater proportion of the ideas attained by these faculties are acquired.

At a later period the reflective faculties become more active, and the susceptibility for perceptions more sluggish. Hence the old man can depict the events of early life much more vividly than he can what has transpired in later years. During the first period the knowledge we acquire consists principally of facts, at a later period of principles, facts being retained only as they are referred to principles.* By the first set of faculties we are gathering the material which the second will at a later period use. During the first we sow the seed,—during the second we reap the harvest, and we naturally conclude that the fruits of the harvest will be in proportion to the care and culture bestowed at seed-time.

It would seem, then, that in forming our theory of a true education, we must not lose sight of this two-fold nature of the mind itself, and must perceive that the same theory can not apply to both periods. The notion that the mind is a kind of vacant receptacle, which needs to be filled, as applicable to the first period, is not very far from true, but very erroneous when applied to the second. The mind during

* For the development of these ideas in their application to the study of language, see page 178 of INSTITUTE LECTURES.

this first period is like the fallow earth, mellow, and ready for the grain.

That the mind consists of a set of active growing faculties, which must be trained and stimulated to action, which need to have correct habits engrafted upon them, and taught to become skilled in curious workmanship, is true when applied to the second period. If education during the first period corresponds to the fallow earth receiving the seed grain, during the second it corresponds to the careful cultivation bestowed upon it by the husbandman, wherein the soil is shaped and opened to the sun, and stimulated to produce from its own latent resources the abundant fruit.

If, then, these views be correct, the business of education during this first period of development should be to furnish the mind with the material of thought; and to this end the perceptive faculties and consciousness should receive careful culture, and be stimulated to vigorous healthy action. Upon the activity of these faculties, and the accumulations thus early made, depends in a great measure richness of thought in after years. Many a one is born, walks through the world with his eyes open, and makes his exit, without ever seeing what is constantly above, around, and beneath him. Beauty is in the landscape, incense upon the gale, glory in the heavens, but he knows it not!

Object lessons, then, which shall quicken the perceptions of the child, which shall wake up his drowsy senses and attract his attention,—which shall fix the habit of minutely attending to the deliverances of consciousness, is a kind of training that is peculiarly adapted to this, the earliest period of development. And it is with the utmost pleasure that we hail every attempt to introduce and popularize this species of instruction.* The dumb and senseless methods of primary teaching which formerly prevailed, have too long disgraced our systems of popular education. The fossils embedded in the rocks of Scotland, and scattered along the chalky shores of England, were more intelligent and inspiring teachers to the soul of Hugh Miller, than were the schoolmasters who crammed his mind with dry formulas, and, to him, senseless jargon. Let children be taught the concrete during the first years of school life. Let them have some mental aliment that they can relish, some material for thought that they can comprehend. Give them the kind of knowledge that they naturally crave, and which they will receive with exceeding joy.

---

* Since preparing the manuscript of these pages, we have been informed that Prof. Welch, of the Michigan State Normal School, has a work on "Object Lessons" in course of publication, especially designed for use in the school-room. The eminent ability and philosophical turn of mind of Prof. Welch, together with his experience as a teacher, combine to create the expectation of a work from his pen of rare merit. A good practical work on this subject would be received with delight by every earnest-minded teacher.

But there is another fact, in connection with this system of primary instruction, which must not be lost sight of. Although the perceptive faculties are in the ascendency during this first period, still they are not in exclusive control of the mental energy. All the higher faculties are beginning to operate from earliest childhood, and are used with remarkable quickness and readiness, though with comparatively feeble power. This early period is but the preparatory state for their vigorous and controlling action. Hence the early instruction, while it is primarily devoted to these first faculties developed, should also be devoted to a preparation for the successful action of the higher faculties.

Care, then, should be taken that the early instruction be duly classified, and so arranged that it shall be retained in the memory upon the principle of philosophical association; and that each successive accumulation of knowledge shall take its place in the memory in its appropriate class. Every opportunity must be seized of bringing into judicious exercise the higher faculties, and a beginning must be made of their training. In making this beginning, is required the skill of a master hand. It will not answer for a teacher to talk generalizations to a class of children;* for although it is plain to him, a film is

* What became familiar to him [the teacher] only by severe and protracted effort, seems capable of being learned by his pupil in

over their eyes. It is a difficult task, in giving instruction, to pass from the concrete to the abstract, from the real to the ideal. The most ingenious devices and delicate tests are here in constant requisition.

We must, during this first period, commence the education of the will. For a man's success in life depends, after all, upon the efficiency of this power. It is the regal faculty, the monarch of the mind. The power to command our faculties, to put them upon the consideration of a subject, and to keep them employed, is really the great end of education. The power of independent thinking depends upon this. Hence, the habit must be imparted, during the early training, of bringing the mind to act at stated periods, and of patiently and persistently performing tasks. The child must not be suffered to believe that he can have his education done for him, or that there is any royal road to learning. The earth sown with good seed, and most carefully cultivated, will only

---

much shorter time than is actually possible. In these respects, it becomes a teacher to be on his guard. He should consider, not what he can now do, but what he could have done when under the circumstances of his pupils. He should, therefore, be careful to assure himself that what he teaches is understood. He who will bear these things in mind, will not often have to complain of the stupidity of his pupils. When an instructor finds all his pupils blockheads, the indication is certainly ambiguous; there is a blockhead somewhere, but whether it belong to the teacher or the pupil, becomes a proper subject of inquiry.—*Wayland's Intellectual Philosophy*, p. 276.

produce such a crop as the elements in its own bosom are capable of nurturing.

The education of the will leads us very naturally from the first to the second period of development. The will must be educated, not only to enable the pupil to observe constantly, and to engrave upon the tablets of the soul every result of consciousness, but it must also be subservient to making him a patient and independent thinker. *What* we learn is of importance, but it is only important according to the use we make of it by the higher faculties. We may, by careful training, give the mind great acuteness of perception and vividness of idea, but unless the pupil acquires the power of analysis and generalization, unless he can compare and combine his acquisitions, so as to deduce therefrom new and original knowledge, and is able to test the opinions of others by the powers of his own understanding, then his preparatory training has been comparatively useless. The pupil may be taught the profound mysteries of creation, and led by the poet's numbers to the highest heaven of invention; but unless he has a soul capable of appreciating these, vain are the searches of the philosopher and the brilliant fancy of the poet.

During this second period of development, we must attentively consider how much it is proper for the teacher to do for his pupils, and in what way it shall be done. If the pupil is to be made to do all for himself, there would be little need of a teacher, beyond directing and keeping him to his tasks. The wonderful success that has attended the efforts of our self-educated men, and we have many in our midst, would seem to indicate that we may be guilty of too much crowding instruction upon our pupils. Or rather it may indicate, that our efforts should more especially be directed to such methods of instruction as shall successfully exercise and strengthen the will.

The ultimate object, then, of education being to minister to the growth and independent action of a living, acting intelligence, and this growth and action being dependent upon the efforts which itself puts forth in its own behalf, the only method of deciding upon what course a pupil shall be put, is by an inquiry into his mental status.*

And here is needed the greatest skill of the teacher, to know how to classify his scholars, and prescribe for their intellectual wants. They are not to be arranged according to age, or courses of studies they

* What, indeed, are almost all the processes of our schools but the tame retravel of beaten paths, or the rank empiricism of unphilosophical experiment? How uncertain, in any given case, is the result which shall flow from the schooling of our children! Where is the school that is not in some part, and to some extent still, a Procrustean bed; the pupil that is too short must stretch or be stretched; the pupil that is, unfortunately, of too tall a growth for the ordinary course of puerilities must lose his head, or take to his heels. How many ruined intellects, spoiled in the training, lie scattered through the land, telling of the fatal mistakes made in the school-rooms!—*Address of Hon. J. M. Gregory, Superintendent of Public Instruction, Michigan.*

claim to have pursued, but according to mentality. For, of all things, we are to avoid putting a scholar to learn what he can not understand. Like a person attempting to ford a river beyond his depth, he will be submerged. In no particular have our teachers more signally failed, and in none do they need more careful training, than in the ability to classify. The study to be pursued must be suited to the capacity. It is vain to put a scholar to work upon a branch requiring the vigorous exercise of the reflective faculties, if he has not come to that period when these faculties are in the ascendency; and hence he must be kept at his primary or preparatory courses till that condition has been developed. To a large portion of the human race this period never comes, though, probably, nearly all could be educated up to that point, were their primary instruction properly conducted.

When the studies have been assigned after due classification, the main purpose should be to lead the pupil to independent thought, and to original investigation. The danger is, that he will merely learn what is found in the book, without fathoming its bearings and the extent of its purport. It is impossible for the writer of a text-book to fully develop and enlarge upon the various parts of his treatise. He can do little more than set forth, in the briefest possible manner, the elements of the science. It is but a skeleton of the subject, whereas volumes might perhaps be written upon a single branch of what he has treated. The teacher, then, must be able to take this skeleton and inspire it with life, and lead his pupil not only to think the thoughts of the text-book, but to branch out, and understand fully all its relations, and be independent of and far beyond it.

The true theory of instruction is to pass from the application of principles in a particular case, to the generalization for all cases of that class—or to the rule. All sciences proceed from the simple to the more intricate. From a few definitions or axioms, we develop, by degrees, all the abstruse principles of the science. It should be the aim to accustom the scholar, at every step in his progress, to use what he has already mastered, in developing and discovering for himself the principles which must follow. By cultivating and fostering these habits of mind, scholars have been enabled to make plain that which is intricate, to discover new truth, and to greatly enlarge the boundaries of knowledge.

To establish a course of instruction which shall secure these results, it is proper that the teacher should know what plan of conducting a class recitation will prove most effectual. Of the manner in which class recitations are conducted during the second period of development, an analysis may be made into three classes, each of which has some advantages and defects.

The leading feature in the first method consists in

requiring the pupil to so prepare himself for recitation, that he can, without any aid or hint from book or teacher, state the topics and develop the principles of the whole or any part of the lesson,—can give a complete *résumé* of the author,—while it is the study of the instructor, if he asks any questions, to be sure that the pupil shall gather from it no clue to the answer. In pursuing this method the teacher exercises a stern censorship, and holds his pupil to a strict account for the preparation and proper understanding of his lessons. By this course the scholar learns to depend upon himself,—a habit invaluable in the subsequent pursuit of learning, in the practice of any of the learned professions, and in fact in any of the duties of life. But this system possesses many radical defects, and its virtues are only of the negative character. It is the old stereotype method of *hearing* classes say their lessons, which a wooden man might do nearly as well. "We can easily conceive," says Dr. Huntington, "of all the bare *material* of instruction being conveyed into a school-room through a mechanism of pipes in the wall, or maps let down by pulleys, and its discipline administered by a veiled executioner, no heart-relations being suffered to grow up between teacher and taught."

A teacher of the second class pursues a course entirely different from this. His system of instruction consists in pouring out a profusion of knowledge upon every subject broached in the class-room.

Filled with enthusiasm himself, he is impatient to inspire his pupils with his own conceptions. Without waiting for the pupil to tell in an indifferent manner what he can dilate upon so well, and unable to command the impartiality of a judge and the patience of a listener, he tells every thing, he explains every thing, and rising with the feelings which his subject excites, he glows with an eloquence which reaches the coldest heart, and awakens the feeblest mind. If a question be proposed, he does not ask it so as to elicit the cold naked fact, but in such a manner that the pupil can not fail to answer it correctly; or he includes the answer in the glowing statement of the question, and concludes with "Must it not be so?" or, "Can it be otherwise?" "Does not that logically follow?"

The advantage of this method consists in the opportunity it affords for every member of a class to acquire some knowledge of the subject, and to appreciate its spirit. No scholar completely fails. Each takes in what his capacity and inclination will allow, and though in a portion of almost every class it will be very moderate, yet with this grade of students it will be likely to be something more than would be acquired by the first method. For, when a pupil without capacity is compelled to con for recitation what he can not understand, or the pupil with capacity is compelled to do the same thing without fully comprehending, or feeling the force of what he has prepared to recite, the advantage is very slight.

There are some evils connected with this second method of instruction. The pupil is not trained to habits of accuracy and self-reliance. He fails to acquire a control over his faculties, and the power of thinking how and when he pleases; but he must wait for a favorable moment—for the lucid interval—and his efforts are desultory and governed by fits of enthusiasm. The effect upon his habits of study is even worse. It has a tendency to render the efforts of the best scholars irregular in the preparation of their lessons, to make the irregular still more erratic and careless, and to lessen the incentives of the dull and heedless to improve even the feeble talents they have.

The third method of instruction is a combination of the former two. The representative teacher of this class first rigidly exacts of the pupil a systematic and lucid statement of the lesson assigned, and critically examines him upon the opinions which he has acquired from it, and the grounds upon which they are based. He then opens to him the stores of his own mind, and dilates with all the fervor of his nature upon the relations, the beauties, and the glories of the subject. This method combines the excellencies of both the former, without embracing many of their defects. The pupil is in the first place encouraged to make all the discoveries he can upon the subject, by the exercise of his own unaided powers of understanding, and to set them forth to the teacher as best he can. He thus gets credit for all that he is able to do, and is encouraged by every day's success to do the best possible. There is at least the stimulus of fair opportunity, with an attentive instructor able to weigh and duly appreciate every consideration presented. But the system would be imperfect were this all. The teacher now takes up the subject, and is able from his familiarity with it to elucidate and explain the matter from a different and a higher stand-point. His information is not confined to the mere skeleton of the science presented in the text-book; but he has read extended treatises upon it, and can pour forth from the treasuries of his knowledge what will imbue the subject with new life. He can view the matter as a whole, and at each step has the advantage of the accumulated light of that which is to come, as well as that which has been passed over by the class. He is able to perceive, too, the poetic relations of the science, and the relation which this particular branch sustains in a system of complete development.

As this system of conducting a class recitation is by far the most complete and philosophic, it is recommended above all others, and he who adopts and pursues it with enthusiasm, who feels the moral dignity of his calling, and the value of his work, can not fail to win victories in a field where the opportunities are constantly recurring, and where skill and bravery are sure of success.

We can not close these considerations upon the Theory of Education, without observing that no system is worthy the name that does not provide for the physical and moral training, as well as the intellectual. The worst product of our school-system is that of an educated villain, and the next remove from it is that of an educated invalid. From the earliest point in education the moral and the physical energies should be the subjects of careful systematic culture, and it is hoped that the day is not far distant when text-books in each of these sciences will be in as constant and regular use in all our schools, as those upon any other branch.

THE END.

www.ingramcontent.com/pod-product-compliance
Lightning Source LLC
LaVergne TN
LVHW020116110826
845151LV00001B/173

9781425542474